A KIND OF
GENIUS

A KIND OF
GENIUS

HERB STURZ
AND SOCIETY'S
TOUGHEST PROBLEMS

SAM ROBERTS

PUBLICAFFAIRS
New York

Published in the United States by PublicAffairs™,
a member of the Perseus Books Group.

PublicAffairs books are available at special discounts for bulk purchases in the U.S. by corporations, institutions, and other organizations. For more information, please contact the Special Markets Department at the Perseus Books Group, 2300 Chestnut Street, Suite 200, Philadelphia, PA 19103, call (800) 810-4145, ext. 5000, or e-mail special.markets@perseusbooks.com.

Designed by Pauline Brown
Text set in 11.25-point Berling

Library of Congress Cataloging-in-Publication Data

Roberts, Sam, 1947–
  A kind of genius : Herb Sturz and society's toughest problems / Sam Roberts.
— 1st ed.
     p.   cm.
  Includes bibliographical references and index.
  ISBN 978-1-58648-471-2 (alk. paper)
  1. Sturz, Herb. 2. Businesspeople—United States—Biography. 3. Social entrepreneurship—United States. I. Title.
  HC102.5.S78R63 2008
  361.7092—dc22
  [B]

                                                            2008044847

First Edition
10 9 8 7 6 5 4 3 2 1

For Mike and Will:
The future is theirs to define

Contents

Prologue: Herb's Children   1

Part I   *The Outsider*

1 Only Connect   11

2 *Boys' Life* Goes to Jail   25

3 The Feminine Form of True   35

Part II   *The Innovator*

4 Vera's Bailiwick   47

5 Summons to the Bowery   81

6 Beyond the Bowery   101

7 The Wildcats Strike   121

8 In the Summer of Sam   147

Part III   *The Insider*

9 Politics and Poker   163

Part IV   *The Social Planner*

10 The Process Broker   193

11 Planning the Visionary City   205

Part V   *Tackling Times Square*

12 The Longest-Running Joke
in New York   223

13 The New Times Square   245

Part VI   The Benefactor

14 A Planner Faces Reality   257

15 A Winter's Tale at the Bonfire
    of the Vanities   273

16 "As Long As I'm Doing
    Something That Matters"   297

    Epilogue: Always Connect   313

    ACKNOWLEDGMENTS   325
    A NOTE ON SOURCES   327
    INDEX   333

Herb's Children

Imagine that you're a graduate student at Columbia Teachers College in 1953 majoring in American literature. You've advanced an unconventional interpretation of *The Grapes of Wrath*, John Steinbeck's saga of poor and oppressed migrants during the Great Depression. In contrast to a decade's worth of literary critics, you've embraced the book's undervalued but lyrical inner chapters—those metaphorical ruminations on earth-gouging tractors and on devastating drought and especially the one about the indomitable land turtle's precarious crossing of a treacherous Dust Bowl highway—chapters that endow with epic dimensions and greater purpose a novel that you've just audaciously claimed as your personal manifesto. The professor's sole critique of your hand-written paper dismissively focuses on form rather than content: "Lines not parallel to top edge of paper."

The young student was disappointed by his professor's criticism, but not discouraged. He sought a second opinion directly from the source: John Steinbeck himself. He wasn't just seeking vindication when he wrote to the Nobel Prize–winning novelist, although that would have been sweet. Above all, Herbert Sturz, the tenacious son of a New Jersey saloonkeeper, was constitutionally unable to accept dogma, from an English professor or any other so-called expert, and he was acutely curious about getting to the bottom of any intellectual argument. When Steinbeck answered Sturz, he did so in a poignant essay handwritten on a yellow legal pad, like the original 200,000-word manuscript of *The Grapes of Wrath* itself fourteen years earlier.

"You say the inner chapters were counterpoint and so they were—that they were pace changes and they were that, too, but the basic purpose was to hit the reader below the belt," John Steinbeck wrote. "You are the first critical person who seems to have suspected that they had a purpose."

Critics, Steinbeck continued, have a curious view of writing, an egomaniacal image of authors groping their way up the staircase of immortality. Writing, by itself, without any illusions of imperishability, is tough enough. "Most good writers I know," Steinbeck concluded, "have no time for immortality."

Herb Sturz embraced the great novelist's response as inspiration, as a personal invitation to a lifelong odyssey through the labyrinthine corridors of power and as an opportunity to ameliorate poverty and injustice. It would inspire him not only to write but also to give voice, as Steinbeck had, to the voiceless, to couple the journalist's probing curiosity and irreverence with the novelist's utopian vision. Unlike Steinbeck, however, Sturz would help fashion happier endings than otherwise might have been.

"He was," Sturz says of Steinbeck, "the first person to take me seriously," and so, "I took myself a little more seriously, gained some self-confidence."

Throughout his life, Herb Sturz has been taken seriously by commissioners, judges, mayors, presidents, publishers, philanthropists, scientists, by individuals addicted to drugs and alcohol, crime victims, convicts, bankers, builders and homeless people. Many of the people whose lives Sturz has altered were those with no grasp on power. Or they were people with power they didn't know they had.

Largely as a supplicant seeking financial and political support, Sturz tinkered with, tweaked and finally helped revolutionize bail and other aspects of the criminal justice system, from the outside. As an innovator from inside, he turned government into a vehicle for reform. And, later, he returned to the private sector, first as a critic, then in the trenches again and finally in his most uncharacteristic role, as a benefactor, working for one of the richest men in the world. In every incarnation, he hewed to the same values, and was driven by the same strategy—to lead himself and lure others through imagination.

Most people have never heard of Herb Sturz, even though their lives have likely been touched in some way by his take on society's toughest problems. For more than a half century, Sturz has been largely an unsung hero, a shrewd social engineer and social entrepreneur without a rigid ideological agenda. Armed instead with mastery of process and human nature, of means and motive, of intellect and emotional intelligence, Sturz has profoundly altered the public perception of fundamental issues, has improved the way things get done and made government work more smoothly. As if armed with a divining rod, he could find funding streams in the public and private sectors and combine them to power his visions. And he could intuitively discover and nurture hidden talents that other people rarely knew they had.

As he fostered change, the breadth of the challenges Sturz has tackled, the power of his ideas to reorder the nation's agenda, the scope of his ability to replicate solutions across the United States and in countries as diverse as

Chile, South Africa, Britain and Russia, are virtually without parallel. Peter Goldmark Jr., a former president of the Rockefeller Foundation, has called Sturz "the best social engineer in America."

Gara LaMarche, the president of the Atlantic Philanthropies, sees Sturz as the archetypal social entrepreneur and as living proof that "public policy is a realm where you can have a certain creativity, almost genius."

Aryeh Neier, the president of George Soros's Open Society Institute, says Sturz has made "an enormous difference assisting marginalized people."

George Soros, the financier and global philanthropist, has attributed Sturz's effectiveness to his ability to work with, rather than against, any given system. As Soros puts it, "People with ideas tend to be worn down. He makes the system achieve complete objectives."

That's because ideas, to Sturz, are only the beginning. He would never isolate himself in an ivory tower. The great vice of academicism, the literary critic Lionel Trilling wrote, "is that it is concerned with ideas rather than with thinking."

One of Sturz's underlying principles, according to Jack Rosenthal of the *New York Times*, one of his oldest friends and colleagues, is "using nonprofit, private and even governmental pilot programs and experiments to prove out remedies for wrongs—and using the proof to achieve government funding at scale."

"Some people start with the position that government doesn't work because they don't want it to work," Sturz says. "I had nine years in government. You can do an enormous amount. But to effect real change, why would you expect government to do it alone?"

Sturz's record is laudable not solely on the basis of accomplishment, but also given the constraints of the times in which he achieved success. Describing the "almost languid" decade of the 1950s, David Halberstam wrote: "As younger people and segments of society who did not believe they had a fair share became empowered, pressure inevitably began to build against the entrenched political and social hierarchy. . . . One did not lightly challenge a system that seemed, on the whole, to be working so well."[*] Sturz challenged that system and not lightly. Not head first, perhaps, but strategically. And, considering the political and temperamental and ideological impediments aligned against him, by design or just because that was the way things were and always had been, the results he achieved are all the more astonishing. Even by the beginning of the 1960s, it was still tough to persuade policy makers, to say nothing of their constituents, that many Americans were being denied justice only because they were poor or that alcoholics deserved to be treated as victims not criminals. Those policy makers might have known their own jobs, to one degree or another, but few of them understood the system. Some wouldn't even talk to one another. Sturz remembers Frank Hogan, the Manhattan district attorney in the 1960s, rarely meeting with judges and defense lawyers because he considered such contact "professionally inappropriate."

It was also tough for people to admit that some of the nostrums that seemed so noble when they were embraced early on never lived up to their promise. Sturz succeeded, in part, because he recoiled at the facile and reflexive pat responses that doomed so many other good intentions. In a biting obituary for Lyndon Johnson's Great Society, the Brookings Institution wrote, "Taking refuge in pat, simple answers—decentralize, regulate, coordinate, spend more, spend less—seems unlikely to lead to a workable strategy."

And if it was one thing to get government grants in the heady early years of the Great Society when the reform credo buzzed through the nation, it was quite another barely a few years later, by which point reformers' disillusionment was captured by a wry poster in a welfare office that instructed: "Don't just do something. Stand there." Or, two decades later, when Sturz was faced with wringing support for social programs from the Reagan administration, whose goal was to shrink the government and whose hard-heartedness in achieving that agenda seemed best summed up by the Department of Agriculture's reclassification of ketchup as a vegetable. Or, during the Clinton years, persuading policy makers that it cost money to move people from welfare to work but that the results were attainable and measurable, and again during the Bush administration when he successfully leveraged private dollars to win government investment in an after-school program. Sturz fought on, regardless, tailoring his strategy, but not his principles.

As his long-time friend Robert Hood sees it, Sturz never fails to "fight the good fight even when nobody is watching."

Because not many people were watching and because Sturz typically preferred it that way, "he is well known in certain elite circles, but he has no public profile," says Gara LaMarche. "Herb, in that sense, has a very quiet impact on people. Virtually all the beneficiaries of his vision haven't heard of Herb Sturz and probably never will."

But it is perhaps Sturz's best attribute that he is, as a friend, Jay L. Kriegel, who first recruited him to John V. Lindsay's mayoral team of outsiders, points out, willing to take risks on projects with little chance of return. Kriegel may have summed it up best at Sturz's seventy-fifth birthday celebration in 2006. "Herb," he said, "is not afraid to fail."

And fail he did, sometimes, just because the challenge he faced demanded that somebody do something—almost anything—and because no one else was brash enough to try. "Part of me thinks I can do it," Sturz says. "The other part thinks the only real failure is not trying."

In many arenas, Sturz has not only succeeded but succeeded wildly, igniting a nationwide reformation of costly and unjust bail practices, transforming a faceless court system into one that cared not merely about processing people but also about the victims of crime, sparking a physical and spiritual renaissance of Times Square, creating a pioneering community court and serving citizens without any real clout or constituency.

Gara LaMarche calls him "the good Robert Moses," the benignant twin of the storied Power Broker, one who "dreamed projects up and willed them into being"—without any of Moses's institutional muscle or unbridled obsessions, or his unforgiving single-mindedness. "He is not a manager," LaMarche says. "He is not a fundraiser."

In retelling the history of *The Power Broker*, Robert A. Caro a decade ago wrote that "to really show political power, you had to show the effect of power on the powerless." That is what Herb Sturz is all about. His is not a story about the ancillary impact of power on the powerless. It is about empowering the powerless—and, more often than not, by working with government rather than, as Moses did, flaunting the power liberally invested in him by government.

———

Reared in the optimistic can-do spirit of the New Deal, Sturz was nonetheless chastened by the failings of the Great Society to deliver on the great expectations harbored by many. His legacy would not be a New Deal or a Great Society. But it would, nonetheless, fundamentally alter how much of society—all over America and beyond—

viewed and dealt with people who were alcoholics, drug addicted, arrested but presumed innocent, convicted but unready for release, homeless, jobless and retired but still able to serve. The projects that became Sturz's progeny not only changed perceptions, they profoundly affected countless lives.

The essential vehicle of Herb Sturz's intellectual ferment is the Vera Institute. At thirty, Sturz became its first executive director. By the time Vera celebrated its forty-fifth anniversary in 2006, its progeny evoked a biblical family tree. A bail project begat a summons project, which begat the Bowery Project and Project Renewal. Vera pioneered the first ambulatory methadone program in the nation for die-hard drug addicts and, directly or indirectly, inspired the Addiction Research Treatment Corporation, the Victim Service Agency (which became Victim Services and then Safe Horizon), the Legal Action Center, Mobilization for Youth Legal Services, Pioneer Messenger Corporation, Wildcat Service Corporation, the Neighborhood Youth Diversion Corporation, the Manhattan Court Employment Project, La Bodega de la Familia, the Harlem Defender Service, the Center for Alternative Sentencing and Employment Services (CASES) and the Center for Employment Opportunities—and Sturz himself launched the City Volunteer Corps, the Midtown Community Court, Red Hook Community Justice Center, the Center for Court Innovation, The After-School Corporation and the Center for New York City Neighborhoods.

"They are not Vera's children," Sturz's friend Jack Rosenthal says. "They're Herb's children."

Part I

The Outsider

Chapter 1

Only Connect

Herbert Jay Sturz, the youngest of three brothers, was born in 1930 and raised in Bayonne, New Jersey, a gritty oil-refining town on New York and Newark bays west of Staten Island. Bayonne, he recalled years later, "was a mix between immigrant Slavs and Poles and guys who worked at the refineries. A strong Catholic population. A less strong Jewish population." It was a working-class town that produced middleweight Ernie "The Rock" Durando, the heavyweight Chuck "The Bayonne Bleeder" Wepner (said to have been an inspiration for Sylvester Stallone's Rocky Balboa) and mob enforcer Harold "K.O." Konigsberg.

"I was on the fringes," Sturz says of his childhood. "I never knew poverty."

When his father, Jacob, was nineteen, in 1908, he arrived at Ellis Island from what was then Austria-Hungary. He worked first as a house painter but then was drafted into the U.S. Army as an interpreter during World War I. Herb's mother, Ida, was born in the United States, the daughter of Samuel and Annie Meirowitz. Her father had also left Austria-Hungary. He came to Grand Street on the Lower East Side of Manhattan around 1885 as a boy of fifteen. His first job was as a street sweeper. Neither of Herb's parents got beyond high school. After the war, his father and his uncle opened in Bayonne the Avenue F Saloon, which Sturz says was "literally on the wrong side of the tracks." Not yet a teenager, Herb worked behind the bar dispensing Three Feathers rye and beer to patrons who availed themselves of the pickled tomatoes, hard-boiled eggs, onions and other staples that constituted the proverbial free lunch. Foreshadowing his later obsession with quantifying the results of experiments in social engineering, he would calibrate the precise angle at which to hold a glass and release the tap to produce the smallest head on a beer. He sometimes worked in the afternoons after delivering the *Bayonne Times* door to door and was mesmerized by leaving daylight and fresh air for the hypnotic boozy duskiness of the bar.

Jacob Sturz also started what his youngest son would call "an elementary sort of foreign exchange service"—shipping packages of food, clothing and cash from immigrants to their relatives in Hungary, Poland and Czechoslovakia. His father's passion was Hungarian music, but his personality rarely reflected its vibrancy and intensity. Sturz remembers him displaying strong emotion only once, when he wept on learning that relatives in Europe had been exterminated in the Holocaust. He adored his family but reveled more in their personas than their accomplishments. He never asked to see his sons' report cards from Horace Mann Elementary School or Bayonne High. He told Herb that he loved him best when his face was dirty, and he took particular pride when he saw nine-year-old Herb, sitting on the stoop of their house, as Joe the garbage man greeted the boy by name from his passing truck.

"It was a wonderful acceptance," Sturz recalls. "He never cared about how well I did in school or anything like that. It was much more elemental and, I think, it gave me whatever sense of security I had in my life. It helped a lot. I didn't know it at the time." About the same time, Herb persuaded his mother to take him to the apartment building in Manhattan where Mel Ott, the manager of his beloved New York Giants, lived. The Giants had lost the World Series to the Yankees when Herb was six and again when he was seven. Even then, he was rooting for the underdogs.

As a kid, Sturz was more bully than sissy, tall for his age and usually in charge of choosing up sides for stickball—displaying some of the same skills, but with less of the diplomacy (he remembers saying "awful things" like "He's too fat" or "We don't want him") that would serve him well in later years. In 1944, he delivered an original essay titled "One America" to his eighth-grade assembly (befitting Bayonne's bifurcated culture, his speech was sandwiched between a classical overture and a song titled "The Riveter").

To prepare for his Bar Mitzvah, he attended Hebrew School four afternoons a week, an obligation that interfered with his bartending and hanging out at after-school ball games. He learned to read Hebrew aloud but without understanding the meaning of the words. "In retrospect, a good thing is that I didn't understand Hebrew or have the wit to try to learn what I was reading," Sturz says. "So I didn't know about the negative things I was studying in Hebrew with respect to prejudice, that women are inferior to men, about sin and guilt. All that passed me by. I went to Hebrew School because I had to. It would have been unthinkable not to have gone. But I never thought of myself as religious." As an adult, he would fast on Yom Kippur, the Jewish Day of Atonement, but otherwise didn't hew to tradition. "I'm Jewish when Jews are under attack," he says.

In the fall of his senior year at Bayonne High, Princeton University was courting Herb with the promise of a tennis scholarship. One day, however, when he was playing in the finals of a tournament, something started going wrong: He kept dropping the racket after hitting the ball. "Everyone drops a racket occasionally," he remembers. "I assumed it was nothing." But by January, he would also have trouble squeezing the scoop in the ice cream parlor where he worked after school as a soda jerk.

He had contracted polio. "I had been the captain of the high school tennis team, and we were among the best in the state. I ran track and played other sports. So polio caused me for the first time to think about the fact that I was not immortal." The disease would leave him with a weakened right hand, abruptly ending his affair with tournament tennis and instilling a new discipline and perspective on life's capriciousness. "My family thought that I was going to die. I had to drop out of high school. I received my diploma, but I never went back."

His terrified family reached beyond conventional medicine to practitioners of Jewish Science, a movement that, like Christian Science, emphasized prayer and divine healing. Honey and horseradish were administered; and every day, Sturz chanted the invocation "God is filling my body with health and strength." Sturz's bout with polio infused him with an abiding compassion. (Comparing social entrepreneurs with business entrepreneurs and people employed in "caring professions," Harvard's Lynn Barendsen has found that all three groups considered that they had been outsiders in their early lives, but only among the social entrepreneurs had many experienced some form of trauma at an early age.) Confined to his home for six months, Sturz also honed a tactical skill that would serve him well later: He taught himself mental chess and eventually could calculate a half dozen moves—and their implications—in advance.

In 1948, he enrolled in the University of Wisconsin, at Madison. Both of his brothers had gone there after his mother had met, and been impressed by, a former Wisconsin instructor, Lionel Trilling, on a train. "Wisconsin is the place to go," Ida Sturz was told by Trilling, who, by then, was a professor at Columbia, where Herb would go to graduate school. Wisconsin's program of integrated liberal studies, inspired by Alexander Meiklejohn, the civil liberties advocate, was a major influence on Sturz. "It carried forward in the way I think, the way I connect ideas," he says. "You didn't take a course in English, per se. It was Greek and Roman culture, then on to Medieval and Renaissance culture, then transitioning to the study of industrial society. You looked at literature and economics or history through an integrated lens. It helped me realize how ideas and fields relate to one another, how means lead to ends, how, in order to get from A to B, you had to go to A second and A third—aware in the process that things change."

As one of the first students in the integrated curriculum, Sturz majored in philosophy. "I figured that I could read history and literature on my own, but I wouldn't try to think on my own," he recalls. "Probably that's why I wanted to go into philosophy. Perhaps it was a kind of one-upmanship."

No philosopher inspired Sturz more than John Dewey. "He was idealistic, analytic and pragmatic," Sturz recalled in a discussion years later with Wisconsin students. *"Human Nature and Conduct,* I devoured. I practically underlined the entire book and filled the margins of the page with my scribblings. I learned about the thrust and flow of ideas, facts and relationships." As a disciple of Dewey, he embraced the inseparable bond between human nature and conduct and of the guiding principle that "arriving at one goal is the starting point for another." Ends don't exist without means. Ends change in the course of achieving them. "I learned quickly how the world interrelates even before I read *Howards End* with its two-word invocation: 'Only connect.' I began to connect." For Sturz, "Only connect" became a mantra.

Sturz connected seemingly disparate ideas not theoretically, but practically, embracing William James's definition of the pragmatist as one who

> turns his back resolutely and once for all upon a lot of inveterate habits dear to professional philosophers. He turns away from abstraction and insufficiency, from verbal solutions, from bad a priori reasons, from fixed principles, closed systems, and pretended absolutes and origins. He turns towards concreteness and adequacy, towards facts, towards action and towards power. That means the empiricist temper regnant and the rationalist temper sincerely given up. It means the open air and possibilities of nature, as against dogma, artificiality, and the pretence of finality in truth.

Inspired by James and Dewey, Sturz inevitably plunged into politics. He demonstrated against compulsory enrollment in the Reserve Officers' Training Corps (ROTC) and, with several friends, infiltrated a Young Republicans Club, which then voted to censure the state's junior senator, Joseph McCarthy. He also helped a congregation of Unitarians— including one graduate student he was enamored with— build a stone church designed by Frank Lloyd Wright, a Wisconsin native, outside Madison.

During what he describes as "that period of my life where I wanted to experience stuff" firsthand, one Thanksgiving when he was short of money for the bus ticket home to New Jersey, he rode to Chicago, where he checked into a flophouse but recalls "not having enough guts to get under the covers." On another visit, he talked his way into sleeping overnight at a city jail. One summer, he worked as an attendant in a mental hospital run by Quakers in California—refusing, though, to sign a loyalty oath, which was a condition of getting paid (he waived his salary). Appalled by the use of punishment as therapy, he was handed a negative reference from the American Friends Service Committee for publishing a graphic critique of the treatment, which included using rolled-up newspaper comics pages as gags to prevent patients from biting their tongues during grand mal convulsions. He sat in a cold tub and wore a straitjacket to experience the cruel and terrifying claustrophobia that patients felt.

Ken Marion, his roommate at Wisconsin, who years later would work with Sturz in New York, recalls another episode that might have stimulated Sturz's lifelong interest in criminal justice. To earn some extra money, the roommates ventured into the car-waxing business and printed up flyers that were the same size and color as parking tickets and read: "Here's your ticket for a great Simoniz job." Unfortunately for them, it was against the law to place commercial notices on car windshields. They were driven downtown by the police (Marion remembers Sturz holding the door for the officer when they got to the stationhouse). The experience, Marion suggests half-jokingly, not only cemented Sturz's respect for the police but also planted a seed about what answers from a suspect would qualify him as a candidate for the benefit of the doubt. "After a few words from a sergeant who was sympathetic to our desire to do hard work for spending money, we were released," Marion recalls. "Perhaps Herb realized then that the sergeant's excellent character judgment might be incorporated in a questionnaire."

Sturz believes that, in the long run, it was better that he didn't go to law school. The lack of legal training gave him an awareness of his own vulnerability and helped him turn being an unschooled outsider into an advantage. Not having trained in the law, moreover, did not stop him from serving as "counsel" to a legal advocacy group.

————

After graduating in 1952, Sturz returned to New York and rented a room from the mother of friends from Wisconsin. He worked in the mailroom of Hearst Advertising Service and then as a bill collector for a finance company, where his supervisor offered the following bit of inspiration: "Knowledge *is* power *if* directed and used honestly, wisely and aggressively. Our sincere wish is that your wishes come true, and by hard work and mutual cooperation between us, success will be assured. There is no other way." There had to be. Sturz hated the job and left after a month.

At Wisconsin, Herb had gotten to know Ruth Herschberger, a poet and sociologist who wrote *Adam's Rib*, an early feminist tract, and in New York he plunged into the world of poetry. He applied for a job at the Gotham Book Mart but didn't get it. He went to Dylan Thomas's readings and to the Welsh bard's binges afterward at the White Horse Tavern, and he attended the poet's funeral.

He had planned to enroll at the Sorbonne when he left Wisconsin, but by chance he met a young woman in the elevator of the Manhattan building where he was living who referred him to an artist friend named Natalie d'Arbeloff, who was hoping to work as an illustrator on a screenplay with Norman Mailer. Sturz and she ended up writing another screenplay, "The Peacemaker," about the world's richest man, Quincy Wilbur, who leverages his fortune to achieve global prosperity and peace. Louis de Rochemont, who has been called "the father of the docu-drama," optioned their scenario. "The amount offered was very small but we were too inexperienced and too delighted to argue so we accepted and split the fee between us," Natalie recalls. "We never heard any more from Hollywood after that and the film was never made."

Years later, Natalie was asked what she had made of the lanky young man in his early twenties:

> What I remember of the young Herb was that he was easy to get along with, creative, inventive and adaptable. There was a childlike quality about him which I liked (being a never-quite grown-up myself). He didn't seem to have any fixed idea of what he wanted to do or where he fitted in society but neither was he the type to be the typical rebel/dropout. I believe his family background was conventional and I don't think he would have wanted to break entirely with that and become a beatnik (hippies hadn't been invented yet!). In a sense we were both interested in "doing good" (which "The Peacemaker" was about), but in a quite naïve way. At the time, I certainly could not have predicted that Herb would become such an effective and dynamic force in humanitarian enterprises. There was something awkward and unsure about him, which, evidently, the years transformed into assurance.

Natalie's parents lived in a five-bedroom penthouse on East 72nd Street in Manhattan, in the same building, it turned out, as the Steinbecks. Her mother was French, her father a Russian-born filmmaker, industrialist and philosopher who would publish a book-length Christian spiritual meditation.

"Natalie, my collaborator, had a kid brother who the family thought was quite literally the Second Coming of Jesus," Sturz recalls. "They were going off to Brazil. The family invited me to serve as a sort of spiritual attaché to the young Jesus." Sturz was twenty-one, and Christopher was eleven. En route to Rio de Janeiro, the vessel, the *Rio de la Plata*, was rechristened the *Eva Peron*, to honor the "spiritual leader" of Argentina who had just died. As the ship passed the Equator, the pollywogs among the passengers who had never crossed the line before were initiated during a typically raucous shipboard ceremony into the Kingdom of Neptune. "Herb was with my brother and, in what I guess was a playful gesture, threw him into the pool," Natalie recalls. "My brother couldn't swim." He "was rescued immediately, but my parents were indignant and poor Herb was instantly fired."

"I ended in Brazil, penniless," Sturz recalls.

Herb returned to New York, enrolled at Columbia Teachers College and earned a master's degree in teaching English. While there, he also wrote the obligatory graduate student's novel, taking the title, "Before the Mellowing Year," from John Milton's lament for a friend drowned in the Irish Sea, "Lycidas":

> *I come to pluck your berries harsh and crude,*
> *And with forced fingers rude,*
> *Shatter your leaves before the mellowing year.*
> *Bitter constraint, and sad occasion dear,*
> *Compels me to disturb your season due:*
> *For Lycidas is dead, dead ere his prime*

After Teachers College, Sturz became a cottage father in a Jewish Child Care Association shelter for disturbed adolescents in Pleasantville, New York, and practice-taught at Haaren High School in Manhattan. "I never seriously thought about teaching," he admits. "I wanted to write."

And what better place to write, or to be inspired, than Europe? Buoyed by the modest payment from de Rochemont, Sturz sailed in 1954 on the *Saturnia*, which called at Lisbon, Casablanca, Barcelona, Cannes, Genoa and Rome before docking at Naples. From Ravello, after failing to connect with editors at the *New York Times*, he reported on a landslide for the *Bayonne Times:* "The survivors are stunned, quiet, and beginning the impossible job of clearing debris. There is no weeping, no philosophizing."

In Positano, he was smitten with a woman he met in a bar. He saw her again a few days later at a chamber music concert and introduced himself. She was Elizabeth Lyttleton, a Texas-born former circus acrobat, aspiring poet and the divorced mother of a nine-year-old daughter, Anna. "He was standing in the door of the bar," Elizabeth recalls. "It was like a thunderbolt."

While Sturz was in Positano, Steinbeck and his wife were visiting the Amalfi coast. Sturz sent him a note. "He invited us down for a chat, coffee," Sturz recalled. The two couples met in a café. Steinbeck gave Sturz the name of his literary agent.

Herb and Elizabeth, who would marry in 1958, moved to a tiny Andalusian village on the Malaga coast, still scarred by the civil war and reverberating with "the cry of the blood-soaked ground, the whispering of ashes." They would spend fourteen months in the village they called La Farola—Spanish for streetlight—researching what Sturz would later call a nonfiction novel. It had begun as a dispassionate assessment of the regime of Generalissimo Francisco Franco drawn from interviews with local fishermen and from the gray notebooks Sturz and Lyttleton gave them to use as diaries. As they did their research, the couple were defying the Spanish authorities, who tried their best, as Sturz put it, "to prevent any light being shed upon the miseries of the poor."

As Sturz and Lyttleton later wrote, their path "led into the lairs of every caste and class, and branched into the district and provincial capitals, into churches, convents, schools, hospitals, clinics, jails, prisons and brothels." Subjected to daily interrogations by the secret police, they faced a moral dilemma: whether they could betray and abandon the people whose confidences they'd secured or continue to misrepresent their true intentions. In the end, the couple was left with little choice other than to lie to the authorities and, as they saw it, "cultivate friendships among informers, torturers and murderers."

A London tabloid published their work, which appeared as a novel, *Reapers of the Storm,* in 1958. In the *New York Times Book Review,* Herbert Matthews wrote that *Reapers of the Storm* portrayed the region's grinding poverty without becoming "sentimental or shrill," and the *New York Herald Tribune*'s reviewer invoked Dostoevsky. In the *New Statesman,* V. S. Pritchett called *Reapers of the Storm* "an intimate and concentrated" analysis of social conditions, an account rendered authentic because the authors "listened and listened" and "at the point where most foreigners turn away, they have diligently pushed the matter further."

Eventually, they returned to the United States, where Sturz sought full-time work. He joined the staff of *Boys' Life,* the national Boy Scouts magazine. On his own time he wrote a get-out-the-vote pamphlet for John F. Kennedy's 1960 presidential campaign and drafted a speech for Kennedy proposing a Youth Service Corps.

With the nation still gripped by the paranoia engendered by Joe McCarthy, Sturz conceived and drafted the text of an illustrated *Boys' Life* supplement, an accessible, richly nuanced series that examined and championed the Bill of Rights for a new generation of Americans. Published as "America's Heritage: The Bill of Rights," it received the American Bar Association's Silver Gavel award, was translated into several languages and distributed around the world by the United States Information Agency. Ultimately "America's Heritage: The Bill of Rights" led the thirty-year-old editor to an eccentric millionaire émigré from Ukraine, who would become Sturz's first benefactor.

If John Steinbeck was the first person to take Sturz seriously, Louis Schweitzer was the first to invest in Sturz's uncanny talent to think an idea through to fruition. Their first collaboration, a proposed foundation for youth, was, more or less, a flop—long on good intentions, though considerably shorter on concrete, measurable and attainable goals. The good intentions, however, would eventually prevail. A second project, inspired by Schweitzer's concern about the shocking disconnect between Sturz's utopian vision of the Eighth Amendment ("Excessive bail shall not be required, nor excessive fines imposed, nor cruel and unusual punishments inflicted") and the everyday realities of making bail, would not only produce fundamental reform in record time but would become the model for a durable and ingenious framework for social engineering and entrepreneurship.

Chapter 2

Boys' Life
Goes to Jail

On April 3, 1959, Vito Genovese, a New York Mafia don and the boss of the Genovese crime family, was convicted in federal court of narcotics conspiracy charges. The prosecutor demanded that Genovese await his sentencing in jail, but three days later, a judge released Genovese on $150,000 bail. That same day, Big John Ormento, a fugitive who had evaded the authorities for nine months before arrest in the same conspiracy case, pleaded with a judge to halve his $150,000 bail. When his bail was reduced to $100,000, he left the Manhattan courtroom muttering that he could "never make it," only to return fifteen minutes later with his lawyer to post bail.

A few months later in a Bronx courtroom, a lawyer charged with attacking his estranged twenty-three-year-old girlfriend with lye was released after making bail of $105,000, which, at the time, was said to be the highest ever posted for an individual in a Bronx criminal case. The lawyer, Burton Pugach of Scarsdale, had pleaded not guilty. The victim, a secretary, was left blinded in one eye, her sight severely impaired in the other. The bond cost Pugach $3,210, which he guaranteed with real estate and securities. (Bail and bond are often used interchangeably. Bail is typically paid in cash; bond is a guarantee from a bonding company that a defendant will appear.)

Not long after, two members of the Gallo gang were arrested in Brooklyn, charged with collateral damage in gang warfare with rivals over control of jukebox and vending machine operations. The charges included the shooting of a police officer, the murder of one gangster and the garroting of another, but the judge was persuaded not only to release the two, who were in their thirties, on bail, but to reduce their bond from $25,000 to $10,000. They were released until their trial.

At the same time, two teenagers were being held in the Brooklyn House of Detention, unable to make minimal bail. One, a seventeen-year-old, was accused of armed robbery. The other, eighteen, was charged with grand theft auto. Ultimately the armed robbery case was dismissed, and the second young man was eventually acquitted, but both spent more than a year in jail awaiting trial.

The cases may be extreme examples of unequal justice, but they were not aberrations. In 1961, some 118,000 men and women were held in detention jails in New York City awaiting trial or the disposition of charges against them because they were unable to make bail. That's more than twice the number who were actually incarcerated after they were sentenced. Nearly a thousand of the detainees were behind bars for more than six months. And at the Brooklyn House of Detention, a maximum-security lockup for males between sixteen and twenty-one, the average wait behind bars before trial was forty-five days.

It didn't take a constitutional lawyer to identify a disconnect between the Sixth Amendment, guaranteeing "speedy" trial, and the Eighth Amendment, guarding against "excessive" bail, that had been idealized in Herb Sturz's illustrated supplement in *Boys' Life* and their everyday application in America's courts. Accompanied by a vivid drawing of a nearly naked prisoner hanging by the heels, illustrating the kind of cruel and unusual punishment banned in the Eighth Amendment, "America's Heritage: The Bill of Rights" informed its young readers that "prisoners, both those convicted and those waiting trial, were housed in filthy underground caverns." The Eighth Amendment declared that "excessive bail shall not be required," but, as the supplement pointed out, that safeguard applied only to federal courts, because the framers of the Constitution were determined not to usurp states' rights: "State courts were allowed to make their own decisions on how much bail was 'excessive'!"

———

The concept of bail originated as a practical necessity centuries ago in the development of English common law. Judges usually did not preside full time or in fixed places, so the potentially lengthy intervals between arrest and trial proved to be a burden not only on the accused, whether they were presumed innocent or not, but also on the local authorities who were footing the bill for their imprisonment. As a pragmatic, cheaper alternative to burdensome incarceration, the Anglo-Saxons devised a surety system under which a relative or friend would offer up valuable goods as a guarantee that the defendant would satisfy the system's primary goal at that point in judicial procedure: that he would return for trial. The system was built on trust, not on any legal guarantee that if the accused fled and the friend forfeited the goods he would be reimbursed.

In the United States, a more mobile, rootless society, bail evolved into a profit-making business. Trust was still implicit in the transaction, but an intermediary might play a greater role than the judge in determining whether the accused was a "good" financial risk and would be indemnified by an insurance company if he fled.

Concerns about inequities in the system had been percolating at least since the 1920s, when Arthur Lawton Beeley identified flaws in Chicago's bail procedures. In the 1950s, Professor Caleb Foote and his students at the University of Pennsylvania Law School found similar gaps in the idealized vision of the Sixth and Eighth Amendments and the manner in which they were being implemented daily in the courts of Philadelphia and New York. Their studies revealed similar conditions in both cities.

Being released usually meant putting up only $1 for each $10 in bail set by a judge. But in New York, Foote found, more than a fourth of defendants could not even afford $500 bail. Nearly half could not make bail of $1,500, and almost two-thirds were unable to advance the roughly $250 they needed to make $2,500 bail.

The Constitution, after all, did not define what was meant by "speedy" trial or "excessive" bail in the eighteenth century, much less in the twentieth or twenty-first. But it was becoming increasingly apparent that many judges were determining bail solely on the basis of a defendant's charges and record, not necessarily on the likelihood that he would flee, and that some were employing it preventively, to keep defendants from committing additional crimes, or as punishment. Bail policy primarily affected people gripping the lowest rungs of the economic ladder, who were presumed innocent but were nevertheless being punished for being arrested. The policy was set at the very top of the criminal justice system.

On February 15, 1961, Justice William J. Brennan Jr. of the United States Supreme Court warned that the high court itself was failing to sufficiently protect individuals against the abuse of power by states in criminal prosecutions and was letting the principles of federalism dilute the Bill of Rights beyond the First Amendment. "Far too many cases come from the states to the Supreme Court," he said, "presenting dismal pictures of official lawlessness, illegal search and seizure, illegal detention attended by prolonged interrogation and coerced admission of guilt, denial of counsel and downright brutality."

Brennan spoke at New York University Law School, where he delivered the James Madison Lecture on the Constitution and the Bill of Rights, a series that had just been permanently endowed by a gift from a Ukrainian émigré named Louis Schweitzer.

———

Louis Schweitzer, by his own definition, was an oddball. He was also a millionaire. "Sure, I'm eccentric," he once shrugged. "If you're poor, you're only crazy." Schweitzer, who had been brought to the United States from Europe at the age of four, was schooled as a chemical engineer. He inherited a fortune from his father, whose company manufactured cigarette paper, and presided over the company after it merged with Kimberly-Clark in 1955.

He was serious about the business and about his other passions, which, arguably, produced a greater return to society. But he was also blessed with a whimsical view of the world, one that as a millionaire he was in a position to indulge. He and his wife, the Off-Broadway producer Lucille Lortel, lived most of the year in a suite at the Plaza Hotel (and later in the Sherry-Netherland) in New York.

They spent a month or more in late winter on their two-story, eighty-by-thirty-foot houseboat anchored off Miami Beach, which a Havana hotel owner had spirited out of Cuba a few weeks before Fidel Castro closed the country's ports. The living room walls were bedecked with *Playbill* theater programs, which, Lortel said, made her "feel close to Sardi's."

He helped his wife create the White Barn Theater on their estate in Westport, Connecticut, and bought her the Theatre De Lys in Greenwich Village as a wedding anniversary gift. A legendary revival of *The Threepenny Opera* by Bertolt Brecht and Kurt Weill opened there in 1955, starring Weill's widow, Lotte Lenya, and ran nearly seven years.

Because of that long run, Lortel was wondering whether she should have a chauffeur to ferry her to and from the theater downtown, but Schweitzer found a more ingenious solution. One of his secretaries came to the office one day and announced that she had been driven downtown by a cabbie with the providential name of Louis Schweitzer. Lortel's husband decided to buy the driver a gray Mercedes, purchased a taxi medallion for $17,000 and agreed to split the earnings with the cabbie if he would chauffeur Lortel to and from the theater when necessary.

The taxi was fully equipped, like any other New York City cab, except that its built-in radio could only receive WBAI-FM, which Schweitzer had bought in 1957 and later donated to Pacifica because he liked the jazz and other music and preferred public policy discussion to commercials. Another unique feature of the cab was an interior sign that advised passengers: "When in Venice, ask for the gondola Lucille." For an investment of $1,000, Louis had persuaded the venerable gondoliers' cooperative not only to breach a 450-year-old rule against outside ownership of a gondola but also to name it Lucille instead of assigning it a number, as was customary. Unable to find a gondolier named Louis Schweitzer in Venice, he settled on one named Bruno and advised him that if any of Schweitzer's American friends dropped his name while hiring the gondola, Bruno should "charge them double." In Brittany, where his company had a paper factory, he bought a one-star restaurant so he could be certain when he visited he would have someplace good to eat. Back in New York, Schweitzer also bought a shop for his favorite barber on the subway level of the Chrysler Building, to ensure that he could get his fringe of hair trimmed after hours and that the customary promise of "no waiting" would, in his case, be redeemed.

Schweitzer endowed a number of scholarships and professional awards (one, commemorating his friend, Meyer Berger, the *Times* columnist who wrote about ordinary people struggling to survive; another in honor of a New York high school teacher who dedicated her retirement to improving city government). His one self-confessed outside love interest was his passionate affair with the Bill of Rights. In the 1950s, defenders of the Bill of Rights, like Schweitzer, Herb Sturz and other civil libertarians, focused largely on the First Amendment rights to free speech, press and assembly, which, arguably, faced the greatest challenges at home during the McCarthy era. Schweitzer was also anxious about threats to the Eighth Amendment, anxiety, perhaps, rooted in the Ukrainian ghetto that his family fled when he was a child, an anxiety revived decades later at a Manhattan dinner party in 1960, when a friend told him that there were more than 1,000 boys "who had been in a Brooklyn jail ten months or more just waiting for trial."

Schweitzer was appalled. Every one of the young men was presumed innocent under the law, but they were being detained largely for one reason: They were too poor to pay private businessmen—bail bondsmen—modest sums to be released until the court system could adjudicate the accusations against them. Determined to investigate for himself, Schweitzer recruited a man half his age who shared his progressive views and had already made a modest, but unique mark in the annals of social philanthropy.

―――――

Emboldened by the astounding success of his ten-part series on the Bill of Rights, Herb Sturz decided to explore the possibility of a foundation that would address the hopes and challenges confronting American youth, youth not that much younger than himself. He began, as he put it, to look at what kids should be thinking about.

The *Boys' Life* series had opened many doors to Sturz, doors that prominent people might have been more reluctant to open a few years earlier when McCarthyism was at its height. Still, Sturz believed his tenure at *Boys' Life* was threatened because of an article he published on individualism, "The Little Yellow Dog." The article provoked a letter-writing campaign suggesting that the magazine was feeding communist propaganda to impressionable young Americans. The author of the article was Stringfellow Barr, the former president of St. John's College in Annapolis, an educator who, Arthur Schlesinger Jr. wrote backhandedly, was not a communist but rather what he called a "Typhoid Mary of the left . . . bearing the germs of the infection even if not suffering obviously from the disease." Sturz figured his days there were numbered. "I left before I was gone," he recalls.

By the end of the 1950s, American values were becoming viewed at home less as principles to be reluctantly sacrificed to preserve the nation from subversives and more as a propaganda weapon to persuade the world that American freedom was unique. Moreover, the series was published on the eve of a presidential campaign that focused increasingly on how much the nation had deviated from the visions of equality embodied by the Bill of Rights and the subsequent amendments.

It was through W. H. Ferry and Frank Kelly at Robert Hutchins's Fund for the Republic and also through the Center for the Study of Democratic Institutions in Santa Barbara (a Ford Foundation think tank created in 1951 to defend civil liberties in the overheated climate of anticommunist witch hunts) that Sturz first learned about the man who would become his philosophical soul mate. "I was thinking about creating some sort of youth foundation, but I was basically broke," he recalls. Still, Sturz had convened an impressive exploratory committee, especially impressive for a foundation with no money, the vaguest of agendas and largely the good intentions of a twenty-nine-year-old associate editor. The Youth Foundation advisers included the anthropologist Margaret Mead; the Columbia and Amherst College historian Henry Steele Commager; Senator Harrison Williams, a New Jersey Democrat; Dorothy Pope, head of the American Red Cross and *New York Times* correspondent Harrison Salisbury.

To raise money for travel expenses and to rent a room for the exploratory meeting, Ferry and Kelly referred Sturz to Schweitzer. Their first meeting was not promising. Chain-smoking and gruff, Schweitzer fired questions at Sturz but finally wrote a check for $500. Good intentions, even coupled with $500, weren't enough. It would be one of the few times in his life Sturz had embarked on a project without a definable goal. Nothing came of it. Not long after, Schweitzer begrudgingly granted Sturz a second audience. Sturz delivered an accounting of how Schweitzer's grant was spent before returning $250, the unused portion.

Schweitzer was stunned. "I assumed you were just coming back to ask for more," he said.

Louis Schweitzer was also impressed. When he decided to see for himself whether that appalling story about boys languishing in detention cells for months was merely uninformed dinner party gossip or really horrifically factual, it was no surprise that he recruited Herb Sturz to investigate.

Chapter 3

The Feminine Form of True

The wave of crime and what was quaintly called juvenile delinquency in the wake of World War II was inundating the nation's jails and prisons by the late 1950s. During the 1930s, America's prisons and jails generally housed fewer than 200,000 inmates. Less than thirty years later, the number of those incarcerated was approaching 350,000. In 1945, about 43,000 people a year were sent to jail in New York City alone, but by 1959, the number soared to 111,000, and jails were often as much as 142 percent above their quoted capacity. With the increasingly unyielding municipal budget stretched close to the breaking point by demands for schools and other services for burgeoning baby boomers, the prison population was booming, too, with no end in sight.

In the ten years after 1947, the city's prison rolls rose a total of 5 percent. Between 1957 and 1959, the number of inmates increased by 10 percent. Beginning in 1960, however, the prison population was rising at an annual rate of 20 percent. No expansion program that was remotely

affordable could close the gap. Moreover, diverting precious city revenues to pay for housing and feeding inmates—
instead of hiring teachers and health professionals to help
contain a polio epidemic and expanding the police force—
was just one drawback of the exploding prison population.
To make matters worse, New York City was the only place
in the state required to house prisoners sentenced to as
long as a year instead of transferring them to state institutions. The Board of Correction, the City Bar Association
and the New York County Lawyers Association wondered
whether freeing some defendants without bail would be
preferable.

In the 1950s, Mayor Robert F. Wagner's reformist correction commissioner, Anna M. Kross, was still concerned
about conditions within the prison system and with what
would happen to inmates after they were handed a sandwich and a quarter and returned without any other support
to society upon their release. Overcrowding and idleness
bred tension and violence. Failure to provide remedial education and vocational services all but guaranteed high
rates of recidivism. Segregating adolescents from hard-core
adult inmates, another of Kross's goals, was sometimes
complicated and expensive.

The nearly 1,000 teenagers incarcerated in the Brooklyn House of Detention were held, on average, forty-five
days before trial, but in some cases far longer (the average
was distorted by the one in four detainees released on bail
the day of their arrest). Nearly 20 percent of those inmates had been attending school at the time of arrest. One
twenty-year-old with a history of drug addiction was arrested over the summer for petty larceny and remanded to
Rikers Island, the city's primary prison complex, for violat-
ing parole. He completed his term the following April, but
because the larceny charge had not been adjudicated, he

was transferred to the Brooklyn House of Detention. After awaiting trial for four months, he was released when his mother enlisted a lawyer who had won acquittals for four young men held without trial for up to a year.

When Schweitzer and Sturz visited the Brooklyn House of Detention and the Men's House of Detention in Lower Manhattan, or, as it was known, the Tombs, they were shocked by the Dickensian squalor: the filth, the stench, the overcrowding and the pervasive sense of despair and degradation among people whom the system presumed were innocent. No telephone calls were allowed; detainees could only pass along messages to guards who would make, perhaps, one call a day for them. Rikers Island offered little to justify its designation as a correctional facility. "Temporary" detention facilities offered even less. Some schooling was provided for teenagers at the Brooklyn House of Detention—Puerto Rican inmates were taught English and "American customs"—but too much of their education came informally from hardened criminals. Visiting a crowded day room in the Brooklyn House of Detention with Anna Kross, Schweitzer asked whether any inmates were younger than sixteen. Several raised their hands. New state laws and city policies supposedly separated adolescent inmates from adults. Schweitzer and Sturz regularly witnessed intermingling. Mix-ups happen, Kross explained.

Nobody expected a prison to be pristine, and even some prison reformers had praised Kross's earnest efforts to improve the system she inherited. Nobody assumed a bureaucracy that processed 60,000 people a year—including nearly 13,000 classified as juveniles—would operate flawlessly. Still, after touring what Kross too cavalierly called her "little hotel," Schweitzer and Sturz left convinced that something drastic needed to be done. Not only was bail unevenly applied, its consequences tipped the scales even further against defendants. Some of the costs of being trapped in this inescapable legal limbo were obvious: dissolution of personal and family relationships, interrupted schooling, loss of jobs and income and even housing. Some other, more startling correlations would be confirmed as Sturz probed more deeply.

In December 1960, before leaving for a vacation on his Florida houseboat, Schweitzer offered Sturz the opportunity of a lifetime: to immerse himself in New York's criminal justice system, designing an intensive, personalized, step-by-step post-postgraduate curriculum that would chart the vast disparities between the Bill of Rights as proclaimed in the *Boys' Life* series and as practiced routinely on the streets, police station houses, courts and detention facilities. Sturz reported for work in January 1961 and planted himself in an alcove off Louis Schweitzer's secretary's office near where Schweitzer patiently rotated the dials and sifted through static to chat with other ham radio buffs around the world. "There was no Vera or anything else," Sturz says. "It was just me."

———

All over the country today, law enforcement officials now invoke the 1960s as a desirable benchmark, boasting that crime rates are lower than at any time since then. But even in New York, as comparatively secure as people may have felt, there was a sense that the city's proverbial good old days were already behind it. (In the 1977 mayoral campaign, an elderly woman accosted Edward I. Koch on the boardwalk in Coney Island and beseeched him to "make it like it was." Koch thought to himself, "Lady, it was never that good," but figured that it would have been impolitic to offer that perspective.) Something else was happening, too, something that made the majority of citizens even less sympathetic to the people accused, much less convicted of crime. Not only had the influx of blacks from the South and Puerto Ricans begun visibly altering the complexion of the city's population, but also they were mostly poor and, like previous waves of poor newcomers to New York, they were disproportionately likely to be perpetrators—as well as victims—of crime. The perception of who was prey to criminals was distorted further because so-called cheap crimes—committed by blacks against blacks—were largely ignored by the newspapers or relegated to passing police blotter references on the inside pages.

But these were also, potentially, the best of times for reform. Schweitzer and Sturz heard the barely audible rumble of nascent seismic upheavals that would ultimately transform American society (and subsequently produce their own backlash). For the first time since the election of 1948, Democrats had captured the White House, and the inauguration of John F. Kennedy in 1961 held out the promise that years of deferred dreams of civil rights and civil liberties might finally be realized. The New Deal's grand illusion that government could solve anything had not yet been succeeded by the cynical assumption that government could do nothing well, but a fledgling intellectual faction suggested that government was incapable of doing everything. In 1960, one surefire way to generate support for a program was still to invoke the communist menace. Anna Kross warned that prison reform deserved attention not merely for its humanitarian benefits to the individual and to society but because America's failure to administer justice fairly and equally would result in economic and social costs that the country could not afford in the global struggle against a ruthless enemy that had threatened to "bury" us.

Once they identified the system's flaws and devised potential solutions, Schweitzer and Sturz were blessed with timing. In 1962, voters would approve the most fundamental reorganization of the state court system since 1846. The courts would be unified, simplified and administered more efficiently (the Children's Courts, for example, were merged into the new Family Court, evoking former Mayor James J. Walker's memorably snarky aside that he had appointed his predecessor, John P. O'Brien, to the Children's Court so they could be judged by their peer). Individual judges would retain enormous leeway in decision making but would be subject to more universal guidelines and greater accountability and less autonomy. The reorganization created a five-member administrative board of the state courts. Schweitzer and Sturz immediately enlisted Bernard Botein, the State Supreme Court justice who presided over the courts in the First Department, which covered Manhattan and the Bronx.

"The biggest challenge confronting all the courts today is equalizing the position and resources of the poor man with that of the rich man," Botein would remind listeners in New York's criminal courts, where at least three in four defendants could not afford a lawyer. "The powerful, specifically in the criminal courts, can afford the best lawyers," Botein said. "They have no trouble raising bail and no gnawing anxieties about paying the grocery bills while awaiting the outcome of the charges against them." A radical solution to such injustice was incubating in Botein's brain, one that was planted there by the research of Professor Caleb Foote of the University of Pennsylvania Law School. What would happen if people unable to make bail but with roots in their community could be trusted to return for trial—especially since failing to do so was a crime in its own right? There were risks, of course, not only legal ones, but potential political consequences too. What if the accused was charged with a crime after he was released? What if he failed to appear in court when scheduled? How would judges get and verify background information on a defendant in order to make an informed decision? Justice Botein, his administrative role at the Appellate Division only recently enhanced, had plenty more pressing problems on his agenda. Within a matter of months, though, bail reform was elevated to a national priority, and not by a judge, a politician or even a lawyer but by a layman who insinuated himself into the legal fraternity to mitigate egregious inequities. "I was nudged by an enlightened citizen," Botein said. "Schweitzer."

————

By the time he was recruited by Louis Schweitzer, Sturz was no stranger to investigative reporting. In Spain, under surveillance by agents of the Franco regime, he and Elizabeth had listened to ordinary villagers who for years had struggled to survive against the government. In the case of New York's detention facilities, the government—its already strained budget being sapped by the costs of room, board and security for 1.8 million inmate days of detention a year—was receptive to independent scrutiny, as were the vast majority of police, court and probation officers, defense lawyers, judges, clerks, bail bondsmen, prosecutors, social workers, criminologists and accused criminals, guilty or otherwise, who were accustomed to delivering preconceived answers. Each player, often blind to the perspective of the person next to him, had his personal Rashomon vision of the criminal justice system. And each, through years of gaming the system or circumventing it, or struggling against the odds to make it minimally functional, had accumulated a trunkload of answers to questions nobody had ever thought to ask.

When bail was set at arraignment, what background information about the defendant was available to the court? How much discretion did assistant district attorneys have? What practical alternatives were weighed in the momentary respite granted in the assembly-line proceedings to consider a plea bargain? Did anyone know for certain where he lived, whether he had a job, who and where his relatives were? Did the prosecutors who requested a specific bail and the judges who imposed it know, or, for that matter, care, whether the defendant could afford it? Were they informed whether or not the defendant made bail? Justice was supposed to be blind . . . not dumb.

Sturz's strategy for bail reform was the same one he had pursued in Spain, and the formula he would hone and creatively apply for the next fifty years. His rules of engagement were deceptively simple: No one player had all the facts, each had his or her own agenda and many were confused or ill-informed, prejudiced, defensive or burdened by anachronistic conventional wisdom. He faced another handicap: He was investigating invisible men. "These guys really aren't there," U.S. Supreme Court Justice Abe Fortas said of the defendants languishing in detention, unable to make bail. "They don't exist."

"I learned that when a bail amount was set by the judge," Sturz recalls, "it was actually the bail bondsman, a private businessman, who made the unfettered, unreviewable decision as to whether, for a fee, he would post the required bail amount." Sturz also learned that decades of personal and political connections had endowed self-interested bail bondsmen with the power to hamper meaningful investigation of the process, much less to derail real reform. "If they had taken us on in our infancy they could have knocked us off," Sturz says, "but they had seen various academic studies come and go since the twelfth century. They were sure we would be gone soon."

Sturz would couple marathon personal observation with interviews, repeating the same questions to dozens of sources, evaluating his tentative insights, nailing down elusive leads, feeling the facts, testing them and finally surrounding a fully defined body of truth so, unlike the proverbial blind men, he was confident that he had discovered not only the shape and form but also the inner workings of the elephantine system he was hoping to reform.

"In looking back," he would explain years later,

> one reason Vera was successful, I think, was the inductive way of looking at life. I didn't start with an overriding format. I basically moved Vera along, learning by experience. I learned very early that most of what people tell you is to be discounted. They're either lying to protect themselves or just to sound impressive, or they don't know what they're talking about, or they've vaguely heard something or other. It's rare to get facts that you can count on. To understand the "truth," I learned to rely on my own observations. I learned quickly not to trust so-called important people and what people told you. Many will tell you anything for any reason, if only to seem important, not necessarily to deceive. I absorbed that lesson early in the game.

In February 1961, with Sturz's preliminary exploration generating more questions about the justice system than answers, Schweitzer finally offered him a full-time job at $8,000 a year. (In what turned out to be a "happy misunderstanding," Sturz recalls, Schweitzer was "a little surprised to realize I had quit my job and was showing up for work.") Schweitzer was hiring a non-lawyer with no legal training to reform the law. It was, Martin Mayer wrote in his narrative look at *The Lawyers*, "perhaps the most imaginative gesture" Schweitzer ever made.

Sturz's brief foray into bail reform had already persuaded him that it was a national issue or needed to be made into one, and that some sort of permanent mechanism outside the government was needed to address it. Schweitzer suggested they form a nonprofit foundation. They chose a neutral name without ideological baggage and vague enough to avoid having its agenda prejudged. Schweitzer called it Vera, not an acronym (although for a time, police officers derisively coined their own: the Very Easy Release Agency), but for his mother. As Sturz joked years later: "I've sometimes wondered where Vera would be today had Schweitzer's mother been named Clementine or Samantha." Fortuitously, Vera is the feminine form of "true" in Latin. Its goals, as set forth in its original certificate of incorporation, were ambitious: "To seek and further the equal protection of the laws for the indigent by research into neglected aspects of court procedures, law enforcement and the nature of crime." Schweitzer played the role of a watchful midwife, and Sturz the benevolent father of Vera and its offshoots.

Part II

The Innovator

Chapter 4

Vera's Bailiwick

Early in 1961, Vera had a single goal that seemed sufficiently intractable to consume Herb Sturz full-time. He
had received grudging to tepid cooperation during his preliminary exploration but was now inundated with suggested
solutions. He was savvy enough to know that any proposed
solution would have to be practical, within Vera's capacity
to implement, and politically marketable in a city straining
to reconcile its proud progressive tradition with a nascent
but percolating law-and-order backlash to rising crime.

At first, the most obvious solution seemed to be for
Vera to insinuate itself as a complement or even a competi-
tor to New York's 192 licensed bail bondsmen. The bondsmen, agents of a half-dozen surety companies, charged a
premium of 5 percent on the first $1,000 of bail, 4 percent
on the second $1,000 and 3 percent on each additional
$1,000. They often also insisted on collateral, in the form
of securities or savings passbooks. Good risks were considered defendants with families, long work histories and short
arrest records. The bad risks, or "lamsters," were prostitutes

(shallow roots) and drug addicts (unreliable). "If a person comes in, and I don't know him or the lawyer, we look for collateral," one bondsman, Louis Topper, confided. "If they don't have it, we don't bother with him." That knowledge, Topper explained, was how he had managed to stay in business for nearly fifty years.

The industry, in part perhaps driven by self-interest, adamantly warned Vera against underwriting its own bail fund. The potential drawbacks sounded daunting: How would Vera verify whether the defendant was, in fact, poor? Would Vera conduct an inventory of the defendant's personal property and other holdings? If the bail fund paid the premium, how would Vera persuade a defendant to return? Bondsmen and insurance agents reminded Sturz of the other risks inherent in every bail application: The hiatus between arraignment and trial often stretched to six months or more as prosecutors and defense lawyers requested adjournments; often, what was classified as bail jumping was the result of months elapsing during which the authorities might lose touch with a defendant who left town to visit a sick relative or find work. Moreover, some of the deliberate no-shows, especially teenagers, were not so much seeking to avoid prosecution as terrified by the horror stories they were fed about going to jail. Discouraged, Sturz searched for some alternative.

During the spring of 1961, Schweitzer pulled strings and wangled an appointment with Mayor Robert F. Wagner, a two-term Democrat who was seeking reelection and who, after feuding with the party's regular organization, was hoping to cloak himself in a progressive agenda. Wagner was enigmatic, a machine Democrat whose father, Senator Robert F. Wagner, had been a lion of the New Deal in Congress. Only one of his predecessors as mayor of New

York in the twentieth century had managed to get elected to three four-year terms, and Wagner, a phlegmatic figure with aspirations for higher office, was seeking not only to reinvent himself as a reformer but to position himself to fend off an expected challenge in the fall from a law-and-order Republican, the state attorney general. Wagner was scheduled for surgery but agreed to meet with Schweitzer and Sturz at Gracie Mansion, the mayor's official residence, the night before. The mayor seemed enthusiastic. He grasped the fundamental fairness of what they were trying to accomplish. He appreciated the fact that the proposed bail reform wouldn't cost his administration any money—in fact, it might save city dollars. But he was wary about the political risks. He urged them to consult more judges, the mayoral appointees and elected jurists whose job it was officially to set bail, and who were most politically likely to be held accountable if a defendant absconded or committed a crime after being released. Wagner asked the Gracie Mansion operator to connect him with the city's chief magistrate, Abraham M. Bloch. "I'm here with young Sturz," Wagner said. "I want you to talk to him about bail reform. It seems to me like a good idea." He handed the telephone to Sturz. "What a gift that was!" Sturz recalls. "The chief judge subsequently told me that it was the only time the mayor ever called him at home. About anything."

The jurist whose political judgment Wagner valued most was John M. Murtagh, the city's take-no-prisoners chief justice of the Court of Special Sessions. Murtagh's no-nonsense reputation, already cemented in New York City, would spread nationally a decade later when, presiding over hearings for thirteen Black Panthers accused in a bombing plot, he adjourned the proceedings until the defendants demonstrated a modicum of respect for the court, explaining: "I've been called a pig once too often." In spite of his unforgiving reputation, Murtagh was sympathetic to Schweitzer's argument that the bail system, as regularly practiced, "makes poverty a crime." But Murtagh expressed skepticism about Vera's proposed bail fund. After all, he said, judges were already empowered to release defendants without bail if they were good risks. The problem, Murtagh explained, was that even those judges who were inclined to do so rarely knew more than the defendant's name—and sometimes even that was dubious—and the charges lodged against him. Perhaps, Murtagh suggested, when an indigent defendant was unable to make bail Vera could intervene at that point, conduct an investigation and recommend whether or not to release him on his own recognizance.

Murtagh's suggestion was intriguing. It posed procedural challenges—hearings would have to be rescheduled if deserving defendants were too poor to make bail—and would occur later in the ordinary processing than Schweitzer and Sturz had hoped. Still, virtually no one among all the players that Sturz had interviewed favored the proposed Vera bail fund.

While using Wagner's good offices to build bridges to the judges and other constituencies in the criminal justice system whose cooperation would be required for any meaningful reform, Sturz continued to plumb the primary sources that would always constitute the foundation of his research. In a single conversation, one such source would win Sturz unexpected, potent allies and widen his vista well beyond New York. He called on Caleb Foote, the intellectual father of bail reform.

Foote, the University of Pennsylvania Law School professor, was not just another starry-eyed academic who had never seen the inside of a courtroom. As a conscientious objector, he had once been the target of prosecution himself. Throughout his career he maintained that the criminal justice system committed the worst injustices against poor and unpopular defendants at the earliest stages of prosecution. That, he once told Candace McCoy, a City University of New York professor, was "where the greatest number of people get thwacked."

Foote and his law students had found a troubling corollary to their research, one that was gaining traction among civil libertarians: There appeared to be a possible correlation not merely between poverty and the unlikelihood of being released before trial but also between ability to make bail and the likelihood of being acquitted or, if convicted, receiving a suspended or reduced sentence. In Philadelphia, Foote found that overall only about one in five detained defendants were acquitted, compared to almost half of the ones who had made bail. Among defendants who were convicted, those who had been released on bail were nearly two and a half times more likely not to be sentenced to prison. In New York, a defendant who was convicted was four times more likely to receive a suspended sentence if he had been at liberty before trial. Foote's research did not actually confirm the correlation between sentencing and release on bail. And, in fact, it was altogether possible that, for better or worse, savvy jurists intuitively imposed higher bail on defendants whom they judged more likely to be convicted. Still, it was possible, too, that detention before trial fatally compromised the accused's opportunity to defend himself. And that even a defendant who was convicted might be sentenced more leniently because, while he was awaiting trial, he had demonstrated more reliability by living with his family and returning to work. Foote recommended that Sturz contact David Bazelon, the chief judge of the U.S. Court of Appeals for the District of Columbia. Bazelon was so taken with Sturz's bail reform mission that he invited him and Schweitzer to join two friends at dinner at his home. Sturz and Schweitzer were stunned when Bazelon's friends introduced themselves: U.S. Supreme Court justices William O. Douglas and William Brennan. What impressed the jurists most was the apparent relationship between a judge's original decision about bail and the ultimate disposition of the charges.

"Here it was, 1961," Sturz recalls. "Thirty years old. It was kind of heady. Of course, I wasn't a lawyer. They said we'll each give you a former law clerk to help you think about bail reform, which they did. From there, we organized Vera." Bazelon enlisted Foote and two other law professors, Abraham Goldstein of Yale, who had been Brennan's law clerk and would become dean of the Yale Law School, and Charles Ares, Douglas's former law clerk, of New York University School of Law (and later dean of Arizona Law School). Douglas also gave Sturz some fatherly advice: As a well-intentioned layman, he should leave the major policy decisions to the experts.

But experts about bail were few and far between. Consulting with the law professors and recruiting other advisers, Sturz concluded that one reason constructive answers were in short supply was because nobody was asking the right questions. Nobody was systematically collecting and tracking data that demonstrated the impact of policies so ingrained that they were being taken for granted. And surely nobody was audacious enough to embark on a controlled experiment that could affect the fate of men and women in the criminal justice system. Again and again, Herb Sturz immersed himself and his staff in customized research that would generate an entire new discipline—in this case, the sociology of justice.

In mid-1961, Anne Rankin, who had just completed her master's thesis at Northwestern University, was installed next to Sturz in Schweitzer's ham radio cubicle (her $8,000 salary, the same as Sturz's, was paid for by a grant from the National Council on Crime and Delinquency). Her thesis was "Sociology of the Creative Artist," a subject more akin to a case study of Sturz himself than of the courts. "I knew nothing about courts," she recalled, "and Herb didn't know a whole lot more." They were both about to learn—and teach—a great deal.

Sturz soon parlayed an encounter with David Hackett, a schoolmate of Robert F. Kennedy's, into an audience with the attorney general. "I hope you'll work with other groups active in bail reform," Kennedy urged Schweitzer and Sturz. To which Hackett replied: "Mr. Kennedy, there is no one else working on bail reform." Then came an invitation to address one of the first sessions of the fledgling attorney general's Committee on Poverty and the Administration of Criminal Justice. It was known as the Allen Committee, after its chairman, Frank Allen, a professor at the University of Chicago Law School. The committee's agenda included the right to counsel, an issue that was wending its way through the federal courts (two years later, the Supreme Court would rule in *Gideon v. Wainwright* that state courts are required by the Sixth and Fourteenth Amendments to provide lawyers for criminal defendants who can't afford to hire them). Not only hadn't bail reform been a high priority of Kennedy's committee, it was barely even on the committee's agenda until Sturz made a compelling case and volunteered to deliver a detailed assessment of how the federal courts in the Southern District of New York handled bail. Of course, the data Sturz had promised to deliver didn't exist and would have to be generated expressly for the committee.

––––––

In New York, Anne Rankin agilely shifted gears. She temporarily abandoned the flow charts she had been fashioning that mapped a typical defendant's odyssey through the criminal justice minefield. Instead, she transplanted herself to the Federal Court House in lower Manhattan, where she distilled data from the court dockets, and periodically shipped it to an engineer at one of Schweitzer's paper plants in Massachusetts. There, the information was translated onto computer punch cards, programming a custom-made analysis that largely mirrored Foote's findings about the deficiencies in the state courts of New York and Philadelphia: The U.S. Commissioner set bail without sufficient information about the defendant; defense lawyers provided for indigent defendants played a minor role in determining bail and knew next to nothing about their clients; many defendants were unable to afford even modest bail; and their failure to make bail suggested a correlation with conviction at trial and a stricter sentence.

The research arrangement was a win-win for Vera and the Justice Department. For Vera, working with Washington would provide instant credibility and access to a wide range of participants in the process, from court clerks to judges. For Justice, Vera held out the promise of valuable research provided more nimbly and less defensively than by the federal bureaucracy. In addition to cementing an institutional relationship, the arrangement would pay enormous dividends to Vera for decades through Burke Marshall (then assistant attorney general for civil rights and later an architect of Lyndon Johnson's historic civil rights legislation), Nicholas deB. Katzenbach (later, attorney general under Johnson), as well as Daniel J. Freed and Jack Rosenthal— young and idealistic enlistees in Kennedy's campaign to reform the criminal justice system. Freed, Rosenthal and Sturz became fast friends. Freed, a Yale Law School graduate (like Marshall and Katzenbach), joined the Justice Department as an antitrust lawyer, but became Kennedy's liaison to the Allen Committee because of his personal commitment to its goals. Rosenthal, a Harvard graduate, was a reporter in Portland, where his articles won him the same Silver Gavel Award from the American Bar Association that Sturz had received for his *Boys' Life* series. When his mentor at the *Oregonian* learned that Kennedy was seeking a press assistant, he recommended Rosenthal. The three young reformers ritually lunched at Hammel's, a German restaurant in Washington, that functioned as what Rosenthal would call an officer's club for the Justice Department. There, they conspired to maintain the momentum for Kennedy's criminal justice agenda.

Meanwhile, Sturz learned an enduring lesson from Robert Kennedy by watching him carefully when he spoke publicly. "I would see his hands and think how nervous he seemed," Sturz recalls, "but he just went on and stayed with it."

By late summer, Sturz presented Vera's findings to the Allen Committee, coupled with several recommendations. Sturz proposed that pretrial defendants be segregated from convicted criminals in correctional institutions, that time served in detention be deducted from sentences upon conviction and that a pretrial officer investigate the defendant's background to enable the U.S. Commissioner to make an informed decision about bail. That last recommendation heralded Vera's Manhattan Bail Project.

"It was the first time anyone looked at criminal justice as a system," Rosenthal says. "Herb was in the forefront of this in New York. He saw individual wrongs and created better programs to try to rectify them. The systematic nature became evident to him."

On October 11, 1961, Mayor Wagner announced that under Vera's auspices, New York University law students, privately funded by the Ford Foundation and Louis Schweitzer, would conduct a one-year analysis of bail procedures in the city's Court of Special Sessions and the Magistrates Felony Court. The four paragraphs that constituted Vera's first mention in the *New York Times* were appropriately modest for an organization that had a zero track record, except for producing a single study for the Justice Department that was unusually informative, influential and completed on time. But, within a matter of months, it would become apparent to everyone—even to Sturz, who was terrified that Vera had overreached and would collapse in an embarrassing failure—that the brief mention in the *Times* had not begun to do the organization justice.

———

If the purpose of bail was to ensure that a defendant would return for trial, Sturz and Charles Ares reasoned that wealth was a poor predictor of flight. After all, a defendant with the resources to make high bail might also be rich enough to forfeit his bond. Was there a more reliable measure? More and more, Sturz gravitated toward relying on community ties. But how could the court quantify the emotional and personal cost for a defendant to skip bail? What constituted the most consistently reliable criteria? Could that information be collected quickly? Could it be easily verified? Would it prove dependable? Anne Rankin synthesized a four-page questionnaire that assessed forty criteria, including the defendant's home address, how long he had lived there, whether he was married, had children, supported his family, his job tenure, how much he made, whether he had served in the military, was a member of a union, had any savings or debts, had ever been arrested before, the disposition of that case and if there was a clergyman, employer, relative, creditor who would vouch for him.

Sturz concluded that the most opportune window for Vera to intervene in a bail decision was at arraignment, usually the day after arrest, when the original charges are formally presented and the defendant has the first opportunity to enter a plea. The window is only open a crack, though. Defendants usually arrive at the courthouse from police precinct station houses around nine A.M., and the assembly-line arraignments, lasting moments each, begin about an hour later. Sturz corralled a $110,000 grant from the Ford Foundation and recruited a half-dozen night students from NYU Law at $80 a week to conduct interviews and verify information. They were installed in a two-room office on the thirteenth floor of 100 Centre Street, the Criminal Courts building adjoining the Tombs.

On the second floor, one floor above the courtroom, a cell next to the detention pen was reserved for Vera's interviewers. It was cramped, standing room only. After being briefed on the purpose of the project, most of the defendants who were then invited to be interviewed readily accepted. And most of the correction and court officers, whose opposition could have proved fatal, cooperated.

The forty-question survey took about fifteen minutes. If the interviewer concluded that release on recognizance was warranted, the questionnaire would be rushed upstairs for substantiation by Vera's aggressive and resourceful "verification virtuosos." Virtuosos or not, they were without computers and stuck with primitive instruments like reverse telephone directories that listed people by address. Alternatively, verifiers rushed down to the courtroom to find the defendant's relatives and out into the field to find an employer or landlord or any other responsible party willing to attest to the information on the questionnaire. Within about an hour, Sturz and the staff would weigh whether the defendant's score on Rankin's scale of rootlessness measured against the severity of the charges and prior record merited a recommendation for release on his own recognizance. If the answer was yes, the staff would type out a one-page summary for the judge, the assistant district attorney and the defense lawyer. It did not take long for the process to become so routinized that the judge would automatically ask for the typed Vera recommendation if it had not already been placed before him. "The main thing we've done is to introduce the system to fact finding," Sturz says. "With facts, we can open up options."

One such option, with the bail project on the way to success, was for Sturz to replace himself as director, beginning a pattern that he would repeat again and again as each Vera spin-off started to mature and show promise. (In this case, he hired Roger Baron, who had started as an interviewer while studying for the bar exam and who would manage the bail project until the city took it over in 1965.)

"You don't get trapped running something," Jack Rosenthal says. "You demonstrate its viability."

———

Sturz's goals were clear and well-articulated. His experiment was tailored to be feasible, measurable and replicable. And, before even announcing the project, much less beginning to test his hypothesis, he had tenaciously enlisted every constituent in the court system—and, therefore, every potential critic—as stakeholders in the outcome. Sturz was unabashedly liberal, and Vera's credo was "equal justice under law," but the bail project wasn't promoted as integral to some bleeding heart agenda—even if the political climate in the new decade had thawed some from the chilly 1950s. Rather, he billed it as a pragmatic approach, one that might well make the system more equitable but could also benefit the taxpaying public. Regardless of whether critics shared the bail project's objectives, most professionals agreed that the experiment's empirical design promised a measurable test. At first the defendant pool would be limited to adults too poor to afford private lawyers and exclude problematic defendants charged with sale or possession of narcotics, murder, forcible rape, any sex offenses against children and assaults on cops. The defendants would be randomly divided into an experimental group (for which recommendations were made to the court and the outcomes recorded) and a control group (for which no bail recommendations were made, but for which the outcomes would also be monitored).

Vera's Manhattan Bail Project showed promise almost from the start. With astounding speed, it was elevated to poster child for a national movement. But the reviews were not unanimous. Some lawyers resented Vera's "interference" with their clients (including a pregnant mother of two who had never been arrested before and who, unable to make bail, had already spent two months in jail). Some bail bondsmen complained that the project was skimming off the best risks and leaving them with the worst gambles. And some of the Vera workers were nonplussed by the rigid confines of the experiment: that some of the defendants whom they identified as good risks were dumped into the control group; and that the failure to make a recommendation on bail—because of insufficient staff or the inability to complete the verification on time—would prejudice the judge's disposition. But, generally, the benefits of the project were a no-brainer.

Take the case of a twenty-five-year-old laborer who was arrested for carrying a machete. Vera was still verifying his background when the presiding judge set bail at $500, well beyond the man's means. When a Vera worker completed his investigation later that day, it was determined that the man made $64 a week, lived with his family, had served in the army and supplied references from his boss. The judge recalled the defendant to court.

"Did the officer making the arrest say why this man was carrying the machete?" the judge asked the assistant district attorney.

"No, your honor," the prosecutor replied.

The judge reversed himself and released the man on his own recognizance.

As naysayers had predicted, the most challenging aspect of ensuring that defendants would appear at trial was keeping them informed of the dates that they were due in court. While that sometimes required aggressive follow-through, typically no-shows resulted from illness and miscommunication in a bureaucracy where the volume of cases, the meting out of justice largely by rote and the anonymity and preconceptions of the individuals involved did not make for a people-friendly atmosphere. Sturz insisted that the follow-up telephone calls and home visits to defendants did not threaten the project's experimental integrity. The hypothesis being tested was whether a bail system that discriminated against poor people was the only way to guarantee defendants would appear at trial—not whether people would return entirely on their own. And if they returned as regularly as defendants who were granted

bail and financially able to make bail, the modest investment in verification and follow-up was more than offset by
the savings to society and to the affected families from
avoiding detention.

Because of the ordinary delay between arrest and disposition, the results were slow in coming. After eleven
months, statisticians compiled a sample of more than 700
cases where defendants' roots were sufficiently verified by
Vera workers to qualify them to be released on their own
recognizance. Of those 700, a total of 363 received a Vera
recommendation for release. Judges released 59 percent, or
215, of them. In the control group of nearly the same number, only 14 percent were released. Only three of the defendants released after Vera recommendations failed to appear.
The results demonstrated two conclusions: that the appearance rate was higher than it typically is for defendants
released on money bail; and that 164 defendants who
might have otherwise been detained were spared, saving
taxpayers money and better enabling the defendants to
prepare their defense.

In fact, among those cases that were fully adjudicated
after eleven months, the differences were striking between
defendants who had remained in jail pending trial and those
who were released on their own recognizance. Among
those who had been detained, only 23 percent were acquitted or the charges against them were dismissed. Among
those who had been released, 59 percent were exoner-
ated. A similar disparity prevailed even after conviction.
Among all those who were convicted, fully 96 percent of
those who had awaited trial in detention facilities were
sentenced to prison. Only 21 percent of the released defendants were imprisoned after conviction.

A subsequent analysis of all 135 cases that were closed
in the first eleven months of the project yielded even more

disturbing results. About half of the 135 had been detained pending trial. But only nine of the 135 were convicted and sentenced to prison. Which meant that the chances of a defendant being incarcerated were greater before trial, when they were presumed to be innocent.

Like Caleb Foote's earlier study, though, the Vera results suggested a correlation between the initial decision on bail and the final disposition of the case, but did not necessarily prove cause and effect. Anne Rankin decided to try. Starting with the 700 defendants who had not been released on their own recognizance, she then measured them against three other variables: whether the defendant had been convicted before; whether a private lawyer was representing him; and whether bail was over $500. If all three variables were favorable, defendants rarely were held in bail or imprisoned upon conviction. If none of those variables were favorable, the decisions about bail and sentencing were typically more severe. When Rankin parsed those categories further she reached what for a public policy experiment was considered a reasonably definitive conclusion: Defendants who were released on bail for any period of time before the disposition of a case were less likely to be sentenced to prison upon conviction. Vera's claim that nearly half of those released on their own recognizance were not convicted might have overstated the experiment's success. "I'm not naïve enough to believe that that percentage of the defendants hadn't done anything at all," Sturz acknowledges. "But some of them weren't guilty—not of anything criminal, anyway, or of what they were charged with."

The *New York Times* pronounced the bail project a successful "experiment in human trust." So successful that, even before anything more than preliminary figures had been tabulated, confident court officials expanded the experiment to the Women's House of Detention in Greenwich Village. Botein, the presiding justice, described the results as so compelling that they demanded a complete reacculturation—"a conditioning of judges, lawyers and, most of all, the public to the fact that our society will not collapse if, now and then, a person released without bail fails to appear for trial. Our society has not collapsed when persons who furnished bail failed to appear—'took it on the lam.'" Then Botein offered some advice to his fellow judges that—given the fact they were either appointed by an elected official or had to submit themselves to the voters— was easier for him to offer than to force them to follow. "Our judges must be encouraged not to try to play it utterly safe," he said. "They should not be fearful that, if they make a mistake in a rare case, they are going to be pounced on by the bar and the newspapers." They would be, though, of course. A pattern of lenient bail decisions—mistakes or not—would prompt police officers to derisively dub Justice Bruce Wright as "Cut 'em Loose Bruce" and define Vera itself as an acronym for the "Very Easy Release Agency"—a disparaging nickname that would return to haunt one of its spin-offs in a notorious case in 1977.

In 1964, building on the rave reviews for the bail project in Manhattan and on the alliances Sturz had continued to forge with the Kennedy administration, Vera and Attorney General Kennedy cosponsored a National Conference on Bail and Criminal Justice in Washington. Justice footed most of the bill, and Daniel J. Freed and Patricia M. Wald, who would later be appointed chief judge of the U.S. Court of Appeals for the District of Columbia Circuit, prepared a background briefing. About 450 judges, prosecutors, police and court officials and bail bondsmen attended the conference. Chief Justice Earl Warren delivered the keynote speech. On the basis of Vera's monitoring,

Justice Botein declared that the American bail system had devolved into "an instrument of oppression." Kennedy himself proclaimed the system "not only cruel but illogical" and said whether a defendant remains in custody pending trial usually depends on only one factor. "That factor is not guilt or innocence," he said. "It is not the nature of the crime. It is not the character of the defendant. That factor simply is money."

And, Kennedy continued, Schweitzer and Sturz had helped make society more sensitive to the growing concern among people "who want to ensure that the scales of our legal system weigh justice, not wealth." (The attorney general had just come from a graveside service for his brother at Arlington National Cemetery and recalled: "That was one thing that so concerned President Kennedy, how one man can make a difference to a community.") Eight of the nine United States Supreme Court Justices attended the opening session. "I helped write the chief justice's speech," Sturz says. Rosenthal drafted Kennedy's speech, including a line that Sturz would find appropriate: "'There should not be a Department of Prosecution; there should truly be a Department of Justice.' That," Rosenthal recalls, "was the beginning of a criminal justice revolution in the department."

In the shockingly short time that bail was placed on the national agenda, advocates for making the system fairer and more efficient could point to some progress. Experiments like New York's were being conducted in Washington, Des Moines, St. Louis, Chicago and San Francisco. In just the one year since Kennedy had directed federal prosecutors to emphasize release without bail when warranted, he said, the proportion of federal criminal defendants released on their own recognizance without bail had tripled to nearly one in five. Of the 6,000 released, 2.5 percent were no-shows for subsequent court dates—about the same as under the bail system. And two weeks before the bail conference convened, Senators Sam Ervin, Democrat of North Carolina, and Roman Hruska, Republican of Nebraska, introduced legislation to ensure that no one charged with a federal crime "shall be denied bail solely because of his financial inability to give bond or provide collateral security."

The national conference coincided with another significant benchmark for the Manhattan Bail Project. It was deemed so successful that it graduated from the experimental stage to a permanent fixture in the courts. The control group was scrapped, eliminating an early point of contention in the project because half the defendants eligible for release without bail were not receiving Vera recommendations. By mid-1964, Vera workers had interviewed around 10,000 defendants and recommended 4,000 of them for release. Of the 2,200 or so who had been released without bail, the proportion of no-shows was 0.7 percent—less than one fourth the typical rate when money bail was imposed.

Roger Baron and his bail project workers also tweaked the eligibility qualifications, drawing on their successes and failures to refine the criteria and to systematize them. The gut instinct of individual Vera workers was elevated to an explicit point system, both to avoid inconsistencies by the staff and to insulate them against hostile jurists and prosecutors who might accuse the workers of making arbitrary judgments. If it suggested a false precision—some other variable might prove more compelling in an individual case and the scores were only as valid as the verification of the underlying facts—then the scale was no less reliable either than intuitive guesswork that governed non-Vera arraignments. The scale was divided into four categories (prior record; family ties; jobs or school; residence and other) and ranged in points (1 for no convictions; minus 2 for three or more misdemeanors or two or more felonies; 3 if a defendant lived a year or more at the same address; 1 if he was older than sixty-five). Some cases were unique, of course, but the rating system covered the vast majority. To qualify for a release recommendation, a defendant had to score at least five points. Four decades later, the same framework—with somewhat more weight placed on prior record—was still in place.

"This application of a scientific basis for assessing reliability, ultimately called the 'Vera Point Scale,' was revolutionary," says Jeremy Travis, a Vera pioneer who became head of the federal Bureau of Criminal Justice Statistics and later the president of John Jay College of Criminal Justice of the City University of New York. "The use of a controlled experiment to test the efficacy of the point system—an experiment that showed that the connectedness of poor defendants to their social networks was as important in predicting their return to court as money bail for defendants with resources—established a new way of testing justice reforms and became the defining characteristics of later Vera initiatives."

Within just a few years, the bail project had transformed itself into a courtroom fixture. It was expanded to the courts in all five boroughs and became so integral to the process that New York City government paid Vera the ultimate compliment: By 1965, the pre-arraignment interview process was incorporated into the city's probation department.

Roger Baron, meanwhile, reinvented himself, evolving overnight from an administrator into a national missionary for bail reform. Vera workers went on the road as facilitators, trainers and finally evaluators as scores of jurisdictions strove to replicate the Manhattan Bail Project's successes in reducing overcrowding and budgets for detention facilities and in making the imposition of bail fairer. Baron preached bail reform across the country, in cities big and small. In Plattsburgh, New York, on Lake Champlain, the city's entire criminal court caseload was handled by a single judge. Baron explained the pre-arraignment process, then interviewed several prisoners who were awaiting arraignment. He returned to the judge with his verified reports. "Now what?" the judge asked. To which Baron replied, "You call them in, set a return date and let them go." In Plattsburgh, the bail project was launched the day it was considered.

That same year, Botein calculated, 25,000 defendants had been released through 60 bail projects around the country. Of those, he said, only 400, or 1.6 percent, had not returned for trial. Bail reform was implemented by statewide legislation or administrative court decisions in Alabama, Alaska, Connecticut, Delaware, Florida, Illinois, Maryland, Michigan, Minnesota, New Jersey, Ohio, Pennsylvania, Oregon, Texas and Virginia. Beyond the United States, bail reform was introduced in Canada and London, where Vera would form a partnership with the British.

Public apprehension about rising crime was deepening and the debate generated by reformers over concerns about fairness for indigent defendants was beginning to detour down a decidedly different avenue: to a discussion about fairness for potential victims. In one sense, bail reform opened the door to serious consideration of preventive detention. During the Senate debate over Sam Ervin's bill, many critics of the existing system were recommending that the absolute right to bail be rescinded so that release before trial was solely at the judge's discretion.

In 1966, denouncing the "arbitrary cruelty" of bail practices and a system that weighted the scales of justice for two centuries "not with fact nor law nor mercy" but with money and declaring that from then on defendants would be "considered as individuals, not as dollar signs," President Lyndon B. Johnson signed the federal bail reform bill. In cases not subject to the death penalty, the legislation established a presumption for release without bail. Among the 200 guests in the East Room of the White House, Johnson singled out "one man's outrage against injustice." That man was Louis Schweitzer. Not far away from Schweitzer, but deliberately out of the limelight, stood Herb Sturz.

Five years after the White House ceremony, the Justice Department researched the impact of all the legislation and court directives on actual bail practices. Of twenty major cities surveyed, all but Boston registered dramatic reductions in pretrial detention. In felony cases, the rate had plummeted from 52 percent to 33 percent; in misdemeanors, from 40 percent to 28 percent. Detention had decreased across the board in the sample cities, suggesting that the impact of the Vera-inspired debate about bail had been profound. Although some states eliminated the role of bondsmen and allowed defendants to deposit 10 percent or so of the face value of bail directly with the court, most did not. Their caseload dipped only slightly. Overall a greater proportion of defendants failed to appear for scheduled court dates, but the same was true of those who jumped bail. While no jurisdiction matched the high appearance rates achieved by the Manhattan Bail Project, the failure-to-appear rate in the 1971 sample—defined, perhaps loosely, as those defendants missing for more than eight days—was about 5 percent for felonies and misdemeanors regardless of whether a defendant had been released on his own recognizance or on money bail.

The impact of Kennedy's directive and the 1966 legislation on the federal courts was even more profound. In 1965, about one in five defendants were released without bail. By 1967, three in five were.

"In sheer volume," Judge Botein wrote in 1966, "probably never before in our legal history has so substantial a movement for reform in the law taken place in so short a time."

———

"The average man who is arrested once will be arrested seven times," James Q. Wilson, the Harvard government professor, warned in the 1960s. With all the social services available to potential miscreants, few programs were directed at people when they were arrested or accused of a crime. Vera's Manhattan Court Employment Project sought to satisfy the need. Its goal was to intervene immediately, offer counseling and job opportunities and, if the defendant cooperated, persuade the prosecutor and the judge to dismiss the charges before the case was adjudicated to the point of determining guilt.

The process largely mirrored the Manhattan Bail Project. A screening team would interview the defendant and review his background. If he were deemed eligible and he and his lawyer agreed, project staff would ask the prosecutor to request a ninety-day adjournment and release without bail. If the defendant maintained a constructive relationship with project counselors, when he returned to court after ninety days, the prosecutor would ask that charges be dismissed. Otherwise, a further adjournment might be requested. If the intervention was deemed unsuccessful, the case would be returned to the calendar.

Vera, like Sturz, had already gained a reputation for integrity, professionalism and for being nonideological and generous if and when there was any credit to be claimed. "There is no question," the project's director wrote, "that sponsorship of the project by the Vera Institute of Justice was a deciding factor in our gaining entrée to the court and related agencies. Confidence in Vera inspired them to give us the benefit of the doubt and a trial period in which to prove ourselves." The inevitable institutional rivalries were compounded by the culture clash of the 1960s, when many Americans rallied for change and many more were suspicious of any government initiatives. ("Who's that?" a court clerk demanded when he wandered into one of the project's private offices where a poster of Fidel Castro was defiantly displayed. To which a new staff member replied: "That's our first participant. We got him a job as a prime minister.")

Only about one percent of the cases examined by the Court Employment Project would meet the original eligibility requirements. Among other things, the defendant could not be drug-addicted, could not be charged with a serious violent crime, could not have served more than six months in prison or have more than one other criminal charge pending. (Only males were included because many female defendants were arrested for prostitution, which paid better money than the project could offer.)

Under Sturz's tutelage, the Court Employment Project for teenagers and the Community Service Sentencing Project for adults, both of which began as demonstration programs originated by Vera, evolved in 1989 into CASES, the Center for Alternative Sentencing and Employment Services, which spawned more offspring that would test and promote rehabilitative alternatives even before trial. For example, the Nathaniel Project offers vigorous case management and community-based treatment instead of prison for mentally ill defendants in an effort to disrupt the cycle of recidivism. Parolees with special medical or emotional needs spend 165 days in custody, on average, compared to 77 days for most other parole violators. The Parole Restoration Project expedites the process—among other things, freeing up expensive detention space—by recognizing that the additional time in custody "is not a consequence of greater wrongdoing, rather it is a reflection of the difficulty of finding appropriate treatment and services." CASES also inaugurated a special program to address the growing proportion of female juvenile defendants (who accounted for one in ten arrests in 1960 but one in four by 2000), and partnered with the city's public school system to provide continuing education for students who were regularly attending classes while in custody.

By several measures, these good intentions had lasting results. Participants in CASES programs provided tens of thousands of hours of no-cost labor to neighborhood groups. They refurbished gardens and painted community centers. According to several surveys, participants were less likely to be convicted again and more likely to complete their education than members of control groups.

———

The nationwide successes of bail reform were not being mirrored in New York. One researcher concluded around 1971 that the pretrial process as practiced by the city's probation department bore "little resemblance to the original project." While even the most zealous Vera interviewers might have burned out over a few years in an ongoing program, the city's institutional attempt at bail reform appeared lethargic at best. According to several accounts, desk-bound probation officers, whose primary responsibility was to prepare pre-sentencing profiles and supervise defendants placed on probation, conducted largely apathetic searches for "highly visible good risks" and even they were recommended half-heartedly, without verification and with no promise or expectation of follow-up. The probation officers, Baron complained, "often thought they knew all about the defendants anyway and wouldn't collect any information."

"In a few short years, the credibility of the bail reform effort was severely compromised," Jeremy Travis recalls. "The effort at institutionalization had failed; the Department of Probation, historically understaffed, had other priorities." The probation department's priorities wouldn't change, but the city's did—overnight, by the calendar of the city bureaucracy—after the Tombs erupted in a riot in the summer of 1970. The inmates' complaints echoed the grievances that Schweitzer and Sturz had heard when they visited the eight-story lockup more than a decade before: too many prisoners jammed into cells that were too cramped and too many of them in custody because they could not afford bail. The crowded, filthy facility was built to house 930 prisoners. Its average daily census was nearly twice that. Cells designed for one inmate housed two or three, with one typically relegated to the floor. Whether you were an advocate of bail reform or law and order, one solution would have been swift and certain punishment, but nobody wanted to pay for more prisons or more judges, courtrooms and court personnel (the backlog of non-traffic cases in the Criminal Courts was estimated at half a million) to meet Chief Justice Warren E. Burger's goal of a trial within sixty days of a criminal indictment. Instead, city officials pressed the state to relieve overcrowding by taking responsibility for the 4,000 sentenced prisoners serving time in city prisons following their conviction. Some court reformers, including Judge Botein, even suggested that entire categories of crime be removed wholesale from the courts, including excessive drinking, which accounted for an estimated one third of all arrests, and prostitution.

While unabashedly liberal, the administration of John V. Lindsay would stoop to election-year realities, too. In 1969, Mayor Lindsay demanded that the maximum sentence for muggers be more than doubled, to fifteen years. The proposal wouldn't cost the city anything (those convicted would serve their sentences in state prison), but it appeared unlikely to deter crime (since few muggers were convicted of assault and robbery and many were allowed to plead guilty to lesser charges). Still, the administration was more likely to go against the grain, working with Vera through the mayor's Criminal Justice Coordinating Council, which had been formed in 1967 in part at Sturz's recommendation (and which Professor James Vorenberg of Harvard, former executive director of the president's Crime Commission, hailed for engineering "a quiet revolution"). Now, the administration suggested inviting Vera back to manage a pretrial release program. Through the Coordinating Council, the city and Vera applied for a grant from the federal Law Enforcement Assistance Administration, the agency that subsidized innovative justice initiatives, for a grant to create a Pretrial Services Agency. It was a hybrid, and, as it turned out, a prolific one that would spawn a new generation of quasi-public agencies to improve the delivery of criminal justice and social services. Under the new Criminal Justice Agency, about 46 percent of all defendants would be released on their own recognizance—the same rate that Vera had achieved before. (It would fluctuate, dipping to 37 percent in the 1990s during the first term of the administration of Rudolph Giuliani, then rebounding to about 44 percent.)

Today, 10 percent of the suspects recommended for release by the Criminal Justice Agency miss a court date, but only 4 percent are still missing after thirty days. The system is still far from perfect. But Schweitzer's outrage and Sturz's perseverance combined to profoundly expand the rights of defendants even beyond the U.S. Supreme Court's landmark decisions in the 1960s. "Far more important than *Mapp* or *Escobedo* or *Miranda*, over the long run, will be the bail project Herbert Sturz and Vera launched in 1961," wrote Martin Mayer in *The Lawyers*. "The really significant motion toward decency in criminal procedure comes from reform of the bail system."

————

If so many defendants could be released on bail instead of being held in jail pending trial, as the Manhattan Bail Project proved, then maybe, as Judge Botein had intimated, the criminal justice system could be manipulated another notch to produce a second shortcut. Many of the defendants who jammed the detention pens every morning had been arrested the night before for relatively minor misdemeanors. Virtually all would be released without bail at arraignment anyway. Suppose, Sturz wondered, if many of them didn't have to be arrested in the first place?

The question, in retrospect, seems pretty obvious. There was, he discovered, no legal mandate that someone arrested on a misdemeanor charge be held for arraignment. But, except for minor traffic offenders, people arrested for misdemeanors, like public drunkenness, other cases of disorderly conduct, shoplifting, turnstile jumping and simple assault, were treated much like felons. They were kept in custody overnight, ostensibly to guarantee their appearance at arraignment. The detention facilities were horrific— arguably a deterrent for someone guilty of a minor offense but hardly the place for someone not only presumed innocent, but unlikely to be incarcerated even if convicted. Suicides were not uncommon. Two inmates were fit into four-by-nine-foot cells built to accommodate only one inmate, and on some nights, a third slept on a mattress on the floor. Recreational facilities were converted into makeshift dormitories. Anna Kross, the correction commissioner, forecast "rioting and bloodshed" because the city's jail population was almost 50 percent beyond official capacity. "We shouldn't treat cattle the way we house our inmates," she said.

Apart from the social cost, arrest consumed enormous police manpower; the arresting officer would have to babysit the accused person and accompany him to court—often on overtime—until the arraignment.

In 1963, a total of 206,248 people were arrested in New York City. A majority were booked for relatively minor offenses—more than 68,000 for disorderly conduct alone. Playing the manpower card, Sturz persuaded Michael J. Murphy, Wagner's police commissioner, to conduct a small experiment in one precinct on Manhattan's West Side: Many of those suspects would not be arrested but would instead be issued summonses. How had Sturz persuaded Murphy? According to one account, Vera enlisted Botein to apply pressure and also hinted that it would conduct its summons experiment in collaboration with a more enlightened suburban police commissioner. Murphy finally agreed to try the idea in one precinct. Providing funds, staff and management, Vera began conservatively, selecting only persons with strong neighborhood attachments accused of relatively minor offenses to recommend for release after a summons was issued. Some skeptics would deride the summonses, known as desk appearance tickets, as "disappearance tickets." But the experiment was a success: There were savings in police and court manpower and correction costs, and most defendants complied with the process. Regardless of whether they were guilty, Sturz says, "they didn't want to be fugitives. They wanted to try their case or go back and plead it."

Building on the initial results, the experiment was broadened and institutionalized. The Police Department was transformed from reluctant participant to proud parent and stakeholder. Sturz arranged for the commissioner to be invited to address the National Conference on Bail and Criminal Justice in Washington, where Murphy, in remarks drafted by Sturz, announced the results of the initial six-week test and claimed his share of credit for its early success.

————

In 1964, the 14th Precinct was a gritty, bustling maze of warehouses, office buildings, department stores and transportation terminals in Midtown West. The Manhattan Summons Project occupied one corner of the first-floor muster room at the West 30th Street station house, a five-story granite relic built in 1904 and flanked by showrooms and workshops for dealers in luxury and fake furs. Six Vera workers, students from Columbia, New York University and Fordham, took turns manning a desk there until eleven P.M., six days a week. When a suspect was arrested for disorderly conduct, simple assault or petty larceny, Vera workers interviewed him in a detention cell or at the desk to verify his community ties while the police determined whether he was sought on an outstanding warrant. If the suspect passed muster, the lieutenant on duty or the desk sergeant would issue a summons returnable in court on a specific date. The experiment was based a good deal on trust but was also grounded in Vera's research. "We believed by looking at the rate of appearances that it wasn't about money," Sturz says. It was about faith in the process, about expecting justice.

Between April 2 and May 18, 1964, there were 116 people arrested for simple assault and petty larceny. Sixteen were deemed ineligible for summonses because they were classified as drug addicts, convicted sex offenders or lived out of town. Of the remaining 84 who were interviewed by a Vera worker, 58 were recommended for summonses. The police concurred in all but five cases. (In four others, even though a Vera interviewer was not present, the lieutenant issued a summons.) By the time Murphy delivered his verdict on the experiment, the return date for 50 of the defendants had passed. All 50 had showed up as scheduled.

For anyone sitting through Night Court, the contrast in which defendants are given the benefit of the doubt could not be starker. Take shoplifting, a crime that exacts a price from all consumers, but, depending on how it is handled by the criminal justice system, can be less costly to the taxpayers. Writing in the *New York Times*, Gertrude Samuels contrasted three cases. In one, a police officer and a store detective accused a fashionably dressed blonde of taking a $29.95 dress from Bloomingdale's. The judge set bail at $500, which the woman easily provided with a $25 premium. Later that night, a seventeen-year-old girl in jeans and sneakers stood accused of appropriating two dresses, valued at $26.90, from a small store. The same judge set bail at $500 or $50 cash. The girl couldn't afford either and was remanded to the Women's House of Detention, where she remained for four days pending a hearing. That same night, at the West 30th Street station house, a woman named Alice was charged with shoplifting an $18 dress from a Franklin Simon department store (the dress was recovered) and, in the course of her arrest, with striking a detective. A Vera worker, a twenty-four-year-old senior at Columbia Law School, verified the woman's home address, how long she had lived in New York, her job (a sleep-in maid) and other community roots. She had no criminal record. Les Scall, the Vera supervisor, accompanied by the defendant and the arresting officer, presented the desk officer with a recommendation for release. The arresting officer issued her a summons. Within forty minutes of being booked, she was released. As Samuels would write: "Alice had experienced no personal indignity; she was not searched like a common criminal; she did not go into a cell; she was not taken by police wagon to Night Court. By putting her on her honor to show up in court, the rehabilitation process had already begun."

"If anyone had told me that 90 percent of them would return, I would have been dubious," said Captain James P. O'Brien of the 14th Precinct. "If anyone had told me that 100 percent would return, I would have burst out laughing. But 100 percent have returned—every single one has shown up on the appointed day in court—and that is what is gratifying."

By the end of 1966, following a two-year experiment under Vera's auspices and funded by the Ford Foundation, pre-arraignment in Manhattan was generally freeing suspects—and witnesses, victims and police officers—in one hour instead of eight. By the middle of 1967, it was expanded citywide. Robbery and burglary complaints declined while arrests for those offenses increased. At the same time, victims were treated more humanely and were more cooperative during prosecutions. "Prior to the pre-arraignment processing facility, these victims would have to go down to Manhattan and would have to wait five or six hours, then come back to the Bronx, and, if they were lucky, they may have gotten home without being mugged again," Burton B. Roberts, the Bronx district attorney, said. Under the pre-arraignment process, he said, "they're back home in a half hour and are having their dinner. They're not discouraged with the administration of justice. They come back to court. They cooperate with the district attorney's office in the prosecution of these matters, and we have less trouble bringing these witnesses to court in order to have them testify against those who are charged with the commission of crime." This, he said, "truly is what we mean by law and order."

In 1968, there were 48,159 people arrested for simple assault, petty larceny, malicious mischief, resisting arrest and disorderly conduct. Of the 26,733 eligible, 14,232 received summonses, which saved the city the equivalent of nearly 14,000 eight-hour police shifts. Nearly all of those 14,232 returned to court.

Chapter 5

Summons to the Bowery

The Manhattan Summons Project was so common-sensical, it didn't take a genius to conceive and to implement. It took a *kind* of genius—someone wise and persevering enough to assess what was wrong, quantify the benefits of fixing it to all the stakeholders in the status quo and devising a simple, just, efficient solution. Common sense, George Bernard Shaw said, is instinct. "Enough of it," he added, "is genius." William James described genius as "perceiving in an unhabitual way." The qualifications recalled what Felix G. Rohatyn, the investment banker, once said. After serving for nearly two decades as chairman of the Municipal Assistance Corporation, a novel entity created by New York State in 1975 to bail the city out of its fiscal crisis, Rohatyn was asked why it was finally time to retire. "It's now time for someone who still has illusions," he replied.

No one ever accused Herb Sturz of lacking illusions. He spotted things other people hadn't seen, even things that had been staring them in the face every day. He would pose questions that they hadn't asked, even when those questions seemed mundane. And by peppering participants at every level with even more questions, by meticulously dissecting the responses, by crafting hypothetical fixes and subjecting them to challenging testing and experimentation, he tried his hand at transforming illusions into practical answers. Given the demonstrable results of the summons project in other precincts and his relentless optimism, he was puzzled when he discovered one stark exception on the Lower East Side of Manhattan.

————

The recalcitrant precinct was home to the Bowery, the once fashionable route to rural Manhattan from the city's increasingly congested downtown and lined with the farms of wealthy landowners. But the Bowery's glory days, such as they were, were well behind, even by the late nineteenth century, when it evolved into the bawdy home of honky-tonk bars and entertainment venues and emerged as the last refuge for society's outcasts and self-imposed exiles. By the mid-twentieth century, the mile-long thoroughfare from Chinatown to Cooper Union was synonymous with Skid Row. Lined by cheap flophouses, fleabag hotels and dormitory-style shelters, the street had become a cauldron of human misery. Its most visible regulars were the estimated twelve thousand derelicts and drunks, whose more aggressive successors would, three decades later, become the target of Mayor Giuliani's campaign against squeegee-wielding panhandlers.

In the early 1960s, Bowery "bums" were generally considered less threatening and also less of a social blight than homeless adults would become a decade or two later. They congregated in one self-contained neighborhood. "This is not a dangerous area," insisted the Reverend Michael Allen, rector of the Protestant Episcopal Church of St. Mark's-in-the-Bouwerie, which was consecrated in 1799. "It's a lousy area." But the bums posed a daily nuisance and worse for their neighbors there, and they represented what Mayor Wagner described as "an immovable obstacle in the way of effective resurgence" as huge middle-income housing developments were transforming the Lower East Side. In 1963, about fifty homeless men and one woman died from drinking the denatured alcohol that, while explicitly labeled as poison, had been sold to them at a local hardware store. "Unless you live on the Bowery, you cannot imagine what it is like," the assistant manager of one shelter said. "If you want a sample of human degradation, just walk up the block."

John M. Murtagh, the chief justice of the Court of Special Sessions, whose cooperation had been instrumental in implementing the Manhattan Bail Project, saw the issue of Bowery derelicts as a blight on the city's moral slate and an unimaginable social failing. "Arresting drunks," as he saw it, was "merely society's hypocritical way of discharging its duty to the inadequate. The existence of Skid Row bothers our conscience. We try to salve it by calling on police to arrest the bums." Murtagh's personal exploration into their pathology found that even those who were certifiably alcoholic were "empty, bewildered souls who are the result of early deprivation, lack of maternal or other affection in early life, a deprivation that was never compensated for in later life. We know all too little about the nature of their malady and even less about its treatment. Meanwhile society's answer continues to be: 'Lock the bums up.'"

Sturz was further concerned that the failure to offer an appealing therapeutic program for those who volunteer to participate in one would stiffen the kind of mindset that would culminate in the strict Rockefeller drug laws less than a decade later—indiscriminate mandatory life prison terms for every pusher, regardless of degree—and would be applied to alcoholic derelicts too. They would be involuntarily, and punitively, committed. "It would have been horrible and very expensive and hopeless," he said. At the same time, two federal court decisions in 1966 seemed to suggest that convicting alcoholics for public intoxication was tantamount to prosecuting sick people simply for being symptomatic.

What was it about the Bowery, Sturz wondered, that— uniquely among all the city's police precincts—seemed to be thwarting the best intentions of the summons project? Most of the arrests in the precinct were of hapless derelicts, periodically rounded up indiscriminately in patrol wagons. The cops hated the ritual even more than the derelicts did. But the pattern never changed—until Sturz, who was mulling the reasons for the atypical summons statistics on the Lower East Side, was introduced in 1965 to Rosemary Masters.

Masters had graduated from Harvard Law School in 1964 and, despite her abiding interest in social justice, was steered by Harvard's placement office to a corporate law firm. She was miserable. A sympathetic and civic-minded partner arranged an appointment with Sturz. The timing was perfect. Hiring talented young women was another trend that Sturz helped pioneer. Masters recalls that he "was one of the first to figure out that there were a lot of smart, capable women coming out of graduate schools who could be hired at discount prices." (Another of those women, Patricia M. Wald, remembers: "I was still a housewife with five kids and I could only come up to New York City for several hours a few days a month but back then— this is in the 60s—he was willing to fit my schedule to his.") Masters leapt at his invitation to investigate the issues posed by the anomaly on the Lower East Side. Petite but feisty, she captivated her male-dominated constituency, cops and derelicts, sober or not. For all the gritty, ground-level investigations that Sturz would assign his staff to—and, typically, undertake himself—the Bowery orientation tour would be among the worst.

The city-run Men's Shelter on East Third Street offered a cafeteria and a hellish "big room" that was loosely described as a gym, a mini-infirmary and a one-night voucher for a flophouse, that typically closed at six A.M. "Open those big heavy doors and you were hit by the mingled odors of industrial cleaner, unwashed bodies, vomit, urine, food cooking and the sweet sick smell of Thunderbird wine," Masters recalls. "It was unforgettable." The auditory senses were also assaulted: "Shouts, curses, wails of distress. 'My shoes, my shoes, some son of a bitch stole my shoes!' The orders of the security men. 'Hey! You! You can't go upstairs without a pass!' Men would be arguing over the price of a joint. In the corner some psychotic guy would be carrying on a loud conversation with God or whoever." Masters describes the derelicts as the "invisible maimed." Betty Kiernan, a nurse and another pioneer in Sturz's Bowery Project, says those sensory perceptions were first impressions that were soon subsumed: "Once you get used to it, you start knowing who the people are. And, of course, the staff were often stranger than the clients."

The two cops who flanked Masters in the front of the large panel truck lined with benches that she accompanied one night might as well have had the rank "demoted" affixed to their badges. They glumly complained that their assignment was no picnic, that they were pressured by store-owners to sweep the streets of derelicts and were dissuaded by medical personnel from dumping them in hospital emergency rooms. "Truth is," one officer confided to Masters, "a lot of them are fed up with life on the streets and are glad for a chance to clean up. Sometimes, in really cold weather, these guys ask to get arrested. I'm telling you," the cop continued, "it's stupid to use the courts and jail for this."

But as the police whom Masters accompanied would imply, they were performing a function that everybody else shunned and that nobody else had the authority or the resources to carry out. The cops were literally cleaning up society's mess. Many of the derelicts the cops issued summonses to were not competent enough to comprehend them, let alone meet a court date. Merely handing out a summons and leaving the derelicts to fend for themselves was, if not counterproductive, surely a waste. In *The Lawyers*, Martin Mayer invoked Sturz and his Bowery missions as the cops corralled drunks, writing that he "estimates that half of those arrested (and subsequently lined up in a criminal court) were merely beaten and weary old men, who might have planned to get drunk if they could cadge the price of it but were sober as a judge at the moment of arrest. It is a matter of record that such a police sweep once picked up the father of an assistant attorney general of the State of New York, simply walking down the street and minding his own business."

By arresting them, the police were performing a function. The derelicts were placed in cells until they were sober enough to be arraigned and then transferred to the Tombs for several days more or released back to the streets. Some would opt for an extended stay at Camp La Guardia, the city's alcohol detoxification and treatment program in nearby Orange County, but most would dry out at the Tombs and simply be released back to the Bowery, many before they had really dried out. The migration to Camp La Guardia was customarily a seasonal one. After graduating from Camp La Guardia in late spring or summer, many would get jobs as dishwashers or other kitchen help in the Catskills hotels. "They would never drink up there," Betty Kiernan recalls. "They would save their money, because they were afraid to go to jail up there—it wasn't like New York City. So they would save up this tremendous amount of money, look lovely, come back, blow it all and end up on the street again."

From a law enforcement, medical and legal standpoint, the challenges were formidable (although the practice of arresting drunks was being successfully challenged in courts on grounds that alcoholism itself could not constitutionally be classified as a crime). But the potential impact was enormous. Nationally, nearly one in three arrests were said to be for drunkenness or related behavior, and in New York City officials figured that half of all misdemeanor arrests were related to drinking. But Sturz viewed them as natural extensions of the bail project and the summons project. This wasn't necessarily about saving people's souls. Sturz had no illusions about that or even permanently breaking the cycle of dependency. But could anything break the cycle? Or, at least, prolong the episodic sobriety? "They already suffer from brain damage, enlarged livers and have long ago broken away from any human ties," Sturz explained at the time. "But why not treat them with some level of elemental decency? Sure they'll be recycled through the center again, but why not give them, for a time, a drying-out period and some hot food?" Arrests on the Bowery dropped by 98 percent. "We were smart enough," Sturz recalls, "not to say we're going to turn their lives around."

Sturz's political spadework might be dismissed as cynical, even conniving, or applauded as politically astute and pragmatic. Or both. He successfully sold what might otherwise have been dismissed as another well-intentioned but

pointy-headed scheme as an experiment in police efficiency. "He made it a cop project," Jay Kriegel says, "not a
Bowery mission."

Armed with Masters's research, Vera gravitated toward
a pilot program that was designed to answer whether derelicts would agree to be removed from the street and be
granted a temporary safe haven without being arrested.
The rationale was obvious: Society was unwilling to leave
derelicts lying on the street, whether the motivation was
humanitarian or preserving real estate values, but substituting a medical detoxification program for time in a station
house cell or in the Tombs was more compassionate and
less expensive. Vera was designated by Mayor Lindsay to
coordinate a public-private partnership that would bring
together the resources of four city and two state agencies,
a private hospital and the mayor's Criminal Justice Coordinating Council, to explore alternatives to arrest and detention of Bowery derelicts.

The Police Department's institutional resistance to
change—much less to experimentation—was transcended
by its willingness to be relieved of the burden that the
Bowery derelicts presented, and the ability of police brass
on the Criminal Justice Coordinating Council to bypass the
bureaucratic hierarchy. To avoid a cumbersome regulatory
review, Vera's experiment was launched through the Department of Social Services, which operated the Men's
Shelter. Twelve beds were placed near the shelter's infirmary, and in the summer of 1966, Sturz, Masters, a cop in
plainclothes (to avoid any concern by civil libertarians
about coercion) and a recovered alcoholic who worked
for Vera climbed into their unmarked patrol wagon to learn
whether their hypothesis would work. The first potential
client did not seem promising. He was sprawled on the
sidewalk, barely conscious. Sturz and the Vera worker

shook the man gently to revive him and handed him a cigarette. Once they got his attention, Sturz asked the man if
he wouldn't rather sleep off his hangover in a clean, safe
place than on the sidewalk. "He looked up at us for a
minute, sorting it out, and then just nodded his head,
'Sure,'" Sturz recalls. Not every encounter unfolded as ef-
fortlessly. (As one man was being led into the unmarked
van, his drinking buddy summoned the police to report a
kidnapping.) But the overall response surprised even members of the Vera team. After approaching fifteen men in
half a day, the team filled all twelve beds.

"On one level, it was obvious," Masters says. "Of course,
we knew that these were just ordinary guys in terrible
trouble. But it is hard to overstate how extraordinary the
actual experience was. One day, we saw these beings, who
seemed hardly human, black with dirt, smelling, stum-
bling, incoherent. On the next, they were washed, shaved,
with clean clothes and, above all, so grateful—not just for
the physical care, but for the respectful treatment they
had received. Each man was an individual. He had a life and
a story. The experience changed us, not just the men." On
the third day, if the men acquiesced, they were given beds
at the Bowery Mission, a private, nonprofit shelter nearby.

The experiment was the easy part. Transforming a tiny
pilot project into a full-fledged, ongoing program would require enormous patience, perseverance and diplomatic
skills. Sturz was the chief architect. The implementation
fell to Masters and to R. Palmer Baker, a lawyer at Lord,
Day & Lord, the firm that Louis Schweitzer had hired to
establish the Vera Foundation originally. (Baker's impecca-
ble attire and venerable legal credentials belied a non-
compliant streak that Masters divined on her first visit
to his office. Hanging on the wall opposite Baker's imposing wooden desk was a sensuous Tahitian nude by Paul

Gauguin.) By this time, too, the foundation had been re-constituted as the Vera Institute of Justice. Burke Marshall, the former assistant attorney general for civil rights, a prominent figure nationally, was chosen as chairman. Vera's board included Botein; Orison S. Marden, president-elect of the American Bar Association; and Lloyd E. Ohlin, director of research of the Columbia School of Social Work; Louis Schweitzer and his brothers, William T. and Peter; and R. Palmer Baker.

Baker incorporated the project, drew the detailed road map for winning licenses from various agencies and unraveled the arcana of insurance coverage. Masters took the road map door to door, traipsing through the cycle of approvals during her pregnancy. "I could tell them, 'I really need you to sign off on this now,'" she recalls. "Nobody wanted me to go into labor in their office."

The project opened on schedule in July 1967, within a year and a half after it was conceived. Two-member teams, a plainclothes cop and a recovered alcoholic, began patrolling the Bowery every afternoon, a few hours after the bars opened, in their radio-equipped unmarked van or station wagon. By the end of the first year, the outreach team were patrolling from nine A.M. to nine P.M. every day. The men were brought to the shelter, identified and cleaned up. Six thousand derelicts and drunks were estimated to live on or near the Bowery. Theoretically, if the team successfully approached fifteen a day they could reach 5,500 a year.

Among the doctors recruited to the infirmary of the project, which was located in the Men's Shelter, was Robert Morgan. A gastroenterologist who specialized in liver disease, Morgan had been enlisted by a philanthropist to direct a treatment center for alcoholism in suburban Westchester. After the center was scuttled by local opposition, he began to treat alcoholics in his private practice. One of his patients was connected to the original pilot Bowery project, and Morgan was hired as the medical director. "I told him that physicians and social welfare people with whom I had discussed the idea of a voluntary medical detox had told me I was crazy," Masters remembers. "The men would refuse to come or if they did they would get violent, die of delirium tremors, and so on. He listened to me rattle on about my concerns and then responded quite simply in that deep baritone voice of his: 'A little kindness, a few smart nurses and the right medicine should handle most of it.' And that was that." (Morgan retired from medicine in 1999 after calcification of his spinal cord left him a paraplegic. He died in 2008, as did Palmer Baker.)

Even the original expectations with the Bowery Project were audacious, but, as Sturz would consistently remind his patrons and supporters in every Vera venture, they were couched modestly. The derelicts had no hope and had bought into the assumption that their lives were irredeemable. They were treated with respect. They were empowered for the first time, armed with a modicum of self-confidence that could affect their own destiny. "The men showed the Bowery staff, in microcosm, what homeless alcoholic people need," Masters says. "Together with the staff they created a template for realistic help: uncompromising respect and a network of support services—group therapy, supported housing, introduction or reintroduction to the workforce, medical follow-up and assistance in managing the bureaucracies that could give them temporary or permanent financial assistance."

Sturz had chosen the highest concentration of derelicts in the city, and, predictably, the project proceeded slowly and selectively. Nearly a year elapsed before all 48 beds were filled. Among the initial 150 patients, the vast majority of patients were white. Their median age was almost 50.

About four in five men who were approached by the out-reach teams agreed to voluntarily dry out. "The purpose of the Manhattan Bowery Project," Sturz declared in 1967, "is to develop a decent and workable alternative to dealing with these men by the usually unsuccessful cycle of ar-rest, trial and jail." Typically, he avoided hyperbole or rais-ing expectations beyond his hopes of delivering. The project, he explained, was not about rehabilitation. It was not about how many of the men he recruited actually quit drinking. "I feel it will be a success," he said, "if we find a civilized alternative to the expensive and wasteful way we presently deal with the derelicts." By the second year of op-eration, alcohol-related arrests in the Bowery area had plummeted by 85 percent. But the project's statistical legacy, as impressive as it was and as enduring as it would prove to be, was only part of the story.

The Manhattan Bowery Project was the first Vera pro-gram to function completely outside the court system. It required the cooperation, regulatory approval or financing—sometimes, all three—from as many as eighteen distinct city, state and federal agencies (vehicles were provided by the police, real estate by the Department of Social Ser-vices, medical beds from the Hospitals Department and funding from the city's community mental health pro-grams, the state Bureau of Alcoholism and the U.S. Justice Department). The dividend that investment paid would be incalculable in human lives. It would also solidify Vera's stature as an independent organization with proven capac-ity. Vera had aggregated resources of like-minded public and private agencies to create no-frills programs, whose suc-cesses could be authenticated and replicated, and whose oc-casional failures avoided. The Manhattan Bowery Project would be the first member of an extended family of Vera spin-offs managed by a separate, nonprofit corporation, originally conceived to insulate Vera from legal liability. The Bowery Project's board considered homelessness its primary mission and would not be distracted by other priorities—sometimes competing ones—that Vera's criminal justice agenda might impose. "This commitment," Masters says, "gave the Bowery Project a kind of momentum, a mandate to develop services for homeless alcoholics even after the initial aims of the project—getting deteriorated alcoholics off the street—had been met. Perhaps most importantly, the separate corporate structure gave the project staff independence that permitted, even encouraged, a degree of enthusiasm and innovation that a more hierarchal organization would not have fostered."

That management model avoided competition for funding within Vera, attracted talented people who otherwise might have been buried in middle management to visible jobs and provided programmatic and legal insulation. It also inspired innovation and raised expectations. At one point, after Bob Goldfeld succeeded Masters as manager of the Bowery Project, ten of the forty-eight beds were occupied by men who had overstayed the several-day limit but whom the staff were reluctant to discharge. Some were suffering from chronic medical problems and needed to be stabilized. Others were psychotic, awaiting transfer to a mental hospital when space became available. The chokepoint created an internal crisis over how to reconcile the project's street rescue mission with the welfare of its clients. Goldfeld's solution was to reevaluate patients on the third day of treatment and discharge them if doing so was medically safe. But the staff objected. What the bottleneck demonstrated most clearly was the scarcity of options for longer-term placement. Goldfeld would later explain that he encouraged the development of alternative placements both for the sake of the patients and staff.

"These were idealistic, committed people and they were finding it very discouraging just to put people through detox and then send them out to start drinking again," he says. "I didn't have any illusions. You can't wave a magic wand over people who have been drinking for twenty years and expect that they'll stop. But we had to do something to create the possibility of hope."

Hope was as vital to maintaining the morale of the staff at the infirmary as it was to motivating the patients themselves. Recycling the same pool of alcoholics into temporary custodial care was, arguably, better than leaving them to their own devices. But it was not what the most socially conscientious of the Manhattan Bowery Project's workers were about. The challenge was to avoid the temptation to grasp at magic bullets, at therapies or pharmacological concoctions that appeared to hold great promise but, in the end, left the staff and their patients disillusioned. Most of what passed for rehabilitation hadn't worked. Detox, coupled with counseling, was a simple and relatively inexpensive hardy perennial, but it seldom proved effective long-term. After all, people typically drink to escape some daily irritant. The project gravitated toward an evolving mix of group living (away from the Bowery, in Brooklyn), counseling, peer-group support and modest, programmed work (from raking leaves, which the fiscally strapped Parks Department could no longer afford itself, to making wooden toys for sale in Macy's) for modest pay. The results were indeed modest, but measurable.

Meanwhile, the Bowery Project was wrestling with a profound identity crisis. In part, the project had become a victim of its own success. It had proved the efficacy of detoxification and had effectively prodded government to redefine alcoholism and drug addiction as diseases, not merely as moral failings, which meant that they could, and should, be treated in hospitals. That left the Bowery Project to choose whether to limit its clientele to alcoholics with only minor medical problems or sacrifice its independence by affiliating with a local hospital.

Times had changed since the original bail project had spawned the summons project, which, in turn, had inspired the Bowery Project. Promising medical advances conspired with budgetary pressures (and civil libertarians with fiscal conservatives) to empty mental institutions. Beginning in the late 1950s, the state had begun disgorging tens of thousands of patients but unconscionably failed to provide them with housing or the support they needed to survive. Most were ill-equipped to survive on their own. To whatever extent miracle medicines could mitigate schizophrenia and other disabling mental illness, there were no guarantees that the released patients would take their medications regularly. Moreover, they were discharged to return to neighborhoods that had been gentrified, where single-room-occupancy hotels had been razed or remodeled into luxury apartments. Housing subsidies had evaporated and many found themselves on the streets. The vagrants who had once been largely invisible except on the Bowery proliferated to other parts of the city, encroaching on public spaces and threatening the stability—and, in some cases, the security—of entire neighborhoods. Meanwhile, the population of the Bowery had changed. The older alcoholics—no longer subject to arrest for simply being drunk—were supplanted by a younger, more racially diverse and vulnerable population that was more likely to be drug-addicted and homeless. Flophouses in the Bowery were being converted into artists' lofts and apartments. While the thoroughfare might not recapture the cachet it boasted of centuries ago, it managed to achieve another benchmark in the 1990s, when the first million-dollar apartments were offered in glitzy buildings wedged between dilapidated nineteenth-century tenements and warehouses. Reaffirming Vera's faith in the Bowery Project and reflecting its expanded scope, in 1994 Sturz and the board rechristened it Project Renewal.

Instead of confining its mandate to alcoholics with only minor physical ailments or merging with a hospital to provide more sophisticated medical services, the Bowery Project could capitalize on nearly a decade of knowledge honed on one of the city's seediest streets. By the mid-1970s, Renewal House was operating two residences and providing maintenance services at 100 municipal playgrounds. After five months, the men who remained alcohol free were referred to private housing and employment. By 1977, of the 218 men who had gone through the program, 48, or 22 percent, had graduated to independent living, although within a month 16 of them were drinking again.

Edward Geffner, a Yale Law School graduate and a protégé of Vera's chairman, Burke Marshall, was recruited as the project's administrative director. "Even though I knew he was born and raised in Brooklyn I kept picturing him on the porch of some Southern country store," Masters remembers. "It took awhile for me to learn that he had studied philosophy in Israel, worked in the civil rights movement in rural Alabama during the sixties when it was incredibly dangerous to do so and gotten arrested several times demonstrating against the Vietnam War in various draft board sit-ins."

Geffner and Bob Morgan, the medical director of Project Renewal, agreed on several guiding principles. Morgan's experience on the Bowery taught him that while no one-size-fits-all model could be applied to every homeless person, they all needed hope. And to whatever extent hope could be instilled, the process would require a sustained personal relationship with compassionate staff. Breaking the cycle of homelessness would demand three other requisites: services that were readily available and provided incentives; supervised and supported housing; and the training, supervision and psychological underpinning for employment.

R. Palmer Baker, the lawyer who by then had become the board chairman of Project Renewal, jump-started the homeless initiative by sending Geffner a newspaper clipping. On the eve of the 1980 Democratic national convention, city officials were justifiably concerned that out-of-towners confronted by hoards of homeless people (or, to use the then current term, bag ladies) and panhandlers in midtown Manhattan would make New York seem more like New Calcutta. With Palmer providing legal advice and Sturz paving the way politically, Geffner approached the city's Times Square Development Corporation and offered to help. Project Renewal would expand its outreach operation to midtown. Homeless people would be encouraged to visit a drop-in center, where they would be referred to shelters or to housing. "We were making it up as we went along," says Susan Dan, who would become Project Renewal's chief of mental health programs. Workers identified the vacuum in services, offered alternatives and persisted in persuading homeless people to avail themselves of those services. "Sometimes it would take three years to convince someone to come into the drop-in center. We'd start with a sandwich and a conversation," she says. "Ultimately, that person might accept a shower or just a quiet place to sit and have a meal."

Two yawning service gaps were immediately evident. Even if the project's workers could persuade a homeless person to get off the street, not enough housing was available. Medical care was scarce, too, for untreated illnesses and for mood-stabilizing medicines. In emergency rooms, the wait could easily last six hours. ("You don't have to be crazy to find that intolerable," Dan says.) To meet the medical demand, Project Renewal dispatched a mobile medical van to places where homeless people congregated.

Housing was harder to produce, but by 1986 Project Renewal had embarked on its own transitional residence, where, after health problems were stabilized, residents could be referred to nearby low-cost apartments. The first, Clinton Residence, opened on the West Side. A few years later, New Providence opened in a former convent on the East Side. The project began housing programs in the Kenton and Holland Hotels. And in 1990, Project Renewal came full circle, returning to its roots in the Bowery when the city asked it to operate the Men's Shelter. The detox program was retained, transitional housing was provided, the medical clinic was remodeled and the hellish "big room" on the first floor that Masters had first encountered years earlier was renovated for screening and counseling. In 2004, Project Renewal opened St. Nicholas House in Harlem and the Tinton Avenue Residence in the Bronx. What distinguishes the two publicly funded programs are not only the staff, which offers recreation and social services on site, but the fact that among the residents of both buildings are people who were not homeless but were simply seeking a better place to live.

––––––

Over time, Project Renewal workers understood that some of their clients would always need support of some kind and might never be able to lead fully independent lives. Still, the project was moving closer and closer to fulfilling the sequence-of-care model originally envisioned by Geffner and Morgan—a continuum beginning with street outreach, immediate medical assessment and care, respite drop-in centers, treatment programs and housing. The next challenge was to find jobs for formerly homeless alcoholics and drug addicts, who, if they recovered, could potentially live by themselves and who, if they had a dependable income, would be less likely to revert to their addictions.

The Mayor's Office of Midtown Enforcement, which was run by Carl Weisbrod, approached Project Renewal to suggest that residents of its Brooklyn residences be hired with privately raised funding to supplement the city's efforts at street cleaning in midtown. Outfitted with distinctive red uniforms, they were immediately recognized as one small, but highly visible, symbol of Times Square's revival. Other ventures like Shamrock Construction, which rehabilitated apartments, did demolition work at the Brooklyn Army Terminal and renovated Project Renewal's own offices and other facilities, were organized through Project Renewal. Ernie Talbot, a former police officer who ran Shamrock, encouraged the recovering alcoholics— moving them from temporary to permanent work, to more skilled jobs that came with health insurance and retirement benefits—and referred those who strayed back to the detox program downtown. For those who had the potential for self-sufficiency, employment was crucial and Project Renewal conceived and executed a wide range of job-generating spin-offs, including one that taught computer skills and helped men earn their high school equivalency diplomas, before they were referred to employers. With the Men's Shelter kitchen no longer feeding hundreds of homeless men, one part of it was converted into a Culinary Arts Training Program, which taught basic skills. Another program guided the homeless to jobs in the suburbs, which often paid more, and still another, Job Links, focused on preparing people with serious mental illness to compete in the private sector. Even a portion of Camp La Guardia was transformed into a farm where the formerly homeless could raise food and plants to sell.

Not every program delivered on expectations. Not every client turned out to be a success story. Still, Sturz and his colleagues in the Bowery Project were pioneers. Long before alcoholism was considered a disease rather than a moral failing, they helped recast societal attitudes toward addiction, homelessness and mental illness as a set of behavioral symptoms that could be treated and largely decriminalized. Because one man began asking questions, a costly policy that sapped police manpower, degraded everyone who came in contact with it and accomplished virtually nothing was replaced by a $100,000-a-year program that started off by serving 48 men with five days of medical detoxification and now employs 600, provides mammographies, chest X-rays and primary medical care through three mobile clinics and operates on a $33 million annual budget. Echoing Sturz, Masters says, "It is the decent thing to do, but more than that it is the practical thing to do and the possible thing to do."

Decades later, when Sturz was asked to identify one indelible image that, for him, epitomized what made Vera and her progeny distinct, he immediately reached back to the Bowery. "For me, it's Bob Morgan," Sturz replied, "leaning over the bed of a patient who probably had never been cared for, certainly not since his youth, and with immense patience and intelligence, asking the guy how he was, what could he do for him, looking at him. That, I think, at least for me, marked what Vera is about."

Chapter 6

Beyond
the Bowery

The Men's Shelter on East Third Street, which inspired Sturz's Project Renewal, also triggered another Vera housing initiative. When officials of the city's Human Resources Administration saw applications for housing rising, they asked Vera to investigate. When first-time applicants were asked to fill out a simple questionnaire, half noted that they had become homeless because of a calamity in their building, its abandonment by the landlord or its conversion into higher-priced housing. Vera's proposed long-term solution for people in similar circumstances was that they eventually become landlords themselves. While the proposal was anathema to some tenant advocates, its appeal—home ownership—spanned the ideological divide. R. Palmer Baker would provide expertise on tax incentives for private investment for half the cost of a model single room occupancy (SRO) hotel, and the city would extend a low-interest loan for the balance. City officials had reservations—would homeless people adapt to permanent housing? Would investors pour their money into tax shelters to develop homeless housing? Would nonprofit groups overcome their reluctance and agree to manage the buildings? One sure way to find out was to try.

The Cecil Hotel on West 118th Street in Harlem was once the home of the celebrated jazz club Minton's Playhouse. Like many properties in Manhattan, Brooklyn and the Bronx, it had been seized by the city in the mid-1970s for long-overdue property taxes. In the mid-1980s, Vera bought the vacant and vandalized ninety-apartment building for $25,000 and formed the Public Service Action Center, to develop the property with $2 million from a private investor, a $300,000 loan from the Harlem Urban Development Corporation and a $1.7 million loan from the City's Department of Housing Preservation and Development for renovations.

The Cecil would define the model of a "supportive SRO"—a single room occupancy hotel that delivers social services instead of room service. Tenants would be placed in furnished rooms, and social services would be provided on the premises, with referrals to medical and mental health programs. After what seemed like insurmountable delays over the terms of tax incentives, the city stepped in to front the money originally designated from the private investor. The project was finally completed in 1998 (the jazz club reopened in 2006) and is now home to ninety adults, some of whom had spent up to five years in the city's shelter system. The Cecil is another example of Sturz's uncanny talent for tapping and pooling diverse public and private funding streams to pay for innovative, cost-effective programs. The same resident who costs less than $12,000 a year to house in the Cecil would cost taxpayers nearly $20,000 to maintain in a city shelter, $170,000 in a state psychiatric hospital and more than $400,000 as a patient in a medical hospital.

The Public Service Action Center evolved into Housing and Services, Inc., which filled a void for those community-based nonprofit groups that were willing to own and manage housing but did not want to act as developers. Housing and Services identified sites that could be developed without zoning variances, community partners to manage the projects, finances to build or rehabilitate housing, and an operating budget that often depended primarily on the $215-a-month allowance that public assistance has granted single individuals since 1975. Housing and Services also leveraged loans from the city to create specialized housing, for low-income members of the Actors' Fund including retirees, young performers and actors with HIV and frail and poor elderly people. It established a residential health care facility for families with AIDS, the first of its kind in the country eligible for Medicaid funding that offered medical, social service, substance abuse care and child care.

Overall, Housing and Services was instrumental in the development of more than 2,000 housing units valued at over $200 million. And it helped preserve affordable housing under the subsidized Mitchell-Lama Program, which allowed owners to convert buildings into market-rate co-operatives. In 2005, Housing and Services engineered the transition of a Mitchell-Lama complex in the Soundview section of the Bronx into affordable co-ops where maintenance costs were kept comparable with previous rents. The complex, with 1,865 apartments, was the largest to preserve Mitchell-Lama housing in New York State. In 2008, on Housing and Services' twentieth anniversary, Robert V. Hess, the city's commissioner of homeless services, said: "Thousands of New Yorkers have a better life today in large part thanks to your efforts."

———

Nearly all of Vera's ventures were cooperative. They nudged the system, pointed it in new directions and raised awareness about people whom government should have been serving anyway without prodding from the private sector. Vera initiatives identified common ground and focused on shared goals; they tested and perfected the means to achieve ends by working with and within the system. Sometimes, as some outsiders complained about the Victim Service Agency, Vera's programs seemed more like the system itself than an affiliate.

Vera's Legal Action Center was never mistaken for part of the system. The seeds of the center were sown in 1972, when Sturz hired Elizabeth Bartholet as the Vera Institute's counsel. While working at the NAACP Legal Defense and Education Fund, Bartholet had identified a vacuum in the advocacy world. Lawyers' advocacy groups had rallied around a wide range of issues, such as racial discrimination, civil rights, fair housing, poverty law and access to public accommodations. But no one, as far as Bartholet could see, was advocating for the rights of recovering addicts, former criminals and those stuck in the criminal justice system's maws. Within a year, the Legal Action Center was established independent of Vera (so that each could fulfill its mandate unencumbered by the operational imperatives of the other; Vera, working in collaboration with government, would be inoculated against a backlash that in challenging the government it was biting the very hand that fed it). Bartholet was named the center's director.

In hindsight, the timing seems almost preordained. In 1972, with *Setting National Priorities: The 1973 Budget*, the Brookings Institution had delivered a convincing epitaph for Lyndon Johnson's Great Society. The autopsy by Brookings economists and social engineers revealed symptoms that Sturz had detected more than a decade earlier. It wasn't just about money. Not when federal social spending jumped from $30 billion to $110 billion in a decade and when the budget for Great Society programs ballooned from less than $2 billion to more than $35 billion. Brookings blamed the programs' failures to meet early expectations on overreaching, poor preparation, lack of information or an embarrassing reliance on flawed information about the underlying problems and a complete lack of accountability. "It was not immediately recognized that the new demands required that attention be paid to *how* federal programs were carried out," the Brookings authors concluded. "The idea persisted that if one could identify a problem and allocate some federal money to it, the problem would get solved."

It was one thing for the government to provide a structural engineer with the specifications to build a bridge, and quite another to direct a social engineer to build a Great Society. Brookings gave voice to a challenge that only a handful of people and organizations—Herb Sturz and Vera perhaps most prominent among them—had managed to overcome. "It was not possible to hire an educator and say, 'improve reading achievement in poverty schools,' because educators did not know how," Brookings' book-length analysis said. Its prescription could have been taken right out of Vera's playbook: Don't just stand there, do something. But not just anything. Experiment. Take risks. Measure results. Hold people accountable. Fold what fails and replicate what succeeds.

The Brookings Institution's epitaph for the Great Society flatly rejected the "just stand there" approach and actively envisioned programs that tried for lasting change in a flawed society. In this respect, the Legal Action Center was born in a perfect political climate, one ready for change, if new means were employed to achieve it. Over time, the Legal Action Center's mandate would evolve to address new challenges, like AIDS, but its original agenda was relatively simple. If it succeeded, it held out the promise of improving both the lives of ex-convicts and addicts and the society they were hoping to rejoin. The center focused first on what its staff identified as the biggest obstacle to rehabilitation: the challenges its clientele routinely faced in getting and keeping a job. Regardless of whether politicians harbored any sympathy toward former inmates and addicts in general, rehabilitation and reentry into society once they were released or committed to recovery was something that nearly everyone could support purely on the basis of society's self-interest.

Sturz embraced the challenge of prisoner re-entry early on. Society was always ambivalent about it and followed a double standard based, again, on self-interest: Major criminals were less likely to be released, but when they were, it is ironic that they were more likely to receive support than minor criminals were. "If you commit a really heinous crime, society will be careful to try to rehabilitate you, give you some money when you leave," Sturz said in the 1960s. "If you're unlucky enough to commit only a minor crime, you get thrown into a sump hole, and you're given nothing except maybe a quarter when you leave. If you're put in in the summer, and you leave in the winter, you don't have clothes."

From the beginning, the Legal Action Center committed itself to fighting discrimination. The center also pursued legislative remedies that might be quicker, less costly and more encompassing than case-by-case litigation and mounted educational campaigns aimed at establishing and broadening a popular constituency for its agenda.

Sturz's political ingenuity was well-illustrated by his choice of board members for Vera and each of its offshoots.

They were recruited to serve several purposes: to raise money, of course, to keep the project afloat and enable it to expand; to provide practical, professional expertise in its field of specialization; to unlock access to the decision makers in the public and private sector whose support would be instrumental to the project's success and to provide the political insulation from assault by the left and the right. The Legal Action Center was no exception. Sturz persuaded Arthur Liman, a prominent litigator from Paul, Weiss, Rifkind, Wharton & Garrison, and the fiercely independent counsel to the commission that investigated the Attica prison riot, to chair the board. He also corralled a combination of Vera regulars—R. Palmer Baker, Burke Marshall and F. A. O. (Fritz) Schwarz Jr., among them—and broadened its reach, and the pool of prospective members of boards-to-be, with Joseph Califano, the former secretary of Health, Education and Welfare, *New York Times* columnist Anthony Lewis and Basil Paterson, a savvy lawyer and labor negotiator who would become New York's secretary of state and a deputy mayor (and whose son, David, would become governor in 2008). More importantly, Bartholet recruited a talented, and diverse, legal staff.

Bartholet and the staff also successfully enlisted another vital contingent of any public-interest law firm: clients who conformed to the exacting profile of test-case plaintiffs and who, patiently and relatively cheerfully and with next to no promise of sufficient financial reward to justify the ordeal of public exposure and interminable litigation, contributed their time and bared details of their personal ordeals.

Before pursuing clients and cases, the center's staff meticulously drafted a legal strategy that constituted a solid foundation for their challenges and was nimble enough to adapt to adverse judgments. Its basic premise

was that people with a history of addiction or with criminal records deserve to be protected from discrimination in
hiring if they have demonstrated that they are qualified for
the job. The lawyers' arsenal included the equal-protection
and due-process clauses of the Fifth and Fourteenth Amendments, Title VII of the 1964 Civil Rights Law (since a disproportionate number of people with criminal records are
black or Hispanic) and the Rehabilitation Act of 1973,
which prohibited discrimination against handicapped or
disabled job seekers who were considered "otherwise qualified." Armed with grants from the Ford Foundation and
the National Institute on Drug Abuse, the Legal Action
Center filed suits against the United States Postal Service
and the New York City Transit Authority, both of which
were known for their explicit discriminatory policies toward prospective employees who acknowledged having
been drug-addicted (primarily former heroin addicts who
were receiving methadone) or had records of arrest or
conviction.

Typically, class-action lawsuits take years to litigate. In
one case, though, the Postal Service settled relatively quickly,
agreeing to reinstate employees who were on methadone
maintenance and to reimburse them for lost pay. Five years
later, the Postal Service settled most of the second suit.
Three years after that, the Transit Authority capitulated on
the criminal-record challenge. In the fourth case, challenging the authority's hiring policy for prospective employees
being treated with methadone, the Legal Action Center
was vindicated by the Federal District Court. But the ruling was overturned in 1979 by the United States Supreme
Court. While that battle was lost, the war was won. By
the time the high court ruled, the Transit Authority had
voluntarily lifted its blanket prohibition against hiring
people on methadone. And the Legal Action Center had

persuaded the Justice Department to invoke the Rehabilitation Act to protect prospective employees in the future.

While it was aggressively litigating those cases, the Legal Action Center did not indulge in a single-minded strategy that litigation was its sole recourse. It pursued a political solution, too. A member of the center's board drafted a bill that barred employers from discriminating against workers with criminal records unless their crime was related to the job or posed a potential threat to public safety.

Under the Rehabilitation Act, the center broadened its reach beyond employment discrimination. It sued Buffalo, New York, officials for zoning discrimination against an alcohol treatment agency, winning a case that extended legal protections already granted to former alcoholics to the programs that treat them. In another two-pronged challenge, the center sued in federal court to void draconian provisions of the so-called Rockefeller drug laws, which the New York State Legislature had enacted in 1973 while the center was still in its infancy. The goal of Governor Nelson A. Rockefeller and the State Legislature in imposing terms of fifteen years to life, regardless of whether the defendant was a drug kingpin or was caught with an ounce of cocaine, was to clear the streets of pushers and, by eliminating plea bargaining, clear court calendars, too. It did neither. "You can get all the tough drug laws you want," Sterling Johnson Jr., the city's special narcotics prosecutor, explained "but they'll have little impact unless you go back to the source."

Again, the federal district court agreed that sentences of three years to life for the sale of small amounts of cocaine or heroin represented cruel and unusual punishment. The center's board chairman, Arthur Liman, was enlisted to personally argue the case when the state appealed, but an appeals court reversed the ruling. The Supreme Court refused to review the ruling, but compelling dissents by Justices Thurgood Marshall and Lewis Powell helped persuade state lawmakers to amend the penalties and to eliminate life imprisonment for lesser offenses. The Supreme Court intervened in a case against a Veterans Administration regulation that classified alcoholism in the category of willful misconduct rather than disease. Two lower courts agreed that the regulation illegally discriminated against recovering alcoholics (they had been denied additional time to draw on their education benefits under the G.I. bill), but the Supreme Court again reversed.

In 1990, lobbying by the Legal Action Center and other groups led to protections in the Americans with Disabilities Act for victims of addiction. Invoking those provisions, lawyers for the center won the first court victory in the country (against the city of White Plains in suburban Westchester) establishing that the disabilities act barred zoning discrimination against treatment facilities for addicts and alcoholics. (The center also helped successfully challenge a Hawaii law that curbed welfare benefits to addicts and alcoholics.)

When in the early 1980s, the AIDS epidemic engendered complaints of discrimination in medical treatment, housing and the job market, the Legal Action Center had no mandate to respond and no specific funding. In conjunction with community-based service providers, the center rallied to unleash a battery of lawsuits challenging policies and practices of landlords, employers, health care organizations, zoning authorities and after-school programs that discriminated against individuals with AIDS (including the Girl Scouts, after an eight-year-old with HIV was denied admission to an upstate troop).

The center's lawyers also collaborated with state legislators to draft a landmark privacy law protecting the confidentiality information about people with AIDS, a political victory that prompted the center to expand more aggressively into public policy. By the late 1980s, the center had a proven record of accomplishment and expertise not only in court but in preserving and building upon its successful litigation and advocating protections that the courts declined to provide. In New York State, the Legal Action Center lobbied for more resources for additional drug, alcohol and HIV treatment and preventive services. Eventually, the center opened a Washington office to expand its advocacy role, provided training for sister agencies and established the Arthur Liman Policy Institute to conduct research into issues affecting its evolving constituency.

The growing practice of random drug testing in the 1980s posed another threat to employment opportunities for recovering addicts and alcoholics. Lawyers for the center challenged the policy on several fronts. They argued that individuals who were otherwise fully qualified were being fired or were being denied employment when tests found methadone or other properly prescribed medication in their urine; that sloppy procedures produced a disproportionate number of false positives; and that random testing without probable cause raised constitutional questions. In another federal suit against the New York City Transit Authority, lawyers successfully argued not only that the testing procedures lacked sufficient safeguards but that random testing was improperly conducted among employees whose jobs were unrelated to public safety. Another successful suit was filed against a securities company that fired an employee on the basis of a drug test that was unable to distinguish between an opiate and the poppy seeds on a bagel. On the same basis—that the results are unreliable and inadmissible in court proceedings—lawyers challenged the use of polygraph tests by employers. The center also sued the federal government for denying long-term educational benefits to recovering veterans on the grounds that their alcoholism or addiction constituted willful misconduct rather than a disease. (The center lost on appeal but successfully lobbied Congress to overturn the policy.)

"We created the Legal Action Center as another way of effecting change in a way that, because it was a bit of a threat to the establishment, it would not compromise Vera," Sturz says. "Its m.o. was to litigate. Vera's was certainly not." Its game plan of vigorously applying the protections of the Bill of Rights could have been lifted right off the pages of Sturz's special supplement to *Boys' Life*.

———

Even in its early years, Vera programs ran the gamut from alpha—Addiction Research and Treatment Corporation—to sigma—Wildcat Service Corporation (only a few letters short of omega).

What connected many of Vera's initiatives was a finding by Vera's Court Employment Project that one in four of its potential clients regularly used drugs or were former addicts. Officials at one of the progenitors to Wildcat would later recall that the experience "revealed that the city's addiction problem was becoming an inseparable part of its crime problem." And not just crime. The city estimated that addicts were flooding the welfare rolls at the rate of 1,400 or more a month and that they diverted some of the estimated $70 million in public assistance they were receiving to buy drugs. One promising answer was the synthetic chemical methadone. By satisfying an addict's physiological craving, methadone, it was hoped, would alleviate both the demand for another fix and withdrawal symptoms, eliminate the motivation to share contaminated hypodermic needles that spread hepatitis and worse and obviate an addict's compulsion to commit crime to support his habit.

Early in 1969, the state's Council on Drug Addiction recommended that a modest five-year-old state program of methadone maintenance not be expanded because, while promising, its impact appeared to be limited and still highly experimental. But Mayor Lindsay was desperate, facing election-year pressure to rein in rising crime. His frustration was shared by other officials who had to face frightened voters who desperately wanted something done. Lindsay was enlightened and innovative enough to embark on a politically risky experiment. Less than a month after the council issued its recommendation against expanding methadone maintenance, Lindsay, impressed by the initial success of the Bowery Project, invited Vera to help launch the city's first ambulatory methadone maintenance program. Lindsay couched the program almost entirely in terms of crime prevention and the societal cost of addiction. Empowering Vera to oversee the methadone experiment was a political no-brainer, Cyril D. Robinson of Pennsylvania State University later wrote: "Vera's sophisticated approach involved the development of projects in cooperation with a city department, using its own personnel to evolve and run the project, taking any blame for failure (there rarely was any), avoiding publicity and never seeking praise but, instead, amply bestowing it on cooperating city officials. Once Vera had eliminated the administrative bugs, the project would often be turned over to the city." With health and addiction services officials promoting drug-free therapy, Robinson concluded, "Vera, thereby, became the natural agency to launch what must have seemed, from Lindsay's view, a politically risky venture."

The initial methadone maintenance program was considered a marginal success, enough of one to inspire Vera to establish the Addiction Research and Treatment Corporation. It prudently spun off and was chaired, in part for political cover, by former U.S. Attorney General Nicholas deB. Katzenbach, and run by Dr. Beny Primm in Brooklyn, to determine the long-term efficacy of methadone. Methadone was billed as a miracle substitute for high-priced heroin, and the early results were promising. But after five years—and after Primm was threatened by bayonet-wielding black militants who accused him of enslaving fellow blacks through chemical dependency—researchers commissioned by Vera concluded that the impact was limited to the small group of patients who were highly motivated from the beginning. Three-fifths of the patients who entered treatment had dropped out by the end of the second year. But methadone survived as a heroin substitute for some addicts.

In 1971, while the efficacy of methadone maintenance was still being tested, Vera proposed to go one step further: a heroin maintenance program. That proposal provoked a politically untenable backlash, particularly from blacks (one of Lindsay's core constituencies) who denounced it with epithets ranging from sheer callousness to genocide. Nearly a year later, Vera again proposed a heroin maintenance program, this time couching it much more gingerly as an unassuming experiment. "As unlikely-appearing a provider of drugs as could be imagined," the *Times* said of Herb Sturz. He admitted to no addictions himself, not even minor ones, "except, perhaps, for reading." After visiting British heroin maintenance programs several times, Sturz was persuaded that a similar, more rigorously controlled pilot should be attempted in the United States. He came armed with a medical protocol drafted by two Yale psychiatrists who formulated a four-year experiment that would enroll 130 methadone maintenance program dropouts between the ages of twenty-one and forty. Another 100 addicts who failed methadone maintenance would be re-enrolled and serve as a control group. It was, in Sturz's words, meant "as a last resort for people who had failed in everything else." Heroin would be administered in a clinic rather than distributed, patients would be supplied with heroin for a year at the most, and to keep addicts from flocking to New York, only those who had been residents for at least a year when the program began would be eligible.

Sturz paved the way for the heroin program by inviting a half dozen doctors to dinner at the Harvard Club, and by the end of the evening, widespread misgivings had given way to a grudging acknowledgment that the experiment might hold some promise. "It was a remarkable accomplishment and it illustrated Herbert's métier," a friend of Sturz's recalls. "The ability to bring together divergent people, keep the tensions under control and come through with enough guidelines to get things going."

Still, Robinson of Penn State wrote,

> On the face of it, it seems incredible that, at a time when no more than 5 percent of the city's addicts were on methadone and when an addict might have as many as eighteen months wait for admission to a methadone clinic, city policy-makers could be thinking of "luring" methadone "failures" back into a methadone program with the promise of heroin. . . . But city officials knew that methadone patients had a yearly drop-out rate of 10 to 20 percent. They were convinced that those "failures" were the hard-core addicts; those most apt to commit crimes. . . . Given that perspective, it seemed reasonable to look for a method that would lure them into treatment.

At the time, though, the Lindsay administration was more concerned with back-pedaling out of a political firestorm than in long-term results. Sturz explained that the program's goal was to reach the one in five or so addicts who were enrolled in a methadone maintenance program but who proved resistant to treatment and quit to return to the streets and "become a menace to themselves and society." He explained that "social services, supported work and manpower training would be key elements of the program."

The Lindsay administration nimbly promised a full airing of the "medical, moral, social and administrative issues" before referring the proposal to the city's Narcotics Control Council, which buried it. When Sturz sought independent financing for the experiment, he met with overwhelming opposition from black politicians and community leaders, conservative political groups, an army of anti-drug organizations, an ad hoc congressional committee and even skeptics who considered Vera's proposal worthy and well-intentioned but harbored doubts about its efficacy (including whether patients could be stabilized at standard doses and whether they would supplement their habit on the outside). Representative Charles B. Rangel of Harlem pronounced heroin "a killer, not a drug on which a human being should be maintained." A federal drug enforcement official warned that it meant "consigning hundreds of thousands of our citizens to the slavery of heroin addiction forever." Supporting congressional legislation that would specifically prohibit the experiment, President Nixon himself intervened, declaring: "The concept of heroin maintenance represents a concession to weakness and defeat in the drug abuse struggle, a concession which would surely lead to the erosion of our most cherished values for the dignity of man." Even the *Times*, which, editorially, at least, was largely supportive of Lindsay and Sturz, was unforgiving. "Heroin maintenance?" an editorial sniffed. "Only those who don't know anything about addiction can discuss it."

"With so many different enemies," Peter Reuter of the University of Maryland and Robert MacCoun of Berkeley concluded, "ultimately the proposal had no friends. It simply disappeared."

By the fall of 1973, with the Lindsay administration preparing to leave office, the mayor cut his losses by declaring victory in the war against heroin. Robinson concluded,

> From the Lindsay administration's standpoint, the proposal was at no time more than a scrimmage in the battle for the public mind over who had the best remedy for addict-related crime. By the time the project was ready for public display, the city strategy was expressed as "a balanced approach designed to meet the individual needs of each potential client." Therefore, when it became plain that launching the heroin project would require more time and effort than it was estimated to be worth, the idea— and that is all it was at the time—was easily abandoned.

Sturz says he harbored no regrets about making the proposal, only that he was never given the opportunity to try it: "I thought we would learn something about another modality for some people who resisted everything. I didn't think it was a no-go from the beginning, but the question is, could we have done enough groundwork? In retrospect, it was probably a miscalculation of the politics involved."

Politics was less of an obstacle than science was to another Sturz initiative, one that proved that Sturz's curiosity was boundless. In the late 1960s, he stumbled upon a finding that women before menopause had one sixth as many heart attacks as men of a similar age. Could that mean, he wondered, that "the loss of blood through menstruation could account for the statistical discrepancy"? The statistic was not unfamiliar to medical researchers, many of whom attributed it to hormonal differences between men and women. Sturz figured that regenerating blood might produce some health benefit. He was tantalized, though, not simply in terms of a highly theoretical scientific experiment, but with the possibility that merely testing the hypothesis would have immediate practical value. With blood banks paying Bowery derelicts for blood that often turned out to be tainted, encouraging more blood donations from healthy men in general seemed like a good idea.

As it happened, Mitchell Sviridoff, the Ford Foundation's vice president for national affairs, telephoned Sturz around that time to say that a friend of McGeorge Bundy, the Ford Foundation president, was infected with hepatitis from a bad blood transfusion. "Herb, you have all kinds of ideas," Sviridoff said. "Do you have any ideas about bad blood transfusions?" Sturz relayed his hypothesis to Sviridoff, who bounced it off Bundy, who checked with Gordon Chase, who had been an aide to Bundy in the White House.

Bundy's assumption of the presidency of Ford in 1966 was a welcome relief. Ford had been an early supporter of Vera, but when the institute audaciously applied for a million-dollar multi-year grant, Bundy's predecessor, Henry Heald, insisted the research be overseen by New York University's Institute of Judicial Administration (Heald came to Ford from NYU) with Vera playing a subordinate role. Sturz rejected the grant. Heald was furious.

It was presumptuous enough of Vera to seek the grant. It was even more audacious to reject it. Heald said Vera should forget about ever getting support from Ford again and urged Schweitzer "to provide from your own resources more significant support of the work in which you are interested." To which Schweitzer replied that he had given $200,000 to the Manhattan Bail Project compared to Ford's $376,000. "I am pleased to have been able to match funds even to this extent with our country's largest philanthropy," Schweitzer wrote.

By this time, and with Heald having been succeeded by Bundy, Sturz was so gung-ho, respected for his ingenuity and persuasive that Sviridoff agreed to help satisfy his friend's curiosity with a $100,000 grant that same day. "Mike," Bundy told Sviridoff, "if you can come up with an idea like this in half an hour, just think if I'd given you a whole day." (Sounding a bit abashed, Sviridoff explained that Ford approved the grant "really in recognition of Vera's exceptional talent for innovation" and as part of a "natural progression to a decision by Vera to adapt its techniques to other urban problem areas.") By mid-1971, Vera had persuaded 140 men between the ages of thirty and fifty who worked as police officers (they leapt at the opportunity to get extra days off for donating), Wall Street executives, and professionals, to undergo regular bloodletting. The study, which experts said would have to enroll 2,500 volunteers and continue for five years, was conducted at St. Vincent's Hospital in Greenwich Village. The director of blood coagulation, Dr. Leonard J. Stutman, explained sheepishly, "We've been trying to brainwash Herb into giving up that idea, but he seems emotionally tied to the idea." Sturz remembers the experiment differently: "We never had enough money to carry out the project on a sustained basis with enough men." To this day, some experiments suggest that bloodletting and subsequent re-generation of fresh blood might have therapeutic value in some cases. "I always felt that project had a lot of promise," Sturz says.

Years later, when Sviridoff was awarded an honorary degree by Duke University, his friends and colleagues grilled him at a mock press conference before the cere-mony. One question: "You advocated a grant and served personally as program officer for an experiment whose avowed goal was to bring leeches back to the practice of medicine—that is, to bleed therapeutically the citizens of our nation. Beginning with police officers! Would you say that program constituted one of Ford Foundation's principal contributions to crime control in America?" And another: "How much truth is there in the rumor that when you were at the Ford Foundation you granted millions to the Vera Institute of Justice in order to pay off to Vera's di-rector huge gambling debts incurred at the poker table?"

At the very least, the blood-letting project appeared to adhere to the physician's credo of "First, do no harm." It also demonstrated the faith that Sturz inspired. And it was indicative of a personality trait that, more often than not, paid off. As one friend and colleague, Michael Weinstein, puts it, "He has the vision and persistence to go after low-probability interventions that have enormous ramifications."

Chapter 7

The Wildcats Strike

While Vera had been an early innovator in programs to free addicts from drug dependency, few jobs or services were available to them if they succeeded. Most former addicts approached the job market with seemingly insurmountable handicaps. They hadn't worked regularly in years, if ever. Few had marketable skills or even the requisite work habits to be accepted by public or private job training programs. Most had criminal records. Which meant they remained dependent on welfare and crime for income. Tens of thousands of addicts were supporting their habits through robbery, burglary and auto theft, contributing to crime rates that were spiraling out of control. In theory, policy makers reasoned that employing thousands of former addicts (and, later, ex-offenders without a history of heroin addiction) could make a big dent in an epidemic that was costing money and lives and driving middle-class taxpayers from the city.

Working with the city's Department of Sanitation in the late 1960s, Vera began a pilot program on Manhattan's

Upper West Side called Paper Tigers. Former addicts were recruited to remove bundled newspapers left at the curb for recycling. Buoyed by modest but promising results, Vera launched Masonry Cleaners, which sought city contracts to steam clean the grimy façades of public buildings, and Pioneer Messenger Service to serve public and private clients in what was hoped would become a self-sustaining venture. In contrast to the residential programs offered by the Manhattan Bowery Project to mostly older men with alcohol-induced brain damage, Masonry Cleaners, Pioneer and their successors were designed to test the rehabilitative potential of supported employment for workers presumed to have more potential.

Initially, in 1971, Pioneer dispatched nine messengers, referred by a methadone maintenance clinic, from a cheery office in midtown run by Gary Walker (who would later become senior vice president of the Manpower Demonstration Research Corporation and president of Public/Private Ventures). Unlike private industry where the expectations of employers might prove too daunting, supported work programs like Masonry Cleaning and Pioneer Messenger offered a lower-stress environment (the Pioneer and for-profit workers often came from similar backgrounds). As responsibilities increased, so would pay and the more intangible rewards of success. Work was coupled with counseling, assistance with security deposits on apartments and legal services. Tutoring and other services that were not perceived by the workers as job related were generally the least successful.

In the two years that it operated as a commercially competitive company under a small grant from the U.S. Department of Labor, Pioneer grew to 300 clients, and successfully bid for a City University of New York contract to deliver mail among its twenty-three branch colleges (and it developed into a trucking service that delivered everything from a pair of lions to payroll checks). Pioneer would also spawn a supported work program with the Off-Track Betting Corporation (one betting parlor was manned by former addicts). Pioneer demonstrated that supported work was an effective rehabilitation tool for people who might otherwise have been written off as unemployable.

————

Drawing on the same successful formula underwriting Pioneer, Vera launched the Wildcat Service Corporation, a project developed to test whether supported work could assist ex-addicts toward a mainstream life and full-time jobs while reducing welfare dependency and criminal recidivism. Its very name evoked the high stakes—and high risks—of going after big game. "Engineers are out looking for work, and here we are trying to place addicts and men with records," says Kenneth Marion, Sturz's former college roommate, whom he recruited for Vera in 1968 and Wildcat in 1972. "So we decided the best approach was to set up experimental businesses of our own and support them with Vera's counseling and social services." Wildcat would start as a demonstration project, financed largely by federal grants (the Department of Labor, the National Institute of Drug Abuse, the Department of Justice's Law Enforcement Assistance Administration and the Department of Health, Education and Welfare). As with the bail project, a lottery system randomly created two groups of several hundred individuals. One group was hired by Wildcat. The other was not. Rates of employment, welfare dependency and recidivism were monitored for both groups.

Wildcat opened in 1973 in an unprepossessing second-story office at East 39th Street and Madison Avenue, just west of Vera's townhouse headquarters on 39th Street. The unpretentious quarters belied its ambitions as the pioneer in supported work programs in the United States.

Its board of directors, recruited, in part, by Jay Kriegel and other Vera enthusiasts in the Lindsay administration, was peppered with business and labor luminaries, including its chairman, Norborne Berkeley Jr., the president of Chemical Bank, Richard Salant of CBS, William Ellinghaus of New York Telephone, Donald Regan of Merrill Lynch, Richard Gelb of Bristol-Myers, Anthony Scotto of the International Longshoremen's Union and later Bill Bradley, the former Knicks hall-of-famer and New Jersey senator. The directors achieved a social relevance that otherwise might have been beyond their grasp. They, in turn, gave Wildcat political cover and the gravitas that elevated it from another do-good program to a business enterprise.

Credibility was crucial. Early on, administrators became suspicious because a number of Wildcat workers turned out to have Social Security numbers that were nearly sequential. Sturz immediately notified the district attorney's office. He was relieved the next day to learn that the numbers were all valid and had been issued when the workers qualified for Supplemental Security Income (SSI) while being treated for drug abuse. "One of the reasons Herb is able to get things done is that people trust him," Ken Marion said.

Marion was Wildcat's first president (he would go on to become a New York City deputy police commissioner for administration). Under Marion, Wildcat would grow within a few years from a boutique pilot project with a budget of $2 million to a $20 million operation with about 2,000 employees in four boroughs. Heroin addicts were classified as disabled by the federal government, and Wildcat sought and received a waiver of the Social Security Act so their benefits could be funneled into a wage pool to support their salaries. If former addicts had not been considered disabled, New York would have been required to support them through Home Relief, which was funded half by the state and half by the city. Monthly benefits amounted to about 25 percent of what welfare recipients would collect from full-time jobs. But former addicts had little incentive to work. Welfare benefits would be reduced for each dollar earned and would subject them to payroll taxes and other work-related expenses. And their wages would be too high to allow them to remain eligible for Medicaid, thereby subjecting them to significant health insurance costs or having no coverage whatsoever.

Wildcat also derived income from its contractual work. Beginning under Sturz's leadership at Vera, it signed contracts with several municipal agencies to clean up vacant lots and open spaces, to perform clerical work in various city departments, to steam clean city buildings (Masonry Cleaners had been absorbed by Wildcat), to work with the elderly and to survey street conditions. Thanks to welfare diversion and various foundation and government subsidies, Wildcat's cost per worker would be less than an outside contractor's or the city's. Wildcat aimed to provide meaningful employment, but, in theory, only work that would not have been done otherwise by unionized civil service workers or by private competitors whose employees belonged to unions. Supporting Wildcat was city policy. By the late 1970s, Wildcat was generating more than $5 million a year from city contracts.

During that decade, Wildcat also received between $3.4 million and $7 million annually from the city under a contract with the city's Department of Employment, which Sturz negotiated over chess games with David Grossman, the city's budget director. The city's annual grant paid for Wildcat's overhead and the portion of participants' wages not covered by other sources. The Nixon and Ford administrations made it national policy to encourage training and employment for hard-to-place workers, and a number of cities, notably Baltimore, supplemented federal block grants with local funds. In 1975, New York was verging on a fiscal crisis that would bring the city to the very edge of bankruptcy, which made finding money to pay for any nonessential services an incredible challenge, and at the same time, helped increase the appeal of Wildcat's subsidized rates. Grossman theorized that investing in people and in a future workforce could be construed as a capital, rather than an operating, expense. That adjustment allowed the city's Department of Employment to pay for the Wildcat contract with borrowed funds. (It was, to be sure, the kind of gimmick that would leave the city vulnerable to charges of fiscal chicanery and would be specifically barred by accounting rules imposed after 1975.)

By 1977, Wildcat's workforce grew to about 1,500 participants, and operational centers were established in four boroughs. Workers were embedded in more than a dozen city agencies and several not-for-profit organizations in a wide range of jobs—serving as interpreters at Mount Sinai Hospital, shopping for the elderly, removing graffiti from bus shelters, painting warning stripes on the curbs flanking fire hydrants, removing decades of accumulated detritus from the Bronx River and fixing flat tires on police cars. Wildcat's early success, and the peer pressure to keep it accountable, led to the creation of the Manpower Demonstration Research Corporation and the largest controlled social services demonstration project in the nation's history.

Former addicts working with Wildcat generally lasted longer in unsubsidized jobs than ex-addicts who hadn't participated in the program. There were also indications of reduced criminal activity (about nine in ten had arrest records when they entered the program) and reduced drug and alcohol use among the experimental group. But, most importantly, the findings suggested that the return to government in employment and income taxes, the value of labor produced for the public and the reduced criminal justice costs resulting from lower rates of incarceration produced an estimated $1.25 in economic benefits for every dollar invested.

The initial Wildcat model taught generic working habits rather than specific job skills. As a result, the quality of work was not always exemplary. (The foreman of a crew painting yellow lines on curbs in official no parking zones was offering to paint custom no-parking zones for $10. "Although we admired the foreman's ingenuity," Ken Marion recalls, "we let him go.") Emphasis was placed on instilling basic principles that most mainstream workers take for granted: getting to work on time, dressing neatly, not being drunk or under the influence of drugs on the job, following directions from supervisors, acting politely to fellow workers and the public in the workplace. If participants could absorb the generic requirements of working, they would be prepared for training in specific skills by permanent employers who were better equipped to provide it and were more cognizant of which skills were required. Early on, though, classroom and on-the-job programs were introduced to instill work habits and to teach job readiness, General Educational Development diploma test preparation and clerical and basic computer skills.

Today, Wildcat is a dependable vehicle to prepare participants for entry into the permanent workforce. If it was intended to be transformative, it was also transitional. The idea was that participants would move on to permanent employment when they had a solid track record of meeting the generic demands of the workplace—a record that would instill self-confidence and be attractive to full-time employers. That could take two months; it could sometimes take two years. Modest bonuses and pay increases were awarded early and often, but they were capped low enough to encourage people who were ready to move on to more lucrative employment.

Wildcat participants were valued for several reasons, not the least of which was that the public was becoming painfully aware of the increasingly severe decline in municipal services. The jobs were, for the most part, visible, exposing them not only to the public but also to constituencies within the government that might, had the prospect of working alongside ex-offenders been presented hypothetically, been considerably less receptive. Former addicts and police officers working side by side acquired a mutual appreciation that would have been exceedingly difficult to earn under any other circumstances.

In an era before e-mail and faxes, the Wildcat messenger service was not always reliable, whether as a result of the system's design, its supervision or the efficacy of the workers themselves. In 1975, when telephone service was interrupted on Manhattan's West Side, Wildcat boldly stepped in to offer its messenger service corps as a temporary alternative—a well-intentioned but audacious overreach (but a Wildcat auditor assessing the service happened upon one particularly grateful merchant in the affected area, who turned out to be Carl Weisbrod's uncle). Attempting to substitute for phone service under any circumstances would have been implausible, much less given the scope of the challenge in Manhattan, the lack of preparation and the absence of a deep managerial bench to supervise it. Still, Wildcat gamely launched the effort and delivered more than 10,000 messages (some too late, though, to be of value). And the concept of mobilizing an entire organization to respond to a citywide demand would inspire and become the model for the City Volunteer Corps.

———

Given the growing threats to organized labor's virtual stranglehold on municipal government in the 1970s, Wildcat's relatively peaceful coexistence with the city's public and private unions is nothing short of surprising. It was no accident, though. At its peak in 1975, Wildcat was employing some 1,500 workers, mostly in city agencies, with an expectation that the number would double within two years. While the possibility of workforce layoffs was not looming, the city's workforce was shrinking by attrition. In some agencies, municipal employees were already feeling threatened by the influx of federal Comprehensive Employment and Training Act (CETA) workers who, like those from Wildcat, were ostensibly being hired to complement and supplement full-time, and unionized, civil servants.

By dint of personality and political acumen, Sturz and his colleagues were more sensitive to labor's vulnerability. Vera and Wildcat couched their contracts with the city as work that would not otherwise get done. As revenue sources shriveled and creative accounting became more difficult to accomplish, this was true. But much of the work that Wildcat undertook was in fact essential. Even when city officials were pressing them to be more aggressive, Sturz and Wildcat astutely backed off at any hint of a union backlash (and the possibility of wildcat strikes).

But Sturz's sensitivity was not one-sided. It was complemented by the enlightened leadership of municipal unions that, while feeling vulnerable to layoffs for the first time since the Depression, were nonetheless guided by a liberal ideological legacy. They would not tolerate union busting, but they would tolerate a public welfare initiative that pricked their social conscience. Chief among the labor visionaries who welcomed Wildcat was Victor Gotbaum, the executive director of the largest municipal union, District Council 37 of the American Federation of State, County and Municipal Employees (AFSCME). (Gotbaum would later marry Betsy Flower Hogan, who was working for Vera in the early 1970s and would later be elected twice as the New York City public advocate.) Wildcat wisely avoided seeking contracts in agencies or job categories represented by the more militant unions (maintaining police station houses, for example, was within the jurisdiction of District Council 37, not the Patrolmen's Benevolent Association).

And Wildcat shunned work that outside contractors with unionized workforces normally performed. Sturz and Jay Kriegel, his chief patron in the Lindsay administration, were savvy enough to install a muscular union leader on Wildcat's board of directors in the form of Anthony Scotto, the president of the International Longshoreman's Association in New York. Scotto's deep roots in labor and politics provided a valuable imprimatur. When the ambitious son of a Teamsters local president picketed a Wildcat worksite and sought to organize Wildcat workers, Scotto intervened with the man's father and the problem vanished overnight. (Union organizing, whose primary agenda was job security, seemed antithetical to a program whose mission was to provide transitional work.)

———

Wildcat followed Vera's traditional financing strategy for demonstration projects: Start small with foundation and government grants and avoid posing a threat to potential funding competitors. Once the programmatic concept has been field tested and the services embraced by their chief beneficiary, identify and tap into an institutional funding stream (usually from the government jurisdiction that had come to depend upon the service) and spin off the project as a separate entity so it can seek permanent financing without competing against core Vera programs or sister spin-offs.

But just as Wildcat was being institutionalized, it faced several challenges. The first came from Washington. The Social Security benefits waiver was rendered moot in 1974 when Aid to the Disabled was folded into a new federally administered and funded Supplemental Security Income program. Initially, SSI had no provision for demonstration projects that allowed benefits to be diverted into a wage pool. Vera scrambled and successfully lobbied for legislation that would allow already enrolled Wildcat workers to qualify. But the Social Security Administration determined that under SSI, former addicts would no longer be defined as "disabled." Instead, they would be shunted onto the state's Home Relief rolls, with three strikes against them. First, Home Relief was entirely funded by the state and the city, with no federal contribution. Second, state law also did not provide for pilot projects. And, third, Home Relief recipients lost a dollar of benefits for each dollar of earnings, negating any financial incentive to go to work.

———

In the same year, a new mayoral administration with a new mindset moved into City Hall. Wildcat, to the administration of Mayor Abraham D. Beame, must have looked like just another nontraditional nuisance inherited from political

neophytes. To make matters worse, Beame inherited a fiscal crisis of unprecedented dimensions, which would strip
the mayor of his wide discretion over the city's financial
affairs and shift it to the governor and outside monitors.
With full-time municipal employees facing layoffs, Wildcat's innovative financing depended on a capital budget
supported by bonds that no bank was willing to buy.

The very existence of New York City now depended on
transferring municipal obligations to the state and federal
governments. In response, Vera mobilized on two fronts.
First, it won Beame's support, at least in principle, for
Wildcat conceptually, which, in a way, surprised even
Sturz. "We were imaginative and had become important to
them," he says. "We found the right levers." Sometimes,
Sturz was able to find the right levers because he helped
put them there. When David Dinkins (who would later be
mayor) was forced to withdraw as Beame's nominee for
deputy mayor because he hadn't filed income tax returns
for several years, Sturz compassionately, and cannily, bestowed one of the first acts of redemption by arranging
the appointment of Dinkins to Vera's board.

Now, more than ever, Wildcat could argue that its
workers were providing vital services, which would have
vanished with layoffs from a municipal payroll that had
gotten bloated, although nobody was certain by how much.
(Walter B. Wriston, the former chairman of Citicorp, recalled that when he demanded that Deputy Mayor James
A. Cavanagh reveal the exact number of city employees,
Cavanagh fished a piece of paper from his pocket and finally confided the figure: 397,402. But a Citicorp economist noticed that the paper was blank. "That's when I knew
we were in trouble," Wriston remembered.)

Sturz also pursued a second front, redefining Wildcat's
public rationale to build national bipartisan political support

and to capitalize on a new national agenda. Subtly and not so subtly, Sturz altered the contours of the intellectual terrain to conform to the priorities of the Nixon administration and its chief domestic adviser, Daniel Patrick Moynihan. Wildcat, which in New York addressed the reintegration and employment of former heroin addicts, was repositioned as a national vehicle to divert public assistance recipients from welfare to work. What mattered most was that Sturz kept Wildcat alive against the odds and without sacrificing its fundamental goal.

Sturz enlisted Mike Sviridoff, the Ford Foundation's vice president for national affairs and an early Vera advocate (a mutual friend, Stanley Brezenoff, calls them "the two ultimate pragmatists"), to organize a nationwide conference that would not only showcase Wildcat's contribution to meeting that policy goal but elevate the major participants and transform potential adversaries into stakeholders. Beame was invited to deliver the keynote address; Vera virtually drafted his speech. A mayor who was, at best, a Wildcat agnostic, was being transformed into a fan. Once again, Sturz and Vera invoked the very same strategy that Jacob Riis had successfully used at the beginning of the twentieth century to galvanize Americans against the slums. Call it cynical, perhaps, but Riis, the social reformer whose vivid photographs and narrative of urban poverty seared America's psyche in the late nineteenth century, similarly perceived that all the lofty appeals to altruism would carry his fight only so far. "The battle with the slum began the day civilization recognized in it her enemy," Riis wrote. "It was a losing fight until conscience joined forces with fear and self-interest against it."

With the city's financial prospects growing more and more gloomy and its survival increasingly dependent on support from a skeptical Congress and White House, the

Beame administration was presented with a rare opportunity: to showcase a cost-effective New York City program
before a national audience. Like Sturz's earlier convocations
on bail and other subjects, the conference would serve as
prelude to the launching of a National Supported Work
Demonstration Project funded jointly by the Ford Foundation and several federal agencies.

———

Meanwhile, early results from the research into the program's experimental and control groups validated Wildcat's promise. Vera could demonstrate that the city's costs
were far outweighed by savings from reduced costs for incarceration and from the transition of graduates of the program from the welfare rolls to the tax rolls—coupled with
the revenue from payroll taxes paid by participants employed by Wildcat and the value of the public services provided by them. But the sort of imaginative fiscal devices
that Sturz had negotiated with Grossman, Lindsay's budget director—classifying spending on manpower training as
a long-term investment eligible to be financed by issuing
bonds—would come back to haunt the city. (Generally,
the policy was articulated by Julius C. C. Edelstein, a con-
fidant of former Mayor Wagner: "A good loan is better than
a poor tax.") After years of budgetary magic, one official acknowledged, the rabbits were piling up in the hat. Or, as
Frederick O'R. Hayes, another Lindsay budget director,
put it: "The newspapers created the impression that we
had phony problems and real solutions. Actually, the problems were real, but the solutions were phony." Wildcat's
contract with the Department of Employment suffered a
25 percent cut as the city began to shift suspect operating

expenses from the capital budget, but the program overall continued to receive substantial support.

Wildcat still faced another serious obstacle, though: How to keep tapping into welfare benefits once Aid to the Disabled was replaced by Home Relief. City welfare officials were receptive, but state officials believed that diverting benefits to Wildcat on a permanent basis would cost Albany more, since Home Relief recipients typically bounced on and off the rolls rather than remaining continuously. New state legislation would be needed from Albany. To win over the Democrats, Sturz enlisted Robert Steingut, a city council member from Brooklyn, whose father, Stanley, was the speaker of the State Assembly. The elder Steingut was persuaded to support legislation that would authorize state officials to divert Home Relief benefits to support programs like Wildcat, as long as the legislation was introduced by the state's Department of Social Services. The Republican-controlled State Senate was more problematic. There, the legislation would be subject to the jurisdiction of one of New York City's longtime antagonists, Senator William Smith of rural Big Flats, who had earned the moniker "Cadillac Bill" by bashing welfare recipients who bought flashy cars. Smith was hostile to virtually all welfare legislation, especially bills that were seen as benefiting New York City.

But by then, welfare reform—no matter how it was being defined—was emerging as a bipartisan cause. Generally, Democrats were coming to the realization that the system, rooted in the Elizabethan Poor Laws and later adapted to mitigate crisis conditions during the Great Depression, demeaned those it purportedly served. Republicans viewed the program as a lavish giveaway, which encouraged the able-bodied but slothful to collect cash for no good reason. By cultivating opinion makers and encouraging favorable news and editorial coverage, including in the *Wall Street Journal*, Sturz and Sviridoff promoted an alternative with broad ideological appeal—a program that transformed welfare benefits into paychecks for people willing to support themselves by working. Wildcat had also won over New York's two U.S. senators, both Republicans, but from opposite ends of the spectrum, James Buckley and Jacob Javits, who rarely agreed on anything.

With Steingut shepherding it, the Wildcat legislation easily passed the Assembly. But the bill remained bottled up in Senator Smith's social services committee. As the 1976 legislative session neared an end, Sturz appealed to Buckley and Javits to intervene. Both contacted Smith, repeatedly reminding him that the legislation was not only vital to New York but integral to the Republican Party's national agenda. On the last day of the session, Smith caved on the condition that the diversion of benefits for any individual would be limited to one year. But because the Senate version differed from the Assembly's the legislation appeared to be doomed for the session. Sometimes, though, the absolute power vested in the legislative leadership can be harnessed for good ends. Senator Carol Bellamy rushed the bill to the Assembly chamber just as Speaker Steingut was informing his restive members that the 1976 session would finally end after the votes were cast on ten more bills. Naturally, legislation to reconcile the two versions of the Wildcat bill was not among them. But Sturz's lieutenant, Carl Weisbrod, audaciously rushed to the podium to remind Steingut and his counsel, Ken Shapiro, of their commitment to Wildcat. Steingut shrugged, Shapiro requested the number of the Senate bill and then unabashedly announced to the Assembly that actually eleven, not ten, bills would be presented for final passage.

By voice vote, on a bill that no member had seen much less read, the Senate version was enacted.

———

As a national model for a supported work program, Wildcat was a pioneer. Initially no time limit was imposed on how long it took to classify participants as "job ready," but by 1976 Senate legislation changed that timetable, as did the selection of Wildcat as the site of a Manpower Demonstration Research Corporation experiment, which placed an eighteen-month limit on supported work. The prospects for finding unsubsidized employment, meanwhile, were daunting. Private employers weren't recruiting. City government's personnel agenda ranged from hiring freezes to layoffs. Running out of placement alternatives, Wildcat turned to its own board of directors. Norborne Berkeley, the chairman of the board of Wildcat and president of Chemical Bank, prodded his managers to hire a dozen Wildcat workers as teller trainees, a decision that may seem unexceptional today in an era of security cameras and accounting software, but which in its day was revolutionary for a corporation with fiduciary responsibilities. Chemical's confidence in Vera and the success of Wildcat alumni (among them, Peter Cove would go on to found America Works, a private welfare-to-work employment company) provided other prospective employers with the cover of validation.

———

The difficulty in moving large numbers of Wildcatters into permanent employment on an individual basis prompted Vera to establish a job creation unit, under the direction first of Paul Strasburg and later of Claire Haaga. Its mission was to generate jobs by developing new programs that would provide placements and bridge the gap in government services. Well before the adjective "synergistic" became a cliché, Vera's goal was to marry Wildcat's need to generate jobs for its graduates with a broader programmatic agenda—the "double social utility" that Sturz championed. A survey found a vacuum in services available to the elderly and disabled, especially when it came to transportation. In response, one early effort at cross-fertilization was Easyride.

Services were available for the frail and elderly at senior centers and health clinics, but many of those people were isolated from providers. Today, public transit is mandated handicapped-accessible, but no such law prevailed in the 1970s. Medicaid covered van service to certain medical appointments. But there was no provision for transportation to nutrition, recreation, educational or other programs offered by social service agencies. Easyride, initially managed by Betsy Gotbaum, was created by Vera not only to meet the demand for transportation services on the Lower East Side but to provide meaningful employment to ex-addicts and ex-offenders. Gotbaum was working in Washington for the Kerner Commission on civil disorder when Sturz, through a mutual friend, invited her to New York to be interviewed first for a program to hire receptionists in police station houses, freeing up uniformed officers, and then for Easyride. "I came up for the interview all gussied up, very serious and formal," she recalls, "and walked into his office where there was this enormous dog, Trotwood. It immediately set me at ease and I was very receptive to the offer to work in a program that selected, trained and supervised welfare recipients who then worked in precinct station houses to humanize them. That he had the confidence that I could do that—'li'l miss debutante'—was amazing and it gave me my start in New York City."

Typically, funding for Easyride was patched together from sources that never would have collaborated of their own volition. The federal Department of the Aging approved a demonstration grant; the Urban Mass Transportation Association provided matching funds for three vehicles. Customers who were over sixty-five or disabled were eligible for the same half fare they would have paid on mass transit. They could subscribe to regular service for recurring appointments for medical treatment or other services or reserve one-time trips to go shopping or to attend a nutrition program largely at their own initiative and often without an escort.

Easyride hired Wildcat graduates, helped them get driver's licenses and enlisted the Rusk Institute of Rehabilitative Medicine and Hunter College's Brookdale Center on Aging to train workers to maneuver wheelchairs and other devices and to offer basic customer services. For Sturz, double social utility wasn't enough, though. Easyride had still another agenda. It wasn't enough just to help two underserved constituencies help themselves. Sturz also hoped with Easyride to demonstrate that public funds, leveraged, creatively co-mingled and rigorously monitored, could be stretched more efficiently. Easyride generated jobs. It provided accessible transportation by developing a service that was dependable and responsive to its customers. It also improved the efficacy of a public service that had been so fragmented, duplicative and bureaucratic across the board, in everything from booking a ride to paying the bills, that you could drive a paratransit van through the gaps. Prior to Easyride, depending on their destination, customers had to call one of six different services—Medicaid for transportation to medical visits, the city's Department of the

Aging to senior centers, church and community groups to religious and social services. Sturz sought to rationalize the sources of funding and the demand for transportation with a single reliable, affordable program.

One way, as Sturz saw it, was to broaden Medicare's mandate. If the federal program paid for transportation to a wider range of health services, including nutrition, Medicare could eventually save money because the physical condition of its consumers might stabilize or even improve. When a rule got in the way, as one often did, Sturz's first inclination was to bend it (some inflexible rules would actually have to be broken). The most straightforward way was to apply for a waiver. Vera did, under the Social Security Act, but even under a Democratic administration the application languished. When the most direct route didn't work, Sturz resorted to a more public form of pressure. At his urging Jack Rosenthal, by then editorial page editor of the *Times*, wrote a passionate editorial urging Joseph Califano, the Secretary of Health, Education and Welfare, to grant permission for a pilot program that, by expanding Medicare's coverage to broaden the definition of health services to include preventive and other programs, would free countless elderly and disabled Americans from the solitude of their homes. Less than a week later, Califano signed the waiver.

"The funds are there," Sturz said. "It's the way you use them that counts. Medicaid provides $260 for each day spent in the hospital. Why not use that $260 to hire a van, pay an ex-addict to drive the elderly to the hospital and home again? You've kept people out of hospitals while you've created an employment opportunity."

Building on its record for reliable service, Easyride expanded to the West Side of Manhattan. In the early 1980s, it collaborated with the Eastern Paralyzed Veterans Association to lobby for accessible transportation for disabled passengers. In 1984, the Legislature provided for the expansion of Easyride elsewhere in Manhattan and for a feasibility study into making the buses and subways more accessible. By 1990, responding to state mandates to provide more accessible transportation, the city government began a citywide paratransit service called Access-a-Ride. Easyride won the contract for the Manhattan service. Not surprisingly, the city's rules and regulations were more inflexible and less customer friendly. People seeking recurring trips had to submit to a lottery, and one of the losers turned out to be a Holocaust survivor who had traveled to get dialysis three times a week. Not by chance, the absurdity of the rules were brought to the attention of the columnist Jimmy Breslin. The elderly patient, who commented that he had never before been very lucky, got back his regular seat on the Vera bus.

———

By itself and through its offshoots, Wildcat would serve as a national model for training and placing men and women who were classified as difficult to employ. By far, Wildcat's most successful strategy for permanent job placement was the use of "rollovers." Initially, teams of up to ten Wildcat employees were headed by a crew chief. In contrast to the drug treatment programs, which hired former addicts as full-time counselors, Wildcat's crews and crew chiefs were overseen by managers recruited on the basis of their supervisory skills and workplace experience. (Since Wildcat was intended to be a transitional program, crew members were encouraged to find permanent employment outside of Wildcat.) While supported work included support from fellow crew members, as employees were deemed to be nearly ready for outside jobs, they were given more independent work assignments, often in public agencies and not-for-profit organizations that contracted with Wildcat. The arrangement was similar to doing business with a private office-temp firm. Wildcat would be reimbursed for the cost of salaries and benefits for each employee, and the worker would remain on Wildcat's payroll. Eventually, though, more and more Wildcat graduates would be rolled over onto the payroll of the organization or agency, where they would become permanent employees.

By the early 1990s, the rollover model was successfully adopted by the private sector. Over the years, an estimated 70 percent of the 1,500 or so participants in this welfare-to-work model partnership were placed in permanent, non-subsidized jobs. Smith Barney was among the largest employers, and its enthusiastic participation was a coup for Wildcat. Wildcat and Smith Barney conceived and created a job training program tailored to the employment needs of a Wall Street firm, providing sixteen weeks of classroom instruction and help in coping with barriers to employment, including housing, transportation and child care. The company agreed to hire dozens of Wildcat workers as office temps with the expectation that, if their temporary employment was successful, they would be trained as interns and placed on Smith Barney's permanent payroll as research analysts, administrative assistants and in other entry-level jobs. In return, the company received tax credits and a pool of job applicants specifically trained to meet its needs. The program proved to be so successful that Jamie Dimon, who would later become chairman of J. P. Morgan Chase, and Amalia Betanzos, who would become Wildcat's chief executive, would be honored at the White House.

———

Wildcat's success inspired the Manpower Demonstration Research Corporation, which was funded by the Ford Foundation and several federal agencies to implement, manage and evaluate supported work programs. Over the next three decades, Sturz would repeatedly enlist MDRC to test and validate his innovations. MDRC was established in a dozen sites across the country, managed mostly by local nonprofit organizations. William J. Grinker, the MDRC executive director, described Wildcat's approach as work-training rather than job training.

As with Wildcat, there were randomly assigned experimental and control groups to quantify the value of supported work for ex-addicts and offenders (Wildcat's constituency), welfare mothers and teenagers whose records were blemished by relatively minor run-ins with the law. That Wildcat was the catalyst for a national research project was beneficial on several levels. Not only did it help win over the beleaguered Beame administration, it spurred legislation that allowed for the diversion of benefits. Also, Wildcat expanded its pool of participants to include welfare recipients and youthful offenders—becoming not only the prototype for the national demonstration, but also a participant. As a result, millions of dollars flowed to Wildcat, enabling it to survive during the lean years of New York City's fiscal crisis. But the fundamental benefit to Wildcat was research that proved efficiencies for taxpayers (both in cost savings and in the value of the work performed) and statistical declines in recidivism and drug addiction among nearly all the groups targeted for transition to full-time employment. In a field where evidence and emotion often conflicted, MRDC would endure as a respected, nonpartisan nationwide standard for research into what works—and doesn't—in dealing with social welfare challenges. One Wildcat director, Professor William

Julius Wilson of Harvard, hails the marriage of its "passion for rigorous analysis with an equally passionate commitment to improve the lives of low-income people."

———

Throughout its three decades, Wildcat has adhered to its core mission of providing transitional employment to New Yorkers whose route to full-time employment would otherwise have been riddled with insurmountable obstacles. Its driving philosophy is summed up in its credo: "Service is our business. Self-sufficiency is our bottom line." The funding pool expanded, according to the Sturzian metric, with public sources ranging from the city's Department of Education, Department of Small Business Services, Department of Youth and Community Development, Human Resources Administration and the state's Department of Labor and Division of Parole. Wildcat would serve more than 350,000 ex-addicts, high school dropouts, welfare mothers, immigrants, convicted criminals on work release, students with severe disciplinary problems and undocumented aliens caught in a bureaucratic web after 9/11. And job placements (some 100,000 overall) would become more varied, extending to public-benefit corporations like the Battery Park City Authority and the city's Economic Development Corporation, and to neighborhood business improvement districts, industrial parks and development corporations, which hired Wildcat crews to provide street and sidewalk cleaning services. In 2008, Wildcat expected to involve nearly 17,000 individuals in youth and adult programs and was selected by Mayor Michael R. Bloomberg's Center for Economic Opportunity—the city's own antipoverty program—to go well beyond job placement by helping its "customers" increase their incomes and advance their careers.

Across the country, thousands of workers who would have been written off as impossible to employ were placed by Wildcat replicas. Britain imported and adapted its own version of Wildcat (Bulldog), as did Chile. In 1992, Wildcat opened an alternative high school for students suspended from other institutions. Two years later, the Wildcat Academy graduated its first class, fourteen students who otherwise wouldn't have found a way out of, or even into, school. "None of these kids would have made it anywhere else," says Amalia Betanzos, another Sturz protégé who earlier worked in the Lindsay administration and was appointed by Koch to the Board of Education and by Giuliani to chair the city's commission on the status of women. Most were truants elsewhere. About one in four were on probation or parole. In 2000, Wildcat became a charter school, the John V. Lindsay Academy, with campuses today in lower Manhattan and the Bronx.

Patterned on successful programs that Sturz had visited in the Netherlands, Sweden and Britain, Wildcat would itself become the model for supported work experiments in other cities and ultimately for federal welfare revisions in the 1990s. Sturz's initiative paid off, not only in New York, but all across the country, where it was replicated widely, particularly after the Clinton administration made welfare-to-work a cornerstone of its agenda. Celebrating Wildcat's twenty-fifth anniversary in 1998, Mayor Rudolph Giuliani touted his administration's record on reducing welfare dependency. "Thank you for setting the precedent, leading the way, and being such an important partner in the process," he said.

Wildcat would always remain a nurturing sibling, cooperating with other Vera offspring to produce partnerships that were greater than the sum of their constituent organizations. Wildcat would propose a prisoner reentry program with the Center for Employment Opportunities and would later join with other Vera ventures, Victims Service and Safe Horizon, to provide workforce services to domestic violence victims in shelters. "Staying true to our founding values makes partnerships as natural as functional family reunions," Mary Ellen Boyd, Wildcat's president, wrote Sturz in 2008. "All because of you—you must be rightfully proud."

Chapter 8

In the
Summer of Sam

With Vera spin-offs migrating into welfare-to-work programs and other ventures for former offenders, Vera was still concentrating on keeping people out of prison in the first place. Vera's original Manhattan Bail Project would ultimately evolve into the Pretrial Services Agency, which opened for business in downtown Brooklyn in the summer of 1973. It would be monitored, calibrated, refined, but it was no longer experimental. The Manhattan Bail Project had worked, not perfectly but effectively enough to be deemed a success, and to offer its lessons to the new spin-off. To staff the Pretrial Services Agency, Sturz recruited Richard Rykken, a former military judge, as director and Les Scall, an alumnus of the original bail project, as Rykken's deputy. They enlisted an eclectic, committed staff that included Paul F. Lazarsfeld, the Columbia sociologist, Jim Thompson, one of his protégés, and Lucy Friedman, Vera's own research director.

The agency was a new and improved version of the original Manhattan Bail Project. A revolutionary computer system generated letters reminding defendants of pending court dates and lists for agency workers to call—follow-ups that proved very effective. Community representatives were hired to follow up with home visits if the letters weren't answered or the defendant had no telephone. A special unit was created to recommend supervised release for felony defendants who agreed to enroll in social service programs. The agency also experimented with getting a head start by sending its interviewers directly to police station houses late at night, rather than waiting for prisoners to be transported to detention pens near the courts downtown the following morning. But ultimately the effort failed because cops were generally unwilling to chauffeur the workers to each precinct and the workers themselves were reluctant to roam around the dangerous downtown area after midnight.

The agency's research arm, meanwhile, was finding intriguing statistical correlations, but not all of them could be translated into constructive solutions (in part because, according to Jeremy Travis, the agency "found it very difficult to influence the culture of judicial independence"). Researchers found that the no-show rate among defendants arraigned before judges who followed the agency's recommendations for release most consistently—Richard A. Brown, then the administrative judge of Brooklyn Criminal Court and now the Queens district attorney, was the exemplar—was no higher than the rate for the other judges who more often than not rejected the agency's recommendations. Armed with more sophisticated analytical tools and an expanded database, the researchers also found a striking correlation between a defendant's having a phone at home and his appearance in court on schedule. Despite some concern that it would prejudice the poorest defendants, that variable was included in the latest iteration of the point system.

In 1974, Rykken was succeeded by Benjamin Ward, the traffic commissioner (and later police commissioner), then by Michael Farrell, former commanding officer of the Police Department's Office of Management Analysis and Planning, and the Pretrial Services Agency was expanded citywide—all subsidized with temporary funding from the Law Enforcement Assistance Administration. That would evaporate, and other economies would eliminate the supervised release program and the community service officers, too. But Pretrial Services had proven its value. When some city officials proposed that the agency be folded into the Probation Department again, City Hall balked. Instead, with Sturz's guidance and encouragement, the city created a nonprofit public benefit corporation that would contract with the city to provide legal services. It was christened the New York City Criminal Justice Agency (and was chaired by S. Andrew Schaffer, who was later recruited by Police Commissioner Raymond W. Kelly as deputy commissioner for legal matters).

Within weeks of assuming responsibility for the bail program from Vera on August 1, 1977, the agency faced two decisive tests. That it emerged relatively intact—in some ways, even stronger—was a testament to its record and reputation, to the people running it and to people, like Sturz, who stood behind it.

The summer of 1977 was when New York seemed to have collectively lost its mind in a crazed social, political and cultural competition between two competing visions. Years later, standing in a squeaky clean, booming Times Square in the prologue to Spike Lee's *Summer of Sam*, the columnist Jimmy Breslin intoned: "It wasn't always like this. This film is about a different time, a different place, the good old days, the hot, blistering summer of 1977." In 1977, one vision concluded that the real good old days were the 1950s and that in the ensuing two decades the city had passed its prime and grown unmanageable. A competing vision defined New York as a resilient immigrant mecca where, once the crater-sized potholes were filled, the streets would again be paved, if not with gold. Hulking skeletons of half-built schools stood as grim reminders that spending on public works had evaporated. The Bronx was burning—arsonists were torching tenements and apartment buildings for the insurance proceeds. But to save overtime, firefighters were dispatched by car service to relieve colleagues whose shifts were ending. A mountain climber from Queens named George Willig scaled the sheer outer wall of the World Trade Center. Bombs linked to Puerto Rican nationalists exploded at Manhattan office buildings and department stores. The temperature hit 104 degrees, nearly breaking the old record. Studio 54 opened. Abe Beame was struggling to avoid being the first elected mayor in more than half a century to be defeated for a second term. And a psychopathic killer dubbed Son of Sam armed with a .44 caliber revolver held New York hostage.

On the night of July 13, 1977, in the middle of what, by any measure, was already a long hot summer and with New Yorkers already on edge, a Con Ed power failure plunged the city into total darkness. The blackout triggered widespread looting in scattered neighborhoods that resulted in more than 3,000 arrests. It was the biggest mass arrest in the city's history, and the suspects had to be processed by flashlight and even candlelight.

Not only did the city's Criminal Justice Agency succeed in producing background reports on most of the defendants in time for their arraignment, but the verification process yielded a unique demographic database about the suspected looters. This was no mere academic endeavor. The blackout occurred in the midst of a bruising mayoral campaign already defined by debates about law and order and now punctuated by scenes of unrestrained lawlessness. Who were the looters, and what, beyond the lights going out, prompted the looting? Were they disaffected, jobless and frustrated, seizing the moment in protest, or wanton criminals operating under cover of darkness and taking advantage of a depleted police force? According to Jeremy Travis, "Our data showed that a high percentage of the looters were in fact employed, thereby supporting the claims of those who saw this behavior as reflecting a deeper disregard for property and the rule of law."

The data, compiled by Travis and Charles Kuhlman, was a criminologist's dream even though the agency's research was drawn only from suspects who at that point had been accused, not convicted. They found that 45 percent of the 2,700 adults arrested were employed (50 percent higher than the typical rate among criminal defendants, though most took home less than $150 a week) and that 10 percent were receiving public assistance (compared to the typical 15 percent).

The conclusions were leaked to the *Times* by the chairman of the agency's board, Nicholas Scoppetta, the deputy mayor for criminal justice. "At first, the figures seem surprising," he said. "But if you think about it, why should they be? After all, we know the looting involved a lot of people with prior arrest records. And we know that a lot of people just joined in when they knew they could."

It was said that in the lawless mid-1970s, you could get away with murder in New York City, but, with the city still fixated on generating revenue any way it could, you could not get away with parking in front of a fire hydrant. David Berkowitz proved that adage. A few weeks after the blackout, he was arrested as the .44-caliber killer who had held the city hostage for months, taunting the police and the press with bizarre handwritten notes and identifying himself as Son of Sam. Sam, investigators learned, was inspired, as it turned out, by his sixty-four-year-old Yonkers neighbor, who spoke to him through a dog, a black Labrador whose name in real life was Harvey. Berkowitz worked as a mail sorter, giving new definition to the term going postal (and prompting more than one New Yorker of a certain generation to wonder why a young man would not only transform himself into a killer, but also jeopardize a secure civil service job in the post office). Jimmy Breslin, who received bizarre but literate letters from Berkowitz, described him as the first murderer who understood how to wield a semicolon as well as he did a revolver. He was caught because at the scene of his last stakeout he had parked illegally.

After the police remembered to get a search warrant and some of the other formalities that might have been overlooked earlier, they announced his arrest at Police Headquarters. Struggling to avoid being the first elected mayor defeated for a second term in more than half a century, Abe Beame barely avoided the photo op from hell; he mistook Berkowitz for a cop and almost shook hands to congratulate him on great detective work.

Son of Sam's terror spree, during which six young people were killed and seven others wounded, was only the latest in a succession of horrific events during the summer of 1977. As a result of the lawlessness, the mayoral campaign focused, perhaps disproportionately, on law and order, with each of the candidates seeking to outdo the others with proposed remedies.

Berkowitz was being held in isolation. Not long after his arrest, a Criminal Justice Agency supervisor conducted a pretrial interview in his cell. While this was not an average day, the goal was to treat him like any other defendant, regardless of the notoriety of the case. If the goal was admirable—and even that was arguable—then the chances of achieving it in the politically volatile mayoral campaign were virtually nil. By rote, the supervisor tallied up Berkowitz's responses on the agency's dependable community roots scale. He had a job. He had a phone. He had a home (and had lived at the same address in Yonkers for more than a year). He had no previous criminal record. The information had not been verified, though, because Berkowitz asked the interviewer not to contact anyone. Nonetheless, Berkowitz's questionnaire was perfunctorily stamped "Recommended" for release on his own recognizance.

Luckily, the presiding judge at arraignment was the same Richard Brown whose willingness to cooperate with Vera's pretrial release experiment early on proved vital to its success. Brown disregarded the agency's recommendation and remanded Berkowitz (rather than the agency's supervisor) for a psychiatric examination. The Vera recommendation was regarded as so irrelevant that, apparently, it was never even mentioned at the arraignment. But a week later, with the temperature rising in the mayoral campaign, it became public. Nicholas Scoppetta, the chairman of the agency's board and Beame's deputy mayor for criminal justice, called Travis. "Say it isn't so, Jeremy," Scoppetta said, "that the agency whose board I serve as chair recommended that David Berkowitz be released."

"I think I have convinced the mayor not to call for your resignation," Scoppetta continued, "but you had better come up with a good explanation for this because the press have just now left City Hall and are coming up to your office for an explanation."

Beame was apoplectic. "This monumental irony underlines my contention that we must crack down on loopholes in the criminal justice system," he declared. Scoppetta blamed the recommendation on the "apparently absurd result of a mechanical and literal interpretation by the agency of its criteria for recommending bail." And twenty-nine-year-old Jeremy Travis, whose job Scoppetta gallantly saved, attempted to explain: "The court by statute must consider the defendant's character, mental condition, severity of possible sentence, employment, family ties and length of residence. We provide the last three."

The press was mostly unforgiving. "They asked the obvious questions," Travis recalls. "'How can you not consider the charges? Do you mean that someone charged with murder should be released? If you don't consider the charges, how can you expect the judge to take your recommendations seriously?'" The Berkowitz episode, as Travis would later put it, "exposed the soft underbelly" of Vera's point system. Under the state's criminal procedure law, judges deciding on bail are supposed to consider only those factors—including likelihood of conviction, weight of the evidence and community ties—that affect the probability that a defendant would return to court as scheduled rather than the severity of the charges. But with violent crime spiraling out of control, some jurisdictions around the country were redefining the criteria for granting bail. In Washington, D.C., the district's Pretrial Services Agency went so far as to incorporate an assessment of dangerousness into its formal judgment about whether to recommend release.

In New York, the Criminal Justice Agency resisted the trend, arguing against it on a number of grounds: that judges consider dangerousness too difficult for the interviewers to predict and that, except in cases involving mental disorders, criminal law—for better or worse—did not specifically authorize judges to confine someone deemed dangerous. Moreover, the agency's own research identified a complicating variable: Those defendants facing more serious charges were, after being released on their own recognizance, the ones who were more likely to return. "If the failure-to-appear probability was the only consideration," Travis said, "judges would be more likely to release defendants facing serious charges and less likely to release those facing minor charges." In fact, judges customarily considered the severity of the charges. The agency's research demonstrated that, too. Defendants facing more serious charges were less likely to be released on their own recognizance. ("Our point system did not attempt to accommodate that reality," Travis explained, "because to do so would strain our credibility with the system.")

Within a few days, after barely surviving what would prove to be its most embarrassing collision between blind justice and common sense, the agency bowed to political reality. The Brooklyn supervisor who had interviewed Berkowitz and the interviewer's own supervisor were reassigned (they were quietly restored to their positions a month later). Scoppetta announced that henceforth, the agency would no longer make bail recommendations in homicide cases. In effect, the policy represented a return to Vera's political insulation. The agency abandoned its practice of recommending defendants "for release." Instead, it more noncommittally described those whose deep community roots had been verified as "recommended." And even on those questionnaires that qualified as recommended for release the agency rubber-stamped all four copies with a disclaimer that they'd been made "without consideration of all the factors listed in the Criminal Procedure Law regarding release determinations." It was dubbed the "sorry stamp," as a regular reminder of how much the staff regretted the way the Berkowitz case, given its notoriety and the compelling evidence against him at the time of his arrest, was handled. As Travis himself explained, "This agency did not want Mr. Berkowitz released, but felt the information must be provided to the court. It was a strict interpretation of a procedure brought to an absurd conclusion."

A month after the Berkowitz embarrassment, Beame lost the Democratic primary. He would be succeeded by Edward I. Koch, a congressman who represented Manhattan's East Side. Sturz hadn't known Koch; he can't remember whether they had even met. He apparently knew enough about him, though, to have voted for someone else—Mario Cuomo—in the 1977 Democratic mayoral primary. Still, Sturz was sufficiently respected as a connoisseur of criminal justice talent to be recruited by Koch's transition team to help conduct the search for a new police commissioner. Sturz had served on the governing boards of the Police Foundation, the National Drug Abuse Council, the Corporation for Public and Private Ventures. He was treasurer of the Fund for the City of New York.

In New York City, going back at least to Theodore Roosevelt, the most visible job other than mayor is police commissioner. In 1977, choosing a commissioner was even more crucial than ever. Koch was elected, in large part, because of crime, and because of the perception that all of Brooklyn was being ravaged by looters, that the entire Bronx was burning and that city officials had completely lost control. Koch, who favored the death penalty, rode the crime wave into office. But he was viewed, in large part because of his Greenwich Village base, as a liberal. His choice of police commissioner would be the first test of his law-and-order bona fides.

The first choice was Anthony Bouza, the erudite Bronx commander (who would go on to run the New York City Transit Authority force and later become the police chief of Minneapolis). The unconventional Bouza struck a responsive chord with Sturz. After a spate of violent incidents near Yankee Stadium, Bouza sent reporters to their dictionaries when he described the perpetrators as "feral" youth. As Bronx commander, Bouza complained that America was burying the problems of the poor. Later, he would write that the nation's policy toward its "Bronxes" was one of "malign neglect." But in spite of Bouza's charisma, the mayor reached outside the ranks and appointed Robert J. McGuire, a lawyer and a cop's son.

While Sturz did not know the mayor-elect, he was familiar with one of his new deputies, David Brown. They had met a few times at the home of Nicholas Scoppetta, Beame's deputy mayor for criminal justice. Brown informally enlisted Sturz to help find a successor to Scoppetta. After having dinner with one candidate, they both agreed that he couldn't hack it. "I recollect David said, 'Well, would you do it?'" Sturz says. When he and Koch met the next day, the new mayor asked Sturz for his assessment of the five district attorneys. Perhaps reflecting his turf wars with Robert Morgenthau of Manhattan, Sturz said the prosecutor he respected most was Mario Merola of the Bronx. "I pointed out to Koch that I did not favor capital punishment. I didn't want surprises later." On December 31, Sturz's birthday, Koch called him at home to offer him the job.

"I was ready for another experience," Sturz recalls. "I'd been around government so long and here was the opportunity to function within government." He conferred with Burke Marshall, Vera's board chairman, and quickly installed Michael Smith, who had run the Legal Action Center and Vera's London office, as his successor.

That Jeremy Travis and the Criminal Justice Agency endured Son of Sam—that Vera would survive and thrive for more than three decades since then—is testament not merely to the respect that Sturz had earned but to how he had structured Vera's family tree. "I divided Vera into separate corporations with separate names, interlocking boards of directors, so that Vera would be less of a political target," Sturz says. "Vera became a sort of holding company in the nonprofit area."

Vera thrived through thick and thin, financially and politically, because Sturz had also insulated it from knee-jerk pigeonholing. "Part of Vera's value," Sturz says, "is that we didn't set ourselves up as an ideological kind of group. We also cared about victims of crime, we cared about witnesses, that we cared about police officers not wasting their time, just sitting four and five hours in court rather than helping to prevent crime being out in the street, and developed over time a very important relationship that I think separated Vera out from many other organizations. But I don't think anyone questions that basic commitment to fairness and justice, decency that Vera had. We wanted—it was tremendously important—to bring along the agencies and the decision makers and, I guess, we were smarter than probably most, we had a better sense and feel of what was important to administrators of agencies. We didn't assume that police commissioners hated judges."

Structurally, Sturz also kept Vera from ever becoming complacent. He innovatively raised revenue without becoming dependent on an endowment. "People of Vera today probably are not happy that when Herb Sturz was around he never did a thing to build up an endowment," he says. "But I kind of made a virtue of saying, let's earn our way."

On January 5, 1978, Koch announced Sturz as the seventh and last of his deputy mayors, for criminal justice. For the first time in seventeen years of tinkering at the margins, Sturz was poised to promulgate his criminal justice agenda as the consummate insider.

"After seventeen years," he says, "I was ready to think of other things to do. I wanted to test myself in other contexts."

Part III

The Insider

Chapter 9

Politics
and Poker

The tactical skills that Herb Sturz perfected outside the government would prove even more valuable on the inside. He loves poker. Sheldon Harnick's lyrics for *Fiorello!*, the Broadway musical about Mayor Fiorello La Guardia, whimsically drew a parallel between the two pursuits. "If politics seems more predictable," Harnick wrote, it's only because you can stack the deck. The bosses nominate a front man, give him their regards and watch while he learns that in both politics and poker, as the song goes, "you've gotta have / that slippery, hap-hazardous commodity, / you've gotta have the cards."

Every month, in Mike Sviridoff's Upper East Side apartment, Sturz played poker with a regular group of cronies, including Stan Brezenoff, Koch's welfare commissioner and later first deputy mayor and one of several Ford Foundation alumni to find their way into city government during the Lindsay and Koch administrations. Sturz never blustered—"I don't macho it," was how he once described his poker style. But he bluffed, when necessary, to keep the other players guessing and slightly off-balance. He understood how far and fast to push, when to stay in and when to fold in defeat or, better still, compromise and cut your losses. "Sometimes," he explains, "the perfect is the enemy of the good."

In poker, as in what might be loosely defined as politics, Sturz also brought to the table an exceptional talent that would invariably belie his modest demeanor and make him a formidable rival. "He plays tight and moves in when he sees an opening," Bill Grinker says. "He has an ability to understand how people think that is highly evolved," Carl Weisbrod says. "It made him a great poker player—not reading people's minds but their motivation."

Without losing sight of his ultimate objective, he can intuit a potential adversary's response and tailor his approach preemptively. He is a man blessed with the vision to see around corners. "His ability to read people and understand what others are seeking is a reflection of how knowledgeable he is about himself," Weisbrod points out. (Apparently, though, that self-awareness is largely a product of introspection, rather than the result of some kind of intensive therapy. "I saw a doctor for twenty-five minutes, but I never went into analysis or anything halfway there," Sturz admits. "Right or wrong, I never felt that I needed it. I focused on what I was trying to do, rather than why.")

Sturz does not necessarily embrace Niccolò Machiavelli as his guru, but he might have written a self-help primer "What Would Machiavelli Do?" While Sturz would make his case by sheer force, mustering irrefutable facts and summoning his John Dewey brand of pragmatic idealism, he also proved himself a skillful tactician in disarmingly simple ways. When you want something, do you go personally or make a phone call? Do you go with eight people or by yourself? (Weisbrod recalls Sturz's advice

that often "it's much more important to go by yourself—
you project an air of vulnerability.")

Sturz also has near-perfect pitch when it comes to cal-
ibrating compromise and finding common ground, a rare
commodity in or out of government. "He will throw out an
idea, but then quickly incorporate, prudently, the other
guy's problems or objections and try to solve or accommodate them rather than impose or convince them," Patricia
M. Wald, who worked with him at Vera, says. He leveraged
not only political and financial resources in his ventures but
validation. With the police feeling demeaned by both the
mayor and the public, he elevated them as partners in
the criminal justice system. Earl Warren, the chief justice
of the U.S. Supreme Court, literally embraced Police Commissioner Howard Leary at a national crime conference in
a gesture heavily invested with symbolism and undoubt-
edly choreographed by Sturz. Norborne Berkeley Jr.'s
personal commitment to Wildcat ennobled its workers.
Moreover, Berkeley's personal involvement bestowed on
him a welcome credibility within his own family. ("He
wrote out an IOU for $2 million," Sturz recalls. "Was it
legally binding? I don't think so. But was he going to walk
away from it? I don't think so. We understood that a businessman will support you out of idealism, but also out of
wanting to be respected by family, by his rebellious teen-
age daughters and sons.")

Sturz has what Patricia Wald calls a "trenchant sense of
phonies or deceivers or non-producers"—but also more
faith in human nature than Machiavelli probably had. (The
second song from *Fiorello!* was "On the Side of the An-
gels.") "I believe very much in demonstrating that people
are better than they are thought to be," Sturz says, "of
demonstrating the importance of putting former addicts
in an OTB parlor—to entirely run one. I think that said

something. Just like the idea of Easyride, having former addicts and prisoners, most of them African-American and Latino, care for adult women, who, by and large, were mainly white and Jewish—these individuals would climb up four or five floors and carry older persons to a vehicle and bring them to a senior citizen center or for food or to a cemetery, or whatever."

"How do you let people who've rarely been able to give something—to anyone—be generous?" Sturz says. "I was at a school up in East Harlem the other day and there was a young woman—perhaps fifteen—and she was mentoring two six-year-olds and teaching them, helping them with their reading. And I asked her, after observing for a little bit, 'What is this mentoring doing for you?' And she thought a moment and said, 'I think it's making me a nicer person.'"

"Is this Machiavellian?" Sturz wonders. "Maybe. It's a word. What it is, is trying to understand what motivates people. Sometimes it's just getting recognized, sometimes it's acceptance. Individuals will follow their enlightened self interest, if you can help them discover where it might be."

Nick Katzenbach recalls Sturz's approach to bail reform: "The participants had no interest in making the problem easier for others, but they did like making it easier for themselves. The police had no great affection for either bondsmen or those charged. But they were interested in not wasting their own time sitting around waiting. Herb took these parts and found ways of fitting them together so everyone got something."

Aryeh Neier, the president of the Open Society Institute, puts it another way: "He's had a distinctive role in thinking how to address important public policy issues, not doing it in a confrontational manner, always doing it in a way in which he wants the established institutions to go along and see for themselves the advantages they will derive from innovations."

"He just picks up people as resources along the way and never appears to be in charge," says Franklin A. Thomas, who was counsel to Police Commissioner Leary and later president of the Ford Foundation. "The principals never have a feeling of lost control."

Jay Kriegel invokes a similar metric to explain Sturz's success:

> He would come back with results that were empirically tested. No absolutes. No dogma. No principles you had to conform to. I never heard Herb lecture anybody, and he knows more than anyone else involved in the process. That's an extraordinary skill in dealing with very independent, powerful people and persuading them, seducing them, enticing them to become part of the process. And they all became stakeholders. . . . Herb has no mandate. He has no power. He succeeds by persuasion and intellect and information.

And, unlike many well-intentioned reformers, Sturz gets the most out of government rather than treating it as an adversary. "He immediately brings government into the picture," Bill Grinker says. "His is not some precious hothouse effort that's going to die on the vine because it doesn't have the level of sustainability."

"What Herb understands is that government is a crude, timid instrument," his friend Jack Rosenthal notes. "You can't innovate in government. The way you affect government is demonstrating how something can be done and the way you do that is being anonymous so someone in government can say, 'What a good idea I had.' His own career is a lesson in the fact that there's no limit to what you can achieve if you don't take credit for it."

Sturz has always, as he puts it, seen things with his own eyes, smashing through theories and suppositions to form his own picture of reality and piercing façades to discern what motivates the people he is partnering with, employing or hoping to co-opt.

> I tried to get into people's skins and figure out what they really need or want, small tell-tale things, that reveal whether they're full of themselves, whether they're nuanced, whether they have analytical minds, how they treat people, whether they are negative. Are they oppositional—finding what you can't do, as opposed to finding what you can do. Any one of these isn't enough. A guy can be eager and a total jerk. I've always tried to get under where people really live and what matters to them and what they really need in life. Then, finding some common ground, you deliver it back to them, on your terms. You can convey to other people what is important to them, their strengths, insecurities, ambitions, understanding what their values are and where you can get convergence. Someone could think of it as cynical. I don't.

"He doesn't have an agenda of self-aggrandizement," says Aryeh Neier. "Herb is more self-effacing than is customary and is always willing to give others credit. That has helped him a great deal in getting them to buy into the various things he proposes. I think it's probably personality rather than strategy."

In addition to a shrewd judgment, Sturz, his self-effacement and shambling gait notwithstanding, actually enjoys the power. "Herb likes being a player," Carl Weisbrod says. "He enjoys power and its uses." Unlike so many other seasoned do-gooders, though, Sturz doesn't need the spotlight. Sturz followed Nick Katzenbach's dictum: "If successful, disappear into the background and make sure the politicians get 100 percent of the credit. If there are problems, take the blame for them. Nothing endears one more to elected officials."

"A politician, a mayor—they need the credit," Sturz says. "I certainly don't need it." Giving other people credit can sometimes have an ancillary advantage: insulating yourself from blame. "Herb," Weisbrod said, "is very self-protective."

———

New York voters have an uncanny ability to elect the right candidate at the right time, even if he doesn't necessarily turn out to be the right mayor. In the 1950s, the laconic Robert F. Wagner seemed perfectly attuned to the times (his credo was revealed in notes found only after his death: "When in danger, ponder; when in trouble, delegate; when in doubt, mumble"). After three terms of Wagner, Lindsay "was fresh when everyone else is tired." The antidote to eight years of in-your-face freshness was Abe Beame, a former accounting teacher and city comptroller whose slogan was "he knows the buck," but who had the bad luck to be presiding when the credit markets, after decades of profiting from City Hall's profligacy, finally pulled the plug on city borrowing. (Beame's successors would present similarly persuasive rationales: "After eight years of charisma and four years of the club house," Ed Koch offered "competence"; David Dinkins insisted a mayor "didn't have to be loud to be strong" and after one term was ousted by Rudolph W. Giuliani, who was loud *and* strong.) If Koch's election as mayor in 1977 meant anything enduring, it was that New Yorkers were fed up with a city that seemed sliding into chaos. Koch's campaign slogan about competence hit home. Few voters really knew whether Koch was competent, but he sounded as if he would take charge. He talked tough. He favored the death penalty. And on the campaign trail, he delighted in telling the story about a liberal judge mugged by a man whom he had released on bail. Unchastened, the judge insisted he would not have acted any differently. To which an elderly woman among Koch's supporters shouted out: "Then mug him again!"

————

Even before Sturz was sworn in and confronted by that chilly political climate, he was tapped to stand in for Koch, who was out of town, at a police officer's funeral in Brooklyn. The mood was somber with the attendant pomp, but also tense because there was some question as to whether the officer who died had been a rogue cop. "McGuire and I lined up on the street, waiting for the hearse to be taken from the funeral home, when suddenly the television crews pushed in on me asking, 'Mr. Mayor, Mr. Mayor, what are your thoughts on this solemn occasion?' I was bewildered," Sturz recalls. "Was Koch here after all? I hadn't yet realized that in the mayor's absence, the deputy mayor is called 'Mr. Mayor.' For a fraction of a moment, it went through my mind that I could blow it all by saying something truthful about the true nature of the police officer's death. Instead, I said, 'This is a very solemn occasion; I hope that it is the first and last police officer killed in the City of New York this year.'" Later, he says, "I sensed the absurdity of it and sadness as well."

————

As deputy mayor for criminal justice, Sturz inherited a fragmented bureaucracy and a mandate to bring it together. Some courts were funded by the city and some by the state. The district attorneys were state or county officials, but their budgets were set by the city. Jails were under city jurisdiction, but prisons were the state's. Some prosecutors, as Sturz had learned at Vera, considered it all but unethical to contemplate a joint strategy with the police or the judiciary, much less with the defense bar. While it would enable him to create a legacy that would not have been possible from outside government, being deputy mayor, Sturz later acknowledged, was "not an inherently strong position." It didn't necessarily help that Koch, as Sturz put it, was "Peck's bad boy attacking judges," that computer networks were either rudimentary or incapable of communicating with each other and that lawsuits by advocates for inmates had hobbled reform by judicially imposed regulation or endless litigation. Koch, Sturz says, "thought I might have been too liberal. I don't recall his ever saying that, although he may well have thought so."

Most of Koch's retinue of seven deputy mayors worked out of City Hall. If they were not a "team of rivals," as Doris Kearns Goodwin has characterized Lincoln's cabinet, nor were they functioning cohesively and free from competing agendas. "There was a lot of infighting as to who did what," Sturz says. "I was largely immune because my areas were more discrete, something that one could grab hold of." Sturz was also secure enough to be comfortably ensconced across the street, in an oversized (compared to the warrens occupied by most of his fellow deputy mayors) red-carpeted office at 250 Broadway overlooking City Hall. In a refreshingly frank assessment he delivered a decade later for Columbia University's oral history project, Sturz singled out another deputy mayor, Herman Badillo, for one strategic flaw that Sturz himself could not suffer: being clueless about moving from A to B to C. In retrospect, Sturz describes his six colleagues as an "uneven bunch," taking care not to rank himself, but nonetheless distinguishing his mandate from the others: "I had to deal with real criminal justice matters. The other deputy mayors functioned as assistants to the mayor, vying for his attention, creating turf if it didn't exist. Mine existed. The question was, what could I do with it?"

———

Sturz's first hire as deputy mayor was a young woman, "very able and straight," who had worked on Koch's campaign and was referred to him by City Hall. That, he said, was his last political hire. He brought Paul A. Strasburg back from Paris, where he was running a Vera outpost, to inaugurate a new Department of Juvenile Justice and had Ellen Schall from Legal Aid succeed him. He hired Min Schwarz, the wife of his friend Fritz, to focus on education. As counsel he brought in Bob Davis, who had come recommended by United States Court of Appeals Judge Jon Newman as the best law clerk he had ever appointed.

One of Sturz's first acts as deputy mayor was to convene a conference on victims and witnesses. "Too often," he says, "the victim has been left out of the system and is unaware of what's happening or if the case has been plea-bargained away. We have to make sure that he is not victimized again by the system itself." Less than three months later, Koch formally announced the creation of the Victim Service Agency (VSA), virtually the first program of its kind to focus on victims of crime. The mayor's announcement, to the City Bar Association, was drafted by Sturz, who was motivated primarily by empathy for the victims and also guided by an overriding political agenda that he carried with him from Vera. "It was important," Sturz explained later, "that Vera not get tagged as a defendants' do-good organization." (The very pragmatic agenda that Sturz established would be followed assiduously as a matter of self-preservation; at Vera's 2008 fundraising event, the two primary honorees were Roger Altman, the former deputy treasury secretary, and Police Commissioner Raymond W. Kelly.)

The VSA was built on the skeleton of an earlier Vera project developed in Brooklyn. Sturz had found a receptive partner for innovation in Eugene Gold, the Brooklyn district attorney, who embraced Vera's Pretrial Services Agency, a computerized notification system to speed the processing of criminal court cases. "The police and victims were just sitting there in court when there is a technology called the telephone," Sturz says. While he was introducing the system to Benjamin Altman, the chairman of the mayor's Criminal Justice Coordinating Council, Altman wondered aloud whether the notification system could be extended to victims and witnesses. Sturz pounced on the suggestion, and the Victim Witness Assistance Project was born. (It was one of two such programs, the other in Des Moines, funded by the federal Law Enforcement Assistance Administration.) Among its earliest initiatives was providing day care service in courthouses and locksmiths to secure homes and apartments that had been burgled.

"The bail project and the summons project had established Vera as a progressive, compassionate vehicle for protecting the rights of criminal suspects and for giving them the benefit of the doubt," says Jeremy Travis, whom Sturz tapped to run the program. "The possibility of improving the system for victims and witnesses—and speed prosecutions—presented a tantalizing opportunity in the aftermath of the Berkowitz fiasco. We tried everything to make the system less intimidating."

Another hallmark of every Vera project was the ongoing monitoring of how well it worked and fine-tuning—or overhauling it altogether—to fulfill its goals. Lucy N. Friedman, who would become the founding director of the reincarnated VSA (and later president of The After-School Corporation), was ecstatic with the results of research into witnesses who had received no notification of trial dates and those who had. People who were routinely notified were 10 percent more likely to show up for scheduled hearings or other judicial procedures. But when the appearance rate was reviewed again six months later, the project staff discovered that the improvement was short-lived.

After careful probing, it was apparent that the project's original premise was too paternalistic. Moreover, it had entirely failed to take into account prior relationships between victims and witnesses, which almost always precluded candid testimony. "Criminal sanctions proved to be a blunt instrument when dealing with crimes that had a relationship at the core," Travis says. Instead, cases in which the principals had a prior relationship were assigned to the Institute for Mediation and Conflict Resolution, where, as an earlier study had suggested, the process may not have fundamentally changed the relationship but "the sense of procedural justice had tremendous power."

As Travis moved on to transform the Pretrial Services Agency into the Criminal Justice Agency, Friedman, a former Peace Corps volunteer who returned from the Dominican Republic to earn her doctorate in social psychology at Columbia, was named director of the VSA to help deal with the shame, guilt, fear and helplessness of crime victims. "Many victims do not report the crime to the

police," Friedman says. "And since less than one in five reported crimes ends in arrest, for most victims there is no
satisfactory result in reporting the crime. Even when an arrest is made, restitution is rarely ordered or made."

The breadth of services she envisioned to bring clarity
and sanity to the criminal justice system went well beyond the agency's original blueprint—from a foster home
for victims of violence, to counseling and referral programs
in police precincts, organizing block watchers and a twenty-
four-hour lock-replacement service and an experiment in
restitution as an alternative to fines and imprisonment and
other customary forms of punishment in disposing of a
criminal case. Friedman's vision was to provide services to
reduce the trauma and inconvenience associated with being the victim of a crime, reduce crime and fear of crime
through prevention, increase the reporting of crime by improving relations between the police and potential victims, reduce court delays through more efficient scheduling
to rationalize the system for all its participants and increase productivity for the police, prosecutors and the
court system.

Beginning with an initial budget of $100,000 in city
funds, Friedman and her deputy John Feinblatt tapped a
wide variety of public and private resources and myriad
federal tributaries and nongovernment funding streams for
revenue. In what she describes as a sustained surge of "entrepreneurial energy," she enlisted VISTA (Volunteers in
Service to America) volunteers, persuaded a company to
donate locks and then recruited young workers hired under the federal Comprehensive Employment and Training
Act (CETA) to install them. The agency's agenda—to
return dignity to victims of crime and abuse and burnish
the Koch administration's credentials—had been set by
Sturz from the start. Rather than a rigid model of corporate

governance, the agency was a patchwork of programs that responded to needs nimbly. As a hybrid—court-based and working closely with prosecutors, but also an independent entity—VSA enjoyed unique flexibility. And as a growing bureaucracy, it never forgot its grassroots. Feinblatt, a former Legal Aid lawyer who joined the VSA as director of court operations, recalled how exhilarated he felt to begin on the ground floor of a movement that, for the first time, formally elevated victims, individually and as a group, to stakeholders with a legitimate claim on the outcome of criminal cases. "We took on domestic violence and assault, we got victims the right to make an impact statement at sentencing, to have their voices heard," he says.

All of the agency's employees, including senior management, were required to staff the twenty-four-hour hotline. Friedman remembers fielding a call from a woman whose husband had just been murdered. "At the end of the call, I had given her all the information she needed, and I found myself mumbling 'I'm so sorry' into the phone. At that moment, I realized how terribly inadequate the response was, and I decided we needed to focus on what else we could do for families of homicide victims." Friedman enlisted Rosemary Masters to address the needs of victims' families, especially parents.

In 1982, VSA reached out to crime victims from out of town, partnering with the Travelers Aid Society and the Mayor's Office of Midtown Enforcement (run by another Sturz protégé, Carl Weisbrod, who had been the president of Wildcat), to create a tourist victims project in Times Square. (Weisbrod went on to create the City Volunteer Corps, another Sturz innovation, before joining City Planning as its executive director and later heading up the 42nd Street Development Project.) That program rapidly expanded the agency's constituency to foreigners and immigrants and young people. Advice on legal issues, including asylum, avoiding deportation and bringing relatives over was offered in twelve languages, and a twenty-four-hour hotline for runaways was soon fielding calls from homeless teenagers. A Streetwork subsidiary was formed, which sent an outreach staff fanning across Times Square's arcades, movie theaters and fast food restaurants offering counseling and other assistance and a place to clean up. In 1987, those services were expanded to include AIDS education and prevention. After dispatching swat teams to offer counseling in the aftermath of specific acts of violence, the agency also expanded into high schools. "After these assemblies kids would come up to us and ask questions they felt they couldn't ask out loud in front of teachers and peers, like where can I get help because there are problems at home, my parents abuse me or each other—and a lot of what we would hear about was the domestic violence at home," Friedman says.

By the end of the decade, VSA was rechristened as Victim Services ("Agency" was dropped from the name to reflect its emergence as an independent entity) and offered programs at sixty-five sites around the city. The menu of services included programs to unite homeless people with relatives in other cities, safe housing for victims of abusive spouses and parents, counseling for families with children at risk for abuse and neglect and reception centers where witnesses and victims could comfortably await court appearances.

Victim Services mediation centers were opened in Queens and Brooklyn, and mediation and conflict resolution training programs were established in high schools. Mediation often proved less successful in resolving domestic disputes, which more often required the authority of the court to prevent, or respond to, violence. Moreover, the emerging women's rights movement was highlighting and publicizing the threat of domestic violence against women. By the mid-1980s, Friedman and Susan Herman, director of the domestic violence division of Victim Services, concluded that domestic violence resulted in more injuries to women than muggings, rapes and auto accidents combined and accounted for a third of women's visits to hospital emergency rooms and more than a third of all female homicides.

In approaching domestic violence, Victim Services straddled the line between counseling and advocacy and between the law enforcement agenda, which focused on the priorities of prosecutors and dealing with witnesses and victims and the priorities of feminist groups. One unanticipated need was that many domestic violence victims were drug-addicted, and as addicts they were ineligible for admission to halfway houses and shelters for battered women. Victim Services tried acupuncture to quickly detox them. It started a program to help the batterers who were willing to change their behavior.

Victim Services would metamorphose yet again, this time into Safe Horizon. It continues to operate many of the same services, including a twenty-four-hour crime victim hotline in English and Spanish (which averages 2,000 calls a month from battered women), community offices that offer emergency assistance and counseling, a training program to help police officers identify domestic violence and respond appropriately, temporary housing for abused women and their children, an employment program to help domestic violence victims develop work skills, an anti-stalking program and initiatives that respond to emerging priorities, such as refugees from war and torture.

Like Vera itself, Safe Horizon adapted and survived because Sturz ensured that the operating structure was intact, a committed staff had been hired that was loyal to the mission, the funding sources were more or less secure and the governing hierarchy was sufficiently independent to elevate everyone from volunteers to executives into stakeholders in its future. Lucy Friedman would be succeeded by Gordon Campbell, who explained the name change this way: "People would say, 'I'm not a victim, I am a survivor.'" The terrorist attacks of 9/11 de-stigmatized the public and personal perception of "victim" and affirmed the mission's relevance. Safe Horizon headquarters was within view of the World Trade Center, and Campbell recognized the symmetry between domestic violence and the violence inflicted on the domestic front by terrorists. "The local knowledge of New York that the staff of Safe Horizon had was unique among the social service agencies that participated in providing direct services to 9/11 victims," a University of Pennsylvania study concluded.

Early in 1979, following Sturz's road map, Koch proposed the creation of a Juvenile Justice Agency to coordinate the city's strategy toward the 6,000 or so youthful offenders (under the age of sixteen) who passed through the city's detention facilities. He would also shut the Spofford Juvenile Center, which was run by the Human Resources Administration in the Bronx. Spofford was notorious. It was widely considered to be overcrowded and inhumane. For anyone concerned with the fair and efficient administration of justice, the only thing worse than placing someone in Spofford was the ease with which they departed on their own. In 1977, there were 130 reported escapes, although none since August 1978, when, Sturz says, "I enlisted welders from just about every city agency. We went up

there, stayed two days—overnight—and secured the facility in two days." He had visited the facility with "welders
from six or seven city agencies." The welders not only succeeded in keeping the kids from leaving Spofford. Their
success in ending the epidemic of escapes reduced the political pressure on the Human Resources Administration to
shutter Spofford and transfer its residents to Rikers, where
they would have inevitably mixed with adult inmates.
"That would have been a dreadful policy," Sturz says. The
mayor proposed replacing Spofford, as in the plan to dis-
perse detention centers from Rikers, with facilities that
were smaller, provided tighter security and were closer to
the city's courthouses.

With responsibility for juvenile justice divided, no one
was in charge, which meant no one could be held accountable. There was no continuity in case management. The
Department of Probation was running about two years behind in developing a computerized index of youthful offenders that, according to state mandate, was supposed to
have been in place by July 1, 1977. Without it, judges in
one borough might be unaware of crimes committed by a
juvenile in another borough, inadvertently producing what
Manhattan District Attorney Robert Morgenthau dubbed
"born-again criminals." Juvenile crime was increasing, so
much so and so dramatically that Governor Hugh L. Carey
endorsed harsher penalties for youths thirteen and older
convicted of murder and other violent crimes. The influx
of more violent young criminals to detention facilities created a new challenge of how to segregate them from the
youthful offenders who were found guilty of relatively minor offenses.

"Rather than bouncing from agency to agency, we'll
focus it in one agency," Sturz says. Just that sort of juvenile

agency had been envisioned in 1978 by Paul Strasburg, who was then the associate director of Vera. Thanks to Sturz, Strasburg would be named to head the new agency that he himself had proposed. By most measures, the new Department of Juvenile Justice represented a vast improvement over what the administration had inherited. "We don't know if this is going to work," Koch says candidly, "but we know that what we have doesn't work."

———

On August 2, 1979, Sturz was fired as deputy mayor for criminal justice. After nineteen months in office (his appointment was announced on his forty-seventh birthday), the Koch administration cast the sudden reshuffling, the mayor's Thursday morning massacre, as a streamlining from seven diverse deputies to three. "The attempt at demographic representation in government had no impact on anything, including race relations," Koch recalls. He reached Sturz, who was vacationing on Martha's Vineyard, at 10:30 P.M. the night before the firing was announced. As Koch remembers it, he and Allen Schwartz, the mayor's corporation counsel, explained that Sturz would retain his staff and the title of coordinator of criminal justice and would gain the unequivocal authority to hire and fire the correction commissioner, William J. Ciuros Jr.

As angry as Sturz was over what would be perceived as a demotion, he wasted no time in exercising his new prerogative. Two days later, he returned to New York and fired Ciuros. For eighteen months, Ciuros had presided over inmate suicides, accusations of brutality by guards, bad blood with the correction officers' union and the escape from a Bellevue Hospital prison ward of a suspected terrorist who had lost both hands in an explosion. Worst of all, perhaps, he had flatly opposed Sturz's hallmark criminal justice initiative to sell Rikers Island to the state.

Ciuros, a former sheriff from upstate, was a proud man who presided over department ceremonies in full dress regalia, including a sash that proclaimed him commissioner. Sturz and Allen Schwartz fired Ciuros, who made one demand: to see the mayor. That produced an awkward moment. "Ciuros packed a gun in his ankle holster," Sturz recalls, "and Allen and I were afraid that he might take it out and try to shoot someone. This was after the Harvey Milk shooting in San Francisco. And yet we couldn't ask him, we felt, to disarm." They alerted Koch's police security detail about their apprehensions and left the door to the mayor's office ajar. The exit interview was uneventful. Ciuros left. Sturz offered the job to Benjamin Ward, who, he said, was "a very simple, direct guy capable of great loyalty."

Reacting to Koch's City Hall shuffle, the *Times*, echoing Sturz's own anguish, called the demotion of Sturz and his fellow deputy mayor, Ronay Menschel, who were expected to remain with city government but with diminished rank, "a gratuitous insult in return for solid service." Fred Hayes, the former city budget director, accused Koch of having "reneged on the deal that persuaded [Sturz] to leave Vera and simply ignored the return he has gotten on that deal." On the letterhead of a Holiday Inn in Princeton, Howard Leary, the former police commissioner, wrote Sturz: "Keep a stiff upper lip. Things do change and come full circle. Stay the course and win."

But there appeared to be not much of a course to stay, at least not immediately. For the first time, Sturz had became a casualty of bureaucratic intrigue that he seemed either oblivious to or had seriously underestimated. For seventeen years, he had operated as a criminal justice reformer largely on the fringes, set his own agenda and meticulously built a network of friends, confidants and fellow reformers. Being in government provided power to propose, to convene, to deliver, and Sturz had harnessed the power to achieve goals that would not have been possible to realize as an outsider. As deputy mayor and criminal justice coordinator and later as chairman of the City Planning Commission, though, Sturz would be able to point to a litany of other accomplishments on a broadly defined personal agenda that would go well beyond his official portfolio and would have far-reaching implications in and out of government.

He established an Arson Strike Force that would seek to douse the epidemic of fires that ravaged tenements in poor neighborhoods. It was a situation epitomized by Howard Cosell's comment during the second game of the 1977 World Series, when an aerial camera lingered on an abandoned school burning a block from Yankee Stadium. "There it is, ladies and gentlemen," Cosell said soberly. "The Bronx is burning."

Thousands of tenements were not only fuel for the frenzy of arson, but in danger of collapsing, and breeding grounds for crime. Sturz suggested getting the army or the National Guard to demolish them, but the secretary of the army nixed it. "I was probably a bull in a china shop, not knowing at that time as much as I later did about community problems," Sturz says. "But I felt that with no war going on, we had all these army people, and National Guardsmen, doing nothing while large areas in the South Bronx and Brooklyn were filled with vacant, dilapidated, dangerous buildings."

Following the venerable Vera evidentiary formula, though, the interagency strike force Sturz established fought fire with figures, analyzing nearly 12,000 arson fires over two years and identifying likely arson targets: small vacant or partly vacant walk-up corner Brooklyn tenements with a ground floor store and a history of tax arrears, uncorrected building code violations and previous fires. Fire Commissioner Charles J. Hynes flooded arson-prone neighborhoods with red-capped fire marshals, who responded to every call while the evidence was still fresh and witnesses were still around to be interviewed. The city's Arson Strike Force eventually helped stanch the hemorrhaging of salvageable housing, coupled with cooperation from insurance companies, rising replacement costs, which presumably made arson less profitable, and the fact that in some neighborhoods there appeared to be little left to burn.

———

Sturz also tackled another criminal justice challenge that virtually no one else was willing to take on and that required interagency collaboration—and political cover—to address in any meaningful way: the consequences of sending so many people to prison. The United States has the highest proportion of incarcerated inmates of any nation. Each year, 700,000 Americans are released from prison. Another ten million return to their communities from briefer says in jail. Practically since Vera's inception, through his experience on the Bowery and later with Wildcat, Sturz was committed to their successful re-entry.

When Sturz tiptoed into the field, he entered a hostile climate. Few public officials were willing to risk sounding soft on crime by directing resources to the people who had committed it. From the beginning, though, he wisely couched the goal not as another liberal nostrum, not as some moral imperative, but as a matter of enlightened self-interest. Much later, others would embrace the concept of prisoner re-entry and the concept would be endorsed across the political spectrum, as liberals and conservatives recognized the consequences of long sentences and lack of rehabilitation and the prohibitive cost of building more prisons. Among the first was Charles J. Hynes who in 1999, as the Brooklyn district attorney, would start a program to keep the 4,000 or so former inmates who came home to Brooklyn each year from returning to prison.

Sturz would later team up with Michael Weinstein, chief program officer of the Robin Hood Foundation, to support re-entry programs like SingleStop, which ensures that inmates get the federal and state benefits they and their families are eligible for immediately, rather than being tossed into society's unwelcoming arms with only a Metrocard and, perhaps, a word of encouragement. "I told Herb, I don't have a program officer who understands the correction department," Weinstein recalls. "I asked him, 'would you take this under your wing?' Herb poured unbelievable amounts of time and energy into it." As a private citizen with unparalleled access, Sturz visited the city's detention facilities on Rikers Island to personally interview inmates about what sort of help—food stamps, Medicaid, job training, housing—might go a long way toward keeping them out of jail.

"Even though they know we're not likely to help them at all right now, we can engage them to learn more about who qualifies for what," he explained on one such visit. "We're connecting with them and letting them know as part of the process that we care about them."

"When you're released, do you have any place to go?" Sturz asked a fifty-one-year-old man arrested for shoplifting. He had been living on the street and homeless shelters since he was released from prison three years earlier.

"I'll probably wind up back here," he said. "If I can get a job, a carpenter, painter . . ."

"You don't know what you're going to learn," Sturz said after the interview. "What did I learn that I didn't know two hours ago? We're not going to solve everything, no way, but you might be able to find something for this guy. He didn't qualify for anything, but his kids and partner probably do. Some 60,000 different people pass through here in a given year, and maybe 10 percent get discharge planning. About $8 million of the Department of Correction's budget is spent on prisoner re-entry. Sixty-seven percent recidivate within three years. I'd be happy if we cut that to 55 percent. That would be big."

———

"From my experience with the Bowery and Wildcat, I knew that people coming out of jail were extremely vulnerable on the day they leave," Sturz says. "I raised the idea of creating an entity that would connect offenders with temporary jobs, the key being to put money into their pockets the day they left jail." A forerunner of what would become the Center for Employment Opportunities was launched to focus on inmates beginning the day they left detention. Sturz conducted his own research, boarding the Rikers bus at six A.M. to follow detainees, and quickly understood the intrinsic value of getting a job immediately and of getting paid the day of release.

More than two-thirds of parolees are typically rearrested within three years. Over half will be incarcerated again. Research suggests that a meaningful job is among the strongest incentives against a formerly jailed individual's recidivism. In the late 1970s, Vera launched the Neighborhood Work Project, an experiment in day labor to test the thesis that immediate paid transitional jobs would help overcome the barriers—the lack of basic education, employment skills and work history; minimal family or community support mechanisms; criminal histories that limit the options or inclinations of companies to employ ex-convicts. The Neighborhood Work Project spawned the Vocational Development Program, which guided former inmates working as day laborers to full-time employment. In 1996, the combined programs were spun off to the Center for Employment Opportunities (CEO), which over the next decade would place more than 10,000 enrollees in full-time jobs with local businesses and nonprofit agencies. To qualify for those programs, an individual's most recent conviction could not have been for a flagrant violent crime and he or she must be capable of engaging in physical labor. Not surprisingly, the vast majority of participants were men, mostly black or Hispanic, with an average age of twenty-six.

A separate program, incorporating Sturz's goal of double social utility, was begun later specifically for inmates of the city's jail system. The multi-agency partnership's mission was not only to employ former inmates but to focus those services on a specific neighborhood—in this case, the Queens Plaza area where many Rikers Island inmates were released from Department of Correction buses at a local transportation hub and largely left to fend for themselves.

In the late 1980s, with state prisons overflowing and budget coffers dwindling, the state began military-style boot camps for nonviolent felons to reduce the amount of time and space they would occupy in the correctional system but that were rigorous enough to be politically acceptable to a safety-conscious public. The New York State Division of Parole enlisted Vera to help ensure that graduates of six-month so-called shock incarceration boot camps would go straight. As a result, CEO became, in effect, the managing agent for the Division of Parole's transitional employment services. It marked the beginning of a mutually beneficial relationship with government. CEO received a steady stream of clients—former inmates—and parole officers could demonstrate lower rates of recidivism. CEO's record of screening applicants and of supervising them impressed government agencies and private employers seeking to tap into a flexible and reliable (participants are covered under a federal bonding program) labor pool that could be hired at competitive costs

The core principles on which CEO operates echo Vera's time-tested formula. One ingredient is instant gratification. In keeping with the overall theme of seeking social justice through practical solutions, CEO offers immediate employment to former inmates, pays them daily at the minimum wage, gives then four days of training and job search preparation to expose and acclimate them to basic skills like showing up on time, accepting direction and appreciating their fellow workers. Each is assigned a job coach. Over time, CEO, like other Vera ventures, also evolved to provide ancillary services to ease the integration of its clients into both employment and their community. (One is a Responsible Fatherhood Program, which helps reconnect non-custodial fathers with their dependent children. To help keep them out of prison and to instill the values of parenting, the program provides guidance in meeting child support obligations, nutrition, budgeting, personal health and anger management. Another is the Rapid Rewards Program, which provides incentives to clients who are placed in unsubsidized jobs and keep working past monthly milestones for up to a year.) All of CEO's training and employment imperatives are flexible enough to allow clients to meet other commitments, including reporting to parole officers and undergoing drug treatment.

In any given year, 60 percent of CEO's clients who work with a job developer get jobs. Overall, about 30 percent of the clients placed in jobs returned to state prison within three years, compared to 51 percent of the former inmates who were not placed. Among those who were placed in a job and remained employed for six months or more, only 13 percent were re-incarcerated.

In creating a Learning Institute to further its research and to disseminate the results, CEO further modeled itself on Vera. And in 2008, with the stability of some urban communities being undermined by a proliferation of abandoned homes and by the threat of more foreclosures, Sturz was hoping to enlist Wildcat and CEO workers to mow lawns, fix windows and conduct other maintenance and improvements to keep whole neighborhoods threatened by mortgage foreclosures from deteriorating.

———

Sturz also took on a number of other criminal justice initiatives that had been talked about for years, sometimes decades but had defied solution because of competing priorities and political constituencies.

As deputy mayor, he helped lay the foundation for a fundamental change in law enforcement that police commissioners had been lobbying for for ages: the merger of the transit and housing authority police forces into the NYPD as a single operational force. Sturz later developed some second thoughts about the wisdom of merging the transit cops with the larger police force, but it eventually was accomplished under Mayor Giuliani and perfected by Police Commissioner Ray Kelly.

While the city's detention system was ostensibly overseen by the correction commissioner, Sturz had inherited a bifurcated system in which the commissioner had been superseded, in effect, by a federal judge, Morris E. Lasker.

Lasker was virtually running the system after a series of challenges by the Legal Aid Society to overcrowding and other horrendous conditions. After years of what Sturz acknowledged was "stonewalling" by the fiscally strapped Beame administration, he negotiated a settlement that would not permanently resolve every issue but would put much of the acrimony behind the antagonists. "Herb Sturz breathed fresh air into what had been a stale, one might even say rancid, environment," says Michael B. Mushlin, who represented Legal Aid and is now a professor at Pace Law School. "Before he came on the scene, the City of New York was engaged in an all-out defense of indefensible jail conditions." Mushlin recalls Sturz as a patient, skillful negotiator who reached agreement on consent decrees for every city jail. "These decrees resolved litigation that was draining the city's legal resources and causing embarrassment to the city. . . . Without Herb's leadership, who knows what might have happened?" Lasker himself would call Sturz's legacy "a product of the intellect and the heart, both practical and visionary."

———

On a frigid, snowy day in December 1979, Sturz and Koch were returning to City Hall from Harlem, where they had announced an agreement Sturz had arranged with an insurance company for $500,000 in guarantees so minority contractors could bid to build low-income housing. Koch ushered Sturz into his office, where he offered him the chairmanship of the City Planning Commission. "I was totally surprised," Sturz recalls. "I'm not a lawyer. I'm not a land-use planner. But I had done a lot of social planning. I read [Lewis] Mumford, I read [Jane] Jacobs, I went to neighborhoods. I realized it was an incredible learning experience, a challenge and opportunity."

The Bowery, Before: "There were no mourners on the Bowery," Gay Talese wrote in 1963 when more than thirty derelicts died from drinking wood alcohol. The city's skid row in lower Manhattan was home to a revolving population estimated between 10,000 and 20,000 men.

EDWARD HAUSNER / *THE NEW YORK TIMES*

The Bowery, After: White denim men's pants were on sale recently for $298 at Blue & Cream—enough in the old days for a year's stay in a flophouse. Cheaper rooms at the new Bowery Hotel go for $395.

FRED R. CONRAD / *THE NEW YORK TIMES*

Boys' Life: Sturz's illustrated supplement championed and explicated the Bill of Rights when, as now, America was challenged to reconcile national security with civil liberties.

COURTESY OF HERB STURZ

The Letter: More than a decade after "The Grapes of Wrath" was published, John Steinbeck congratulated Sturz for understanding the metaphorical inner chapters. "You are the first critical person," he wrote, "who seems to have suspected that they had a purpose."

Times Square, Before: "We had to learn to negotiate streets full of people shrieking in rage and despair at the top of their voices, and often directing their shrieks at us," Professor Marshall Berman wrote.

NEAL BOENZI / *THE NEW YORK TIMES*

Times Square, Before: One New York City police officer remarked about the worst block on West 42nd Street: "All the losers who can't make it in their neighborhoods come to be losers here."

NEAL BOENZI / *THE NEW YORK TIMES*

Times Square, After: Some critics complained of "Disneyfication," but the Crossroads of the World was revived by teams of tourists, shoppers and workers, and even a place to sit. Said Professor Marshall Berman: "Now it is clearer than ever that there is room for everybody."

DAVID W. DUNLAP / *THE NEW YORK TIMES*

Vera, the 1960s: "I didn't start with an overriding format," Sturz recalled. "I basically moved Vera along, learning by experience."

The Insider: "After seventeen years," Sturz said, "I wanted to test myself in other contexts." Joined by his wife, Elizabeth, Sturz was sworn in as deputy mayor in 1978 by Edward I. Koch.

The Benefactor I: In 2007 Nurcha, a South African housing finance program that Sturz helped foster, built its 200,000th house. The land-acquisition strategy was later replicated in New York and other cities.

SIPHIWE SIBEKO / COURTESY OF THE OPEN SOCIETY INSTITUTE

The Benefactor II: The After-School Corporation was founded with a $125 million grant from George Soros's Open Society Institute. "The important thing," Sturz said, "was to develop something of quality that could go to scale."

JEFFERSON SPADY / COPYRIGHT © 2006 CIVIC VENTURES

A Kind of Genius: A friend says of Sturz's strategy: "It is like Barack Obama's vision of the world. Herb is not a centrist. His is not the Third Way. He's a pragmatist."

Part IV

The Social Planner

Chapter 10

The Process Broker

Wasn't Sturz nervous, someone asked, when his appointment as chairman of the City Planning Commission was announced on December 27, 1979, a few days before his forty-ninth birthday? After all, he had spent nearly his entire career in criminal justice, nearly seventeen years as director of Vera and then nearly two as a deputy mayor whose portfolio dealt almost entirely with the fate of people, not with issues of physical development. One could argue that Vera had successfully served as the Police Department's planning arm even though Sturz was not a lawyer or law enforcement professional or even social worker. What had Sturz known about bail or about the Bowery or about addicts and alcoholics and former convicts before plunging into those challenges, too?

City Planning was something else, entirely, though. Sturz was not an urban planner, a developer, an architect or a design visionary. And, as Carl Weisbrod says, "the intricacies of zoning are like the Talmud." The job not only demanded a quick study but called on some of Sturz's other strengths, his political acumen and his sensitivity to what motivated people. Still, Weisbrod says, "it took Herb a lot of time to get his sea legs there and to understand how passionate people would get about the height or look of a building while the death of five homeless people would go unnoticed."

"I'm going in with modest confidence," Sturz said, smiling, at the time. Privately, he later recalled, "there was a sense of the department being adrift." Also, he would later acknowledge that in his gut he might have been more skittish than he let on. "On the one hand I have a lot of confidence. On the other, an edge of uncertainty."

The Planning Commission was established in 1936 under Mayor Fiorello H. La Guardia to plan for the housing, transportation, business, recreational, environmental and other needs of eight million New Yorkers and millions more commuters and visitors. Sturz was recommended to Koch for the job by Bobby Wagner, son of the former mayor, former planning commission chairman and now a deputy mayor. He was not an obvious choice—over four months, two architects, two lawyers, a former member of the commission and two professors had turned it down or said they weren't interested (perhaps because they were concerned that Wagner would be looking over their shoulder from City Hall). Koch deferred to Wagner's judgment of Sturz as the archetypal Renaissance man.

City planning, in a way, was no different from criminal justice or any other organic enterprise with lots of moving parts dependent on each other, egos that needed to be sated, people with competing agendas and results that might redound very differently to the various players but, nonetheless, could be quantified.

"I could count," Sturz says.

For starters, he had to learn a whole new lexicon. "I barely knew what a cornice was," he says. But he followed a familiar learning curve. "Vera grew inductively," he explains, drawing a parallel with this latest learning process. "It started from something narrow and expanded naturally. I start from a narrow scope of knowledge and learn," adding, unfailingly: "It would be pretentious of me to come in with preconceived notions."

The last thing Sturz ever wanted to be perceived as was pretentious (he liked to run, he once explained, but "to say that I am a real jogger would be pretentious"). "A tall man prone to pushing his hair back with the flat of his hand like a small boy," Anna Quindlen wrote in the *Times*, as Sturz fielded questions from reporters in the rotunda of City Hall the day his appointment was announced. Keeping both hands in his pockets most of the time, the six-foot-one Sturz "was thoughtful, earnest, rather cautious, anxious not to seem presumptuous."

Still, while everyone benefited from the safer, more efficient city that Sturz had envisioned at Vera, development, by the sheer amount of profit at stake, came with a very different built-in constituency. "Construction," said Ada Louise Huxtable, the *Times*'s architecture critic, "is not only New York's most important product but also the key to the quality of its future."

———

As chairman of City Planning, Sturz succeeded one of his most enthusiastic boosters in the Koch administration, Bobby Wagner, whom Koch had promoted to be a deputy mayor. They met at Princeton, where Sturz was delivering a lecture and volunteered some kind words about Wagner's father, himself a former chairman of the Planning Commission and the first of seven New York City mayors whom Sturz would win over to his public policy agenda. While they were both members of the Koch administration, Sturz and the younger Wagner would regularly meet at Monte Carmelo on the Upper East Side over their fixed menu of spaghetti carbonara and veal piccata, accompanied by liberal quantities of Chianti. Wagner was one of the administration's small circle of wise men, as gentle as he was sagacious. Sturz was also skilled at forging consensus, at rarely offending, and if he lacked Wagner's institutional memory he largely shared his vision and his grasp of human nature.

As a city planner, Sturz was neither Robert Moses nor Jane Jacobs. But, in his own way, Sturz altered the city's physical landscape, and harnessed the Planning Commission's broad jurisdictional reach to achieve social changes as well, including the creation of an Immigrant Affairs Office.

Constitutionally and institutionally, Sturz was not a power broker. He never inherited the unfettered prerogatives that Robert Moses, himself a member of the Planning Commission in the 1940s, agglomerated and wielded with impunity through myriad other roles in government. By the 1970s, there was simply less power for any one person to broker. The Planning Commission's historic dominion proved to be fleeting, especially its broad discretion over public works financed by the capital budget, which after 1975 would gravitate to other agencies, including the mayor's office, to community district boards and later to the city council. The council would also inherit more sway over how to develop the city's most vital resource, land. The Balkanization of power to community boards was compounded by the city's fiscal crisis, which crimped its ability to borrow. "At times of growth, City Planning is on the ascendancy," said Carol Bellamy, the city council president. "In times of decline, the Office of Management and Budget is." Huxtable delivered a more severe verdict: "The new chairman has inherited an agency, and a process, that has almost ceased to function." When Sturz was finally sworn in by Koch five months after taking the job, he commented that it was rare to have the honeymoon before the ceremony and added: "I had worked in criminal justice for a good many years, and I suspect, Mr. Mayor, that you may have decided that in appointing me chairman of the City Planning Commission it was time for the transition from crime to punishment."

Moses himself had rendered the power broker passé. In its place, demand had developed for technocrats whose savvy and personal charm could help them navigate the jagged shoals of public opinion and regulatory review: The Process Broker. If anyone fit that bill, it was Herb Sturz.

Given his background, it's not surprising that several of Sturz's most visible contributions as chairman of the Planning Commission had less to do directly with the physical condition of the city than with its tattered psychic fabric. And also with the police. One failed; the other largely succeeded.

Before being sworn in after his election in 1977, Koch visited the city's correctional complex on Rikers Island and was appalled by the conditions in which 7,000 inmates were hidden away in plain sight of La Guardia Airport. With the city too fiscally strapped to respond except cosmetically, the Beame administration kept losing federal lawsuits filed on behalf of inmates. Koch, determined to demonstrate both his progressive and fiscal bona fides, turned to his newly minted deputy mayor for criminal justice. Sturz responded ingeniously and audaciously. Not only were the city's detention and correctional facilities overcrowded. The state's were in even worse shape. Sturz proposed that the city sell Rikers to the state.

"The idea was twofold," he recalls. "It was tough for attorneys to visit their clients. It took hours for prisoners to get to court and back. And it made sense for pretrial detainees who had not been convicted to be in close touch with their families and their lawyers." One result was a new pretrial detention facility next to the Tombs on Centre Street downtown.

City prisoners on Rikers, most awaiting bail, being held before trial or awaiting sentencing, would be placed in smaller detention facilities closer to courthouses, their lawyer and their families, in every borough except Staten Island. The state would modernize Rikers to accommodate 5,000 inmates from jammed upstate prisons who were nearing the end of their sentences and facilitate their reentry into communities by placing them closer to their homes. A $200 million up-front payment from the state combined with about $179 million in city capital funds would pay for the new local detention facilities. Sturz estimated that the city's costs for the initiative would probably be lower, or little more, than what it would have to spend to bring Rikers into compliance with standards being imposed by the federal courts. Decentralization would allow the department to focus fewer resources on transportation; officials estimated that in the previous year, 400,000 inmates traveled 800,000 miles as correction vehicles ferried them on 500,000 trips between detention facilities and courthouses. ("It forces us to move prisoners to and from the courts from sunup to midnight," Sturz said.)

The entire criminal justice system, and virtually all of its constituents, would benefit from a more efficient and humane process. In June 1979, while Sturz was still deputy mayor, Koch and Governor Hugh Carey agreed to a memorandum of understanding that embraced his plan in its entirety. Peter Tufo, chairman of the watchdog Board of Correction, hailed Sturz's leasing plan as "the single most important development" in the correction department's history, adding, "It is clear that it will cost the city just as much to preserve the status quo without any of the improvements the plan will provide."

Nonetheless, a majority of the city's Board of Estimate, including the mayor, walked away from it. "I think ultimately," Sturz says, "the Budget Bureau felt we were spending too much of our money on bad people." With only a year before citywide elections, the consensus seemed to be that the money could be spent elsewhere with a greater political return on the investment and less grumbling from constituents whose homes and businesses abutted the proposed detention sites. The correction officers' union vigorously opposed the plan, too, warning that in place of a secure complex on Rikers Island, the city was proposing escape-prone, "experimental, posh prisons."

The mayor's reversal followed by less than two months the plan's approval by the City Planning Commission. The commission's new chairman was flummoxed, "muzzled and clearly uncomfortable," as Wayne Barrett described him in the *Village Voice.* Twice, he was asked whether Koch had consulted him before abandoning the most ambitious criminal justice initiative of his young administration. "I can only say," Sturz replied, mustering his most magnanimous and steadfast posture, "I was aware that the decision was being considered." Privately, though, Sturz would say later, "I probably would have left government once I knew where things were going with Rikers Island and other matters I cared about."

He had fought so many good fights, having begun with so little. How did he know when to give up and to cut his losses. "Sometimes," he replied, "other people cut them for you. Rikers Island is an example."

———

Early in 1983, delivering what was perceived as evidence of racial insensitivity, Koch had bypassed a black deputy schools chancellor to name Bobby Wagner to the position of schools chancellor (Koch's first choice, Gordon Davis, his former parks commissioner, who is black, was savvy enough to decline; Wagner would be rejected by the state education commissioner because he lacked the academic credentials but would be named president of the Board of Education instead). To make matters worse, a series of fatalities suggesting excessive use of force by the police was provoking accusations of racially motivated brutality, accusations that resulted in congressional hearings into cases that ran the gamut from ambiguous to gross overreactions and which generally proved to be an embarrassment to the Koch administration. With Bob McGuire beginning to mull retirement as police commissioner and the mayor committed to seeking a third term, the choice of a successor for a job that is more visible than any in city government except for the mayoralty itself became paramount.

Koch's early favorite to succeed McGuire was William J. Devine, the able first deputy commissioner. But Devine was ailing and was likely to retire soon, too. So the field was open. In June 1983, Sturz and Frederick A. O. Schwarz Jr., the city's corporation counsel, invited Koch to dinner. "He said, 'Well, come to Gracie Mansion,'" Sturz recalls. "We said we didn't want to go to Gracie Mansion, we would rather go to a restaurant. He was a little taken aback. We said, 'We'll take *you* out to dinner.' He was nervous. I heard later that he feared, not knowing what we wanted, that both Fritz and I were thinking of quitting the administration." Koch was pretty savvy, but it did not take a political genius to divine their agenda. At dinner at an Italian restaurant, the moment he realized that neither of them was resigning or presenting him with some other unanticipated crisis, the mayor broached the subject himself. "So," Koch said nonchalantly, "which black do you want me to appoint as police commissioner?"

Koch had already seconded McGuire's appointment of a black commander of Harlem's police precinct, but commissioner was another dimension entirely in a force—and, even more so, in the patrolmen's union—on which whites predominated. All other things being equal, the case that Sturz and Schwarz presented was compelling. It would be echoed by others, who had a stake in stability. "I think," said Lewis Rudin, the real estate mogul and chairman of the Association for a Better New York, a business-oriented boosterism group, "the message has gotten through that the mayor should be more sensitive to the responsible black community because otherwise we'll get irresponsible black leaders." In the search for a successor to McGuire, Koch deviated markedly from his normal routine. Instead of a collective decision made at City Hall, the mayor considered this matter so sensitive that he met with advisers individually and privately to encourage total candor. "It was clear to me this matter would best be served if every person I spoke with felt total confidentiality," he explained later. "I've never done that before. It's mind-boggling. You do get honest answers."

Sturz and Schwarz wanted Benjamin Ward. They had no second choice. Ward had worked with Sturz at Vera, where he directed the Pretrial Services Agency, and Sturz had delivered him to Koch as a prospective appointee once before. That was in 1979, after Koch, keeping his promise, empowered his newly named criminal justice coordinator with the discretion to hire and fire the correction commissioner. Ward could be headstrong at times, but they all shared a common agenda, which recognized that the jails and prisons were not merely a repository for prisoners but also a potential breeding ground for recidivists. "Maybe it was part of affirmative action, if you will, but I thought it was good for New York City if you had a good person who happened to be black," Sturz says. Koch, Schwarz recalls, "would never allow, in his own mind, to make an appointment by race. So the right way was to stress Ben's résumé."

As a student at the Brooklyn High School of Automotive Trade, Ward, after winning a citywide essay contest, had been appointed "police commissioner for a day." In 1951, he joined the force for real. "Most people tell you they wanted to do service," he would recall later with endearing candor, "but I wanted a good secure job." He remained with the department for twenty-three years, earning a bachelor's degree and graduating from law school while rising through the ranks to deputy commissioner of community affairs, then traffic commissioner. Governor Hugh Carey appointed him commissioner of the state Department of Correctional Services in 1975. After a tenure marked by run-ins with the union representing prison guards, which accused him of being too lenient toward inmates, he resigned in 1978 to head the city's Housing Authority police force. "It was time to return to the police field," Ward wrote Carey, "where one can tell the good guys from the bad guys, at least with more certainty than in corrections."

By late 1983 Ward would have been on his way to what most veterans of the criminal justice hierarchy consider to be their final reward—a judgeship. Instead, Koch named him police commissioner. Publicly, at least, most of the reaction was overwhelmingly positive. With no expe-

rience in prison administration when he was appointed
state correction commissioner by Carey, Ward acknowledged at the time that "my blackness was a factor in the
governor's selecting me." But the same was not true this
time around. As he put it, "My whole background is police.
It's just fortuitous that I happen to be black." That Ward
was black, Koch says, was "an extra added plus after the decision was made."

Ward would serve for six tumultuous years, steadying
a department buffeted by a continuing string of brutality
accusations. He reflexively reacted by defending the force
in general but, when justified, firmly responded to individual cases of abuse (when officers in Queens were accused
of torturing a suspect with stun guns, he delivered an angry tongue lashing to 300 ranking officers whom he summoned to Police Headquarters and fired the entire chain of
command, from the chief of patrol to the local precinct).
During his tenure, the number of blacks, Hispanic officers
and women in the ranks rose (by 17 percent, 60 percent
and 84 percent, respectively to roughly 12 percent each) as
did the education level of officers overall. And he developed a warm personal and professional relationship with
Koch, which solidified the mayor's judgment about Sturz,
the man who had hired him as correction commissioner
and initially recommended him for this job.

Ward could be strikingly frank. When he resigned
shortly after Koch lost the 1989 Democratic mayoral primary to David Dinkins, he expressed one regret, "that the
people of New York may not understand as keenly as I do
the extraordinary contribution you have made to uphold-
ing the law in this city." But, with customary candor, Ward
added: "I think Ed Koch was the right man for the job, the
right man for the times. He didn't win the primary. I clearly
think that David Dinkins is the right man for these times."

Chapter 11

Planning the
Visionary City

·

Since its inception during the Depression, the City Planning Commission rarely had the inclination or the
resources to plan. More often than not, it responded to
political imperatives, to the horse trading among the borough presidents for their priorities in the city's capital budget and to the daily crises that elected and appointed
officials inevitably become inured to—the never-ending
litany of emergencies that come to define their daily routine. (One of Sturz's predecessors in city government, Barry
Gottehrer, Mayor Lindsay's chief troubleshooter, poignantly
wrote that after several years of coping with government
crises, the administration's machinery for responding to
explosive situations of one sort or another had become
so accomplished that "it tended to flatten them out into
toneless similarity.") Planning for something that hadn't
happened yet was a luxury that might be indulged once a
generation, when an existing zoning formula had been rendered obsolete by technology or by a new economic mandate or when visionaries (John Lindsay's ambitious 1969

Plan for New York City, Ed Koch's Commission on the Year 2000, Michael R. Bloomberg's PlaNY2030) momentarily managed to see beyond their cluttered desktops.

Sturz inherited a diminished city struggling with scarce resources to regain its preeminence. From the beginning, he defined planning more broadly than his predecessors had. He was determined to plan not just for the physical city but for the individuals who occupy it. He cast a wide net, perhaps, in part, as compensation for the fact that some of the commission's prerogatives over physical planning had been compromised, preempted or obviated by lulls in development. "I would use—in some cases my position, in some cases my ideas, my access—to get involved in a range of decisions that had nothing to do with city planning."

In 1983, as Planning Commission chairman, Sturz again expanded his portfolio exponentially to include the city's human capital. Going well beyond his job's ordinary mandate or agenda, he created City Volunteer Corps. Within five years, under one of its alumni, Michael Brown, a Harvard graduate who worked for Representative Leon Panetta, the corps would become the inspiration for City Year (which would expand to nearly twenty U.S. cities and to South Africa and become the model for the Clinton administration's AmeriCorps).

Addressing a fundraiser for the Boy Scouts of America, Koch articulated Sturz's vision. Echoing a concerted proposal made earlier that week by Sturz's friend, Franklin A. Thomas, president of the Ford Foundation, Koch said the program would meet multiple goals, including teaching skills, earning high school equivalency diplomas, producing a more socioeconomically balanced armed forces (eighteen-year-olds would have a choice between military and civilian services) and would inspire young people who are disaffected and lack purpose. "Their outlook is narrow," he

said. "Too often, they are out of touch with the spirit of altruism, which is a basic part of every human being."

The concept of nonmilitary public service—universal
or voluntary—was not new, of course, although the opportunities arose only intermittently. In the 1960s, the
Peace Corps and VISTA helped fill the void. Governor
Ronald Reagan's California Conservation Corps also did,
employing and helping rehabilitate wayward youth. Its
success, under Reagan and his successor, Edmund G. (Jerry)
Brown Jr., coupled with the abolition of the draft, prompted
a number of foundations to replicate the corps in other
states and to explore its potential impact on rising crime,
unemployment and high school dropout rates. Koch's vision was colored by nostalgia for Franklin D. Roosevelt's
Civilian Conservation Corps and its reputation for melding
Americans from a range of social strata into a homoge-
neous and harmonious collaboration. Sturz tapped into
Koch's slightly rose-colored recollection of the breadth of
Civilian Conservation Corps membership to extract $10
million for an experimental municipal service program.

Sturz's goal for the volunteer corps was not to create
another employment or job training program, but a miniature experiment in national service. Typically, not *that*
miniature, though, given that its legal name—the National
Service Corporation for New York City—was ambitious
(perhaps even pretentious) and that unlike most of its
conservation corps counterparts across the country it was
operating in a unique urban environment. If it worked,
the pilot project would instill the values of citizenship,
introduce participants to unfamiliar places and people in
the city and deploy them in team-building crews for city
agencies and nonprofit organizations. Participants would be
chosen randomly by lottery. In addition to a weekly stipend
pegged near the minimum wage (about $80, to comply

with the Fair Labor Standards Act), graduates of a full year of service would receive a college scholarship worth $5,000, or $2,500 in cash (participants who had not graduated from high school would receive help in obtaining a General Educational Development diploma, the GED).

Sturz had showcased the original Manhattan Bail Project nationally to help generate buzz about Vera. He promoted Wildcat to a much wider audience beyond New York City, in part, to give the Beame administration, which was grasping for any good news, a stake in Wildcat's success. His promotional strategy for the City Volunteer Corps, as it became known informally, was national in scope, too, but with one major difference: Unlike the bail project and Wildcat, which had already been operating and had compiled proven track records, the volunteer corps was just beginning. Representative Leon Panetta, a California Democrat, organized public hearings in New York to highlight the program, and Koch frequently invoked it before any and every audience, including lunch with William F. Buckley Jr., founder of the conservative *National Review*. Sturz was so convinced of the need for a volunteer corps and of its eventual success that he veered from his standard operating procedure of flying well below the radar until a pilot program had proved itself. A national debate was going on, and Sturz was determined to influence it. (That public colloquium took an unexpected turn at 5:30 one morning when Carl Weisbrod, whom Sturz appointed director of the program, agreed to face off in a televised debate against a professor who opposed national service. The professor was blind and was accompanied by a seeing eye dog named Carl. Every time the moderator turned to Weisbrod and said, "Well, Carl, what do you think?" the dog would loudly thump its tail.)

Once the City Volunteer Corps got going, its progress was more conventional, at least by Vera's standards. It was formally launched in November 1984 in a park in a mostly black neighborhood of southeast Queens. Koch and Sturz, who had been working late at City Hall (mobilizing the Board of Estimate for a crucial vote on a Times Square development agreement with the state), arrived for the ceremony by helicopter. Koch had insisted that the participants be selected randomly, but the board of directors was broadly representative. Bishop Joseph Sullivan of the Catholic Diocese of Brooklyn, a giant in social welfare in the city, agreed to serve as chairman of a board that included Arthur Sulzberger Jr., who would become publisher of the *Times* (his expertise in fostering an urban Outward Bound program was invaluable to the volunteer corps); Fred Wilpon, owner of the New York Mets; and Augusta Kappner, who would become an assistant secretary of education and president of Bank Street, the graduate school of education.

Keeping the cost below $10,000 a year per participant was vital if the corps was to be expanded to meet the demand from applicants and service providers and to be replicated elsewhere. That cost ceiling prevented the corps from providing a residential component, which was integral to many similar programs elsewhere, although housing was included during an intensive, two-week training regime for each new class of volunteers. The training was rigorous and, for many of the participants, unique. Held at a camp upstate, it brought together individuals from diverse racial, ethnic and economic backgrounds, some of whom had never spent a single night away from home and had never been out of town before (later, there were exchange programs with corps in San Francisco and Great Britain). Like Outward

Bound, the training program capitalized on each participant's potential and enabled them to bond into a team
whose primary goal was delivering service to others ("Our
volunteers are providers, not recipients, of service," Weisbrod
would say). The orientation also served to weed out applicants who, for one reason or another, were inappropriate.

New York's random lottery drew and admitted a large
proportion of high school dropouts—and, therefore, black
and Hispanic young. It differed from most versions of the
conservation corps, which were predominantly male and
typically involved physical labor exclusively. New York's
CV's, as they were dubbed, were deployed in distinctive
red caps and sweatshirts to homeless shelters, hospices,
parks, playgrounds. They worked with children who were
born addicted to heroin and with disabled elderly people.
The program's goals were restated repeatedly: This was not
make-work or job training or rehabilitation. This was about
volunteering and public service, a mission that would periodically be instilled when the entire corps (nearly a thousand strong at its peak) was enlisted in a single, signature
project, such as delivering food to homebound elderly New
Yorkers all over the city. But they also learned that, while
giving isn't necessarily better than receiving, the psychic returns can be substantial and so can the ancillary benefits of
the service. Volunteers got basic literacy training so they
could earn their GEDs. High school graduates were eligible to attend college classes, tuition free. (One would go on
to win a Rhodes scholarship and would later be hired by
Lucy N. Friedman at Sturz's The After-School Corporation.)

Within a few months, Jack Rosenthal would wax philosophical in a *Times* editorial notebook: "Giving and receiving: The volunteers' experience offers a twist on the
eternally alternating equation," he wrote. "The more the recipients benefit from the volunteers' work, the more the

volunteers value their work, and themselves." They "dismiss well-meant but empty training programs as 'junk jobs for chump change,'" Rosenthal wrote. "But authentic service makes work authentic."

The corps would survive through the Dinkins administration and offer a model for President Bill Clinton's AmeriCorps. Sturz's creation of the volunteer corps vividly illustrated the wider reach, at least in this case, of a social entrepreneur operating within the government. He could not have created entire agencies devoted to juvenile justice or to victim services as a well-intentioned outsider. "In some areas, you had the power," he says. "With the City Volunteer Corps, there was a confluence of time. I helped prepare the mayor's speech. We got $10 million almost overnight. You don't do that as easily from the outside." Then, Sturz adds, "You don't do that so often from the inside, either."

His commitment to social planning would also manifest itself through two other innovative expansions of the Department of City Planning, whose mandate was largely about buildings and land use. "Planning takes in a lot more than structures," Sturz explains. "To plan for New York City is to look at who lives here, to project who will live here ten or twenty years from now, and to design systems capable of meeting their physical and social needs." Two of the fastest-growing groups living in the city were immigrants and older people.

On the brink of the biggest influx of immigrants since the beginning of the twentieth century, he established an Office of Immigrant Affairs to better serve and integrate newcomers by better understanding why they came, what they needed, and how to capitalize on their contribution. Eventually, the office would be spun off as a charter-mandated mayoral agency.

City Planning under Sturz plunged into another unfamiliar realm, the impact of the elderly (the fastest-growing
segment of the population) on the hospital system and the
lack of services that were available to them upon release. At
one point, invoking initiatives he had first tested at Vera, he
challenged the convention that a permanent underclass
was impervious to employment. Under one pilot project,
eligible poor people who were hospitalized would be allowed to return home and be treated as outpatients with
the savings—as much as $350 a day—diverted to hiring
drivers to ferry them to their medical appointments. Theoretically, the project would produce better health care and
provide jobs for the unemployed. "I like the idea of one dependent population helping another dependent population," Sturz says. He dreamed up the Home Health Care
Project with Lutheran Medical Center, which teamed unemployed welfare mothers as home attendants for elderly
patients who otherwise, because they were unable to care
for themselves and nursing homes lacked space, would cost
Medicare $340 a day in the hospital. Instead, paying the
former welfare recipients for a seven-hour day and providing doctors and physical therapists for house calls would
cost $60 daily.

At his belated swearing in, in June 1980, Sturz delivered a mini-tutorial on what he had already learned during
five months as chief planner of a living city. When he began, he recalled, referring to the Uniform Land Use Review
Procedure, adopted in 1976 to codify the process of public participation, "I had heard of ULURP but I barely knew
what the acronym meant, I'm still struggling with it but, of
course, a lot of others are too. ULURP is the quintessential
bureaucratic word, but planning need not and should not
be bureaucratic. It should be liberating. Planning is the application of common sense and reason to creative pur-

pose." That purpose, he said, must be directed at the city's people and neighborhoods, and, hinting at the philosophy he hoped to apply, he added, "It seems to me that planners should see to it that those who live and do business within the city's embrace are not smothered by that embrace."

———

Ada Louise Huxtable's challenge of what to do about the uncontrolled profusion of bigger and bulkier buildings in midtown Manhattan was one that Sturz would seize upon immediately as director of city planning. The growing mass was attributable to skyrocketing costs of land and construction and abetted by permissive zoning regulations, audacious demands from developers in return for public amenities that were often flouted or perverted. The result of vertical growth was more crowds and vehicular congestion, more windows and sidewalks that never saw the sun, greater demand on city services, public works and private utilities that were already stretched too thin. Nobody expected New York to be bucolic, but the building boom—tall, skinny residential slivers sprouting from vacant lots on the Upper East Side and bulkier commercial behemoths in midtown—seemed to challenge the very definition of livability. "Their collective scale," Huxtable warned, "raises serious concerns about density, pedestrian mobility and air, sun and shadow patterns, and eventual structural gridlock. Even their economic benefits will be over-concentrated, while other areas in need of development go begging."

In less than six months, Sturz had begun to tackle imaginatively the challenges created by the city's skyscraper boom. He converted twenty million square feet of commercial and manufacturing lofts in Manhattan for residential use, expanded cable television networks to underserved

neighborhoods and, most enduringly, established zoning
and planning incentives that would eventually preserve
what was left of air and light on the Upper East Side and
shift commercial development from the congested east
midtown to underutilized parcels on the West Side. Those
zoning changes reduced the buildable floor space in east
midtown by about 40 percent and increased it on the West
Side by 20 percent and further would set the stage for the
Times Square redevelopment that had become paramount
to Koch and would emerge as Sturz's indelible legacy.

Sturz's success in shepherding the new zoning regulations into law was presaged by an earlier compromise on an
equally contentious issue that had bedeviled city officials
for years. In the 1960s and 1970s, new residents, many of
them artists, who were willing to put up with limited
amenities in return for space, began to illegally occupy city
lofts—former commercial or factory space—that had been
zoned exclusively for manufacturing or business use and
was, thus, off-limits for living. By the early 1980s, though,
with space exhausted, developers, manufacturers, organized labor and tenants were pitted against each other as
landlords (or new residents, with a wink from landlords) illegally converted open floors from industrial and commercial to residential use. Officials had to balance pressing but
competing concerns: how to protect manufacturing areas
from incursions by new residents who were likely to eventually drive real estate prices beyond the reach of manufacturers; recognize New Yorkers' pressing demand for more
residential space; provide illegal loft residents with a modicum of legal protections as the space they transformed
into attractive living quarters soared in value; and assure
those loft dwellers that their residences met minimum
health and safety standards.

Sturz's proposed solution was to zone four areas on
the West Side (the garment center, northeast Chelsea, the

nearby graphic arts center and the meat market) exclusively as manufacturing , preserving about seventy million
square feet for business. Existing residential loft tenants in
northeast Chelsea would be allowed to remain, but all others would have to apply for cumbersome individual ex-
emptions from the new zoning rules. New residents would
not be permitted in those zones. In four other areas, residential and commercial lofts could coexist, but developers
converting them to housing would have to make comparable space available elsewhere for commercial or manufacturing purposes. Under Carl Weisbrod, whom Sturz installed
as the arbiter of the loft zoning, Sturz's compromise led to
the renewal of Chelsea and the Flatiron district. When it
was approved by the Board of Estimate in 1981, Sturz
hailed it as designed to "bring a certain regulation to the loft
residential marketplace, create a disincentive for illegal
conversion and ensure the vitality of the city's commercial
and manufacturing areas." It finally defused a controversy
that had simmered for a decade and, in effect, ratified a decision already made by the marketplace.

"There is no way to prove to a skeptical public that the
city will perform in a satisfactory manner," Sturz said at
the time. But the legal tools, market incentives and enforcement mechanisms were put in place "to ensure that
new illegal conversion does not take place and that the
existing illegal conversions are legalized." Each side, he
said, "must pay a price to achieve an equitable policy."

———

Just a month after Ada Louise Huxtable demanded a "complete and radical overhaul" of zoning regulation but worried that the Planning Commission lacked the will, Sturz
unveiled a 200-page blueprint. Begun under Bobby Wagner,
the changes were billed as the third generation of zoning

philosophy, the first being the visionary 1916 code (which encouraged the ziggurat, or wedding cake, structure that narrowed toward the top) and the second the 1961 revision (which inspired giant slabs). Sturz's version was intended to promote architectural diversity and curtail the generous "as of right" height and bulk bonuses buildings that added up to 20 percent to a building's marketable volume for providing public amenities that, in fact, were often illegally gated or deliberately designed to be inhospitable. The *Daily News* dubbed them "phantom parks" that existed largely on official building plans, but not in fact. Some developers all but admitted as much. Responding to Sturz's demand that a so-called plaza on the Upper East Side be made more hospitable, the building owner scoffed that "it would be ridiculous to encourage the use of this space."

Sturz's plan would drive development westward, away from the canyons created by new office towers (including the architecturally distinctive IBM and AT&T—now Sony—office buildings on Madison Avenue). "Much of the criticism of the newest crop of East Side buildings," Richard K. Bernstein, a city planner, observed in his report to the commission, "reflects the concern that, however distinguished each may be individually, they do not respect their context and threaten the quality of ensemble that helps makes their location so valuable in the first place."

In 1982, the seven-member City Planning Commission voted unanimously to revamp the 1961 zoning law, a patchwork that had been subjected to thousands of modifications over two decades, to create a special midtown district. The district would be divided into three parts, where the new rules would reflect the commission's separate priorities—to accelerate development farther west, limit it in some areas and bar it in others. Two months later, the Board of

Estimate's lopsided ten-to-one vote in favor belied the fissures that erupted as developers jockeyed for last-minute advantage and other interested parties lobbied to further revise the most fundamental zoning reform in a generation. In the end, the board approved two amendments. One would preserve forty-four legitimate theaters clustered near Broadway in a compromise intended to balance the interests of preservationists with theater owners, who feared that rigid constraints on demolition and on the sale of so-called air rights to developers of contiguous sites would diminish the value of their property.

The second amendment addressed the concerns of the Museum of American Folk Art, which sought to demolish several brownstones on West 53rd Street on blocks that the Planning Commission had deemed distinct and worth saving. Sturz reconfigured the zoning map to exempt the three brownstones. East Side property owners lamented the hundreds of millions of dollars in lost development potential. West Siders, meanwhile, worried that their neighborhoods would become even more congested.

Developers and property owners mobilized, but Sturz drew a line in the asphalt. "I remember sitting down with the chief lobbyist in the city and saying to him, quietly, 'the Planning Commission wants this to happen . . .' I was sending a clear message that there would be war, that his clients would get hurt down the road. I didn't have the slightest qualm doing this because I believed deeply that we were doing the right thing for the city, and I'd be damned if I would lay back in some sort of ivory tower and let special interests gang up to block it."

Sturz's message resonated with Howard J. Rubenstein, the city's preeminent public relations strategist. Rubenstein represented some of the most belligerent and litigious clients in what could be a cutthroat industry. His greatest service to his clients was entrée and sage advice. "You are better off negotiating a solution," Rubenstein would say, "than being a warrior."

The westward shift that the commission intended to encourage through zoning eventually materialized, although some planners said that given the shrinking opportunities for development on the East Side, it might have happened even without Sturz's initiative. Still, one study found that of the twenty-four million square feet of office space built between 1980 and 1987, sixty-three percent was on the East Side and only nine percent was on the West Side. From 1988 to 1994, the study concluded, eighty percent of the twenty-eight million square feet under development would be on the West Side—a shift "directly attributable" to the new zoning bonuses that allowed for bigger buildings.

———

The commission and the planning department that serves as its operational arm had been widely considered Manhattan-centric, unavoidably, perhaps. Sturz sought to alter that by diverting more urban design capacity to each of the other boroughs, which contributed to a 3,500-acre green belt on Staten Island and zoning incentives that helped spark a revival of downtown Brooklyn by luring Morgan Stanley and Chase to a sixteen-acre plot dubbed MetroTech. Sturz pressed to transplant the Police Academy from its anachronistic building on the East Side to a modern campus in the South Bronx.

Over fifty years, between the bloodletting and heroin experiments and the scuttled state purchase of Rikers Island, Sturz's handful of critics could point to few failures. He knew which causes were worth pursuing and which were hopeless. Even the ones that turned out to be hopeless had accomplished something. As virtually every other example of Sturz's ingenuity did, they forced people to think differently—sometimes, in fact, to make them think at all. His former colleague Gara LaMarche, who has seen his share of philanthropic grants fail to fulfill expectations, says, "usually in social entrepreneurship there's a high probability of failure. If you asked in Herb Sturz's case what the failures are, that would be a harder question." To Sturz, there is no such thing as failure. "The only real failure," he always says, "is not trying."

He picked his fights and cut his losses. He once invoked Groucho Marx: "These are my principles; if you don't like them, I have others." But he was just joking. "The essence of genius," William James said, "is to know what to overlook." And to learn from mistakes. "I learned by doing," Sturz says. "I learned by having to learn."

Comparing Sturz to another do-gooder, a mutual friend, who has been in and out of government, too, but one who has the disposition of a bulldog, Weisbrod says the other guy "would see a problem and his desire is to smash through it with no pretense of subtlety. Herb's strategy is, how do you avoid the roadblock? Like the Germans, just ignore the Maginot Line. He brings disparate viewpoints together rather than mounting a frontal assault on the establishment."

"Working with government, not against it," as Nick Katzenbach puts it.

Robert Moses, unabashedly, sometimes cruelly, broke lots of eggs to make his omelets. Was Sturz more deft at cracking the shells? "When he gets criticized, it's for being too cautious, for not breaking the mold," Weisbrod says. Rather than breaking eggs, Weisbrod says, Sturz's style is more akin to blowing up a balloon—pushing the limits as far as he can while keeping the structure intact. "There are some who would say he hasn't been bold enough, some who would prefer to see him more ideological," Weisbrod says. "He has an ideological streak and a moral compass, but he's not the sort to commit hara-kiri. Ideological toughness is also a component of Herb but not something he wears on his sleeve." (His dog does, though, on his collar; the Sturzes' cockapoo is named Franklin, after the father of the New Deal.)

"When you start, you don't say there is going to be a revolution," Sturz says. "You start by learning." From Sturz's very first investigation of bail, his game plan never varied. "I would always go to the source. I never paid much attention to what something was supposed to be—inductive learning from the inside out. Generally, when I start with something, I don't know where it's going to lead, but I have a feel and sense of the issue and its importance, and, broadly, where it can go. In the beginning, I kind of worried about that a bit. I know now that wherever you start, and if you want it to be dynamic, just like a good book, you don't want a mathematical formula. You want the endeavor to grow, almost intrinsically, out of the experience." Beginning with the liberal studies program at Wisconsin, he looked at literature, economics, history, criminal justice through an integrated lens—moving even from A to B through a series of intermediate steps. (Although Robert Schrank, a sociologist and former union organizer and Lindsay administration colleague, would say "for people like us, we don't have to go through the analytical process from A to Z; we can start somewhere at J.")

His credo evokes Sylvia Nasar's insight in *A Beautiful Mind*, her biography of the Nobel Prize–winning Princeton mathematician John Forbes Nash Jr. "A profound dislike for merely absorbing knowledge and a strong compulsion to learn by doing," she wrote, "is one of the most reliable signs of genius."

Part V

Tackling Times Square

Chapter 12

The Longest-Running Joke in New York

Less than two months into Koch's first term, Sturz reprised an issue that virtually every mayor had grappled with since the twentieth century began. The solutions to how to clean up Times Square were elusive, but, to Sturz, the challenge was not unfamiliar. His mission originated in the late nineteenth century and re-emerged periodically when the square's "nice naughtiness" got out of hand. "'Cleaning up' Times Square," says Carl Weisbrod, "had been the longest-running joke in New York since before World War II." The goal was not to sanitize it exactly, but to make it less seedy and menacing and restore it to a tourist destination that was relatively safe. According to Sturz, "It had been romanticized by people who don't go there as 'funky.'"

It was funky, all right. And, terrifying. It symbolized everything that was wrong with the city and its government. In the heart of Manhattan, Times Square was the epicenter of virulent antisocial pathologies, in the form of crime, pornography, prostitution, that had spread well beyond its borders.

"We were used to photographic images of ragged, distressed people down on the Bowery or uptown in Harlem; we weren't prepared to see them face to face, flooding our own streets and doorways and subway stations, and sleeping out in the cold and rain because they had no place to go," Marshall Berman, a City College professor wrote later in the 1980s. "We were used to walking through streets full of quiet desperation; we had to learn to negotiate streets full of people shrieking in rage and despair at the top of their voices, and often directing their shrieks at us."

Even Koch advised tourists to stay away from Times Square. A mile of Eighth Avenue was dubbed the "Minnesota Strip" because so many hookers, when they were arrested or promoting their wares, identified it as their white bread home state. The block of West 42nd Street between Seventh and Eighth Avenues was notoriously known as "the Deuce." In his *Tales of Times Square*, Josh Alan Friedman quoted the Reverend Robert Rappleyea of Holy Cross Church down the block offering a charitable assessment that perhaps as many as one in twenty of the street people (his estimate probably included undercover cops) might have had a legitimate reason to be there. "After eleven o'clock at night on 42nd Street, 95 percent of the people are there for no good," he said. "You have the strata of prostitutes and transvestites involved in drugs. . . . The police tell me if they had the opportunity to search, 90 percent would be armed. After 11, I wouldn't venture out without a police escort." A thirteen-year-old student at Holy Cross School, petitioning President Jimmy Carter to help rid the area of crime, complained of being kept awake at night by "prostitutes running to get into cars, cursing and screaming when the cars won't stop, getting punched." One officer told Friedman: "All the losers who can't make it in their neighborhoods come to be losers here."

Before being ousted by the voters in 1977, the Beame administration had mounted a two-pronged strategy, coupling an ill-fated citywide zoning change with a harassment campaign against the estimated 167 commercial sex businesses—massage parlors (which were really barely disguised brothels), topless bars, short-stay hotels patronized by prostitutes and stores that sold pornography—identified in the area bounded by West 40th and 59th Streets and by the Avenue of the Americas and Eighth Avenue. "It's a dangerous, ugly Barbary Coast," said Assistant Chief Carl Ravens, "and the police alone can't solve the crime problem unless something is done about the prostitution and porno industries." The police announced that crime in the Midtown South precinct had soared 24 percent over the year before and blamed it on proliferating pornography and prostitution. A pornographic bookstore was transformed with great fanfare into a police substation where Mayor Beame proclaimed that "New York's grimiest is being replaced by New York's finest."

Opponents of the zoning plan, which would have applied citywide, feared it would merely drive sex businesses to other parts of Manhattan or the other boroughs. During the 1977 campaign, Koch floated a proposal for "adult pleasure zones"—combat zones or red-light districts—that might be established in areas considered nonresidential and noncommercial, perhaps the waterfront, but that notion quickly fizzled.

Instead, Sturz, then deputy mayor, and Bobby Wagner, then chairman of the Planning Commission, were drafting zoning regulations intended to discourage the spread of pornography and to introduce competition for storefronts and other space by encouraging more constructive uses.

The regulations would be limited to midtown Manhattan. And, while the city's strategy would include encouraging federal tax investigations of sex-related businesses to close them down, the goal was to restrict the addition of new venues of that sort. They sought to apply the lessons of a Detroit law, upheld in 1976 by the United States Supreme Court, that prohibited new sex shops within 1,000 feet of existing ones. They would also offer property tax abatements to legitimate businesses that opened in midtown, ban "offensive advertising" on marquees and building exteriors and restrict how many times a day a room could be rented, to discourage "hot sheet hotels." "Our goal is not to immediately eliminate every X-rated movie or peep show— that's impossible," Sturz acknowledged at the time. "But we certainly can reduce their number through attrition and through discouraging new ones."

Nobody figured the change would happen overnight. Fortuitously, some changes had already been in the works. Manhattan Plaza, a 1,700-apartment subsidized housing complex for theater people and other creative artists built by the developer Richard Ravitch, opened in 1978 between Ninth and Tenth Avenues. Fred Papert of the 42nd Street Development Corporation, an alliance that included Father Rappleyea, Gerald Schoenfeld of the Shubert Organization, the premier legitimate theater owner, and Jacqueline Kennedy Onassis, would transform former massage parlors into an off-Broadway oasis known as Theater Row.

Within a few months, Sturz and Wagner had completed their battle plans for an eighteen-month campaign against pornography and its impact on midtown. Their strategy included a citywide ban on massage parlors (to get around the rules, those businesses were periodically renamed, as "rap centers" or something equally inventive; the marquees of 42nd Street movie houses were famous for their ingenious X-rated riffs on film titles, too), police patrols augmented by about 100 uniformed officers nightly, and a plan to divert teenagers arrested for prostitution from the criminal court system to rehabilitation programs. They stressed that this was not just another moral crusade, that the environment had a profound impact on the city's image and its economic vitality. "Individuals who perhaps may not be offended by pornography or prostitution nevertheless fear, and consequently avoid, going into areas where they will be mugged, harassed, stared at, forced to accept handbills for massage parlors and propositioned for drugs, sex or small change," the report to the mayor said. "A significant reduction in street crime and street pollution is a critically important objective in any effort to improve the Times Square area."

Carl Weisbrod's Office of Midtown Enforcement was charged with the proverbial "cleaning up" of a centerpiece of the city that had become synonymous with vice and, worse yet, with wanton and random violence. Weisbrod could claim inroads against massage parlors and peep shows. Between 1977 and 1984, the city said the number of sex-related businesses had been halved to sixty and all but two of twenty-seven massage parlors on Eighth Avenue had been shuttered. But the centerpiece of vice and violence, the Deuce, seemed impervious to successive crackdowns against businesses for violations of fire and building codes or of zoning regulations. As Professor Lynne B. Sagalyn of Columbia Business School (and whose father, Preston Beyer, was co-founder of the John Steinbeck Society of America) wrote in her definitive study *Times Square Roulette: Remaking the City Icon*, Weisbrod had concluded "that the street's 'cavalcade of horrors' was impervious to change via traditional approaches of physical and social improvement—law enforcement, municipal service delivery and economic development." Sturz recognized that, too. "Law enforcement wasn't going to make the difference," he says. "You had to have good uses replace bad uses. It seemed obvious."

It didn't take long for good intentions to divide the constituents who favored doing something about Times Square. Nobody was seriously opposed to cleaning up the place, though every suggestion was subject to the good intentions, the institutional agendas, the personal whims of the stakeholders and the fears that cleaning up Times Square would merely shift its pathologies to adjacent neighborhoods. When, a few months after Sturz and Wagner issued their recommendations, an emergency shelter for young runaways sought to expand, it became mired in controversy over whether the expansion would displace some of the legitimate businesses that, it was hoped, would crowd out the porn parlors. The shelter, originally supported by local merchants, including Gerald Schoenfeld of Shubert and the Midtown Citizens Committee, had become what they called a "crash pad," which attracted loiterers day and night. "These kids clearly need his services," Weisbrod said of the Reverend Bruce Ritter, the head of Covenant House, the shelter's sponsor, who would later become embroiled in controversy himself. "But the city has been trying to attract legitimate commercial uses to Times Square," Weisbrod said, "and I would not like to see those merchants displaced."

To translate obvious conceptions into practical solutions, Sturz initiated prodigious research (modestly stopping just short, in this case, of learning by doing). Times Square, especially the Deuce, was analyzed in minute detail. Through the Fund for the City of New York, Sturz enlisted William H. Whyte, the urban anthropologist, who stationed himself on the fourth floor of an abandoned hotel across the street from a prime hangout for pimps and drug dealers. Most of the research pointed to a single, inescapable conclusion: "The public," Sturz says, "had lost control."

"This is the national cesspool," Whyte wrote, "and when people from other cities start talking about their undesirables, the New Yorker has to laugh. They should see ours. Here are the *real* undesirables." He installed a movie camera and two time-lapse cameras. The impact of the additional police presence, he found, was transitory. The moment the cops themselves stopped loitering at any given location on 42nd Street, street people would congregate again. Yet Whyte was also more open-minded than most about to whom the streets of the city belonged. He charitably cautioned against a blanket indictment of street life, at least the less predatory strain, by the businessmen and civic leaders who were so insulated from the street that they reflexively lumped all its denizens together as undesirable. "The time to worry is when street people begin to leave a place," Whyte wrote. "Like canaries in a coal mine, street people are an index of the health of a place." But, he invariably concluded, "the best way to handle the problem of undesirables is to make a place attractive to everyone else."

———

Times Square was figuratively—and, in some cases literally—emblematic of the broken-windows theory that James Q. Wilson and George L. Kelling had advanced in 1982. Largely on a hunch, on a very well-educated guess, rather than on the Sturz brand of empirical proof, they concluded famously that an unrepaired broken window in a building would almost inevitably result in the rest of the windows being broken—that, without any signs of repair, a broken window advertised that nobody gave a damn.

"At the community level, disorder and crime are usually inextricably linked, in a kind of developmental sequence," they wrote. "Window-breaking does not necessarily occur on a large scale because some areas are inhabited by determined window-breakers whereas others are populated by window-lovers; rather, one unrepaired broken window is a signal that no one cares, and so breaking more windows costs nothing." The Koch administration was completely familiar with the Wilson and Kelling hypothesis, having improvised a novel response early in the 1980s: Trompe l'oeil seals depicting six-pane windows, half-closed shades and gray-and-blue louvered shutters were placed in hundreds of abandoned apartment buildings around the city for appearance's sake. Eventually, under Koch, many of the buildings would actually be salvaged.

———

The mythology of Times Square begins with an irrefutable geometric: It is not a square at all. Which is just one more reason that most of the fond memories about its better days, the misplaced nostalgia for its seediest and scariest period among people who deride it today as Disneyfied, and the self-serving claims of credit for having finally sanitized it are all suspect. The very motivation for going to the old Times Square—for people to immerse themselves collectively in the escapism of the theater, to be embraced by an anonymous sea of humanity at the crossroads of the world— evoked limitless possibilities, fired the imagination and therefore distorted reality. Marshall Berman, a City College professor and Times Square romantic, once recalled, rather matter-of-factly, that despite its sordid reputation, the worst thing that ever happened to him there was that "once, when I saw a man crack another man's skull, I couldn't get a cop."

By the time Sturz was thrust into the dynamic as the city's chief planner, a new imperative had emerged in the debate over how to salvage Times Square. This time, it was also being driven by the specter of Westway, a bold vision by utopian urban planners that had devolved into a potential real estate boondoggle and a public relations and political nightmare. Westway originated as a scheme by progressive urban planners—among them, Samuel Ratensky, Craig Whitaker and Richard Kahan—to get the federal government to build a vast new park along 4.2 miles of the Hudson by reclaiming 169 or so acres from the river and tunneling an interstate highway underneath. (To which Jane Jacobs, the urban theorist, retorted: "A bad project isn't worth doing just because you can get money for it.") Instead, it became the latest example of what New York Senator Daniel Patrick Moynihan branded as "entropy," a thermodynamic equation that, in effect, generates more heat than light and little substance.

The brazen accomplishments and excesses of Robert Moses had produced a backlash of such proportions that society had lost its will to build anything monumental. "If the ends don't justify the means," Moses liked to say, "what does?" Virtually everyone except the city's self-styled power brokers were convinced that Westway did not. Decades earlier, in building the Henry Hudson Parkway just north of the Westway route, Moses once explained that "only stubborn leadership availed, not the smoothness of diplomacy." But Edward J. Logue, who headed the Urban Development Corporation where Westway was conceived in 1971 and which would eventually play the major role in Times Square, insisted that Westway had been incubated with Moses very much in mind. "Everybody forgets," Logue said, "that it was designed by us as the antidote to the Moses type of solution."

Moses had persisted into an era when the ten most powerful New Yorkers could still be singled out annually in *New York* magazine. Compiling the list became more and more challenging not because the number of powerful people was increasing but because power itself was dissipating as decentralization and community control and environmental constraints were imposed, often in direct response to the excesses of the Moses era. The influence of the institutions from which many of the formerly powerful derived their power fizzled, too. The power brokers of Moses's day were institutionally endowed with a mantle of supremacy. The qualities people like Sturz could bring to the table—intelligence, wisdom, consensus building, imagination—counted too, of course, but they were not mandatory. As institutional power ebbed, those characteristics assumed a whole other dimension. "If you go to almost any other city and there is a coalition of people, if you gather them together and get them to agree," lamented W. H. James, the former *Daily News* publisher who headed a pro-Westway group, "they can pretty much make it happen."

Not in New York.

———

Westway's roots could be traced back sixty years, when regional planners proposed a grid of highways encircling the metropolitan area and dissecting it in, among other places, lower Manhattan and midtown. They succeeded in ringing Manhattan, but the arteries that would have pierced midtown and downtown never got off the drawing board. A prescient prescription contained in the seminal 1929 Regional Plan for New York had been largely ignored: It cautioned that transportation and other planning challenges would not be solved without "constant cooperation between the different communities and the various officials and civic organizations which are interested in efficient development of the region."

In 1969, making a last-ditch appeal for a Lower Manhattan Expressway, Morris D. Crawford Jr., the chairman of the Regional Plan Association, candidly concluded: "In recent years, we have seen growing opposition to all expressways—well designed and bad, needed and unneeded. It is the reaction to the way decisions about their construction were made by political leaders, highway engineers and administrators." But there was no turning back. Mayor John Lindsay, clawing his way out of the political cellar to seek a second term, killed proposed expressways across lower Manhattan and Brooklyn and flatly declared that "no solution will ever be implemented by me that does not have substantial community support."

Koch, who had inherited the proposed project, was himself not a big fan of highways. He didn't drive. As a Greenwich Village resident and Democratic leader, he had vigorously opposed the Lindsay administration's Lower Manhattan Expressway. He embraced Westway because it was there and would not require wholesale displacement. And while he tolerated its supporters, he mostly despised its opponents. By 1985, government's refusal to adequately investigate the project's impact on the environment finally killed Westway in a confluence of court decisions and congressional legislation. Representatives Bella Abzug, Ted Weiss and a handful of others had conjured up an embraceable alternative—to shift federal funds from highways to mass transit. If the Lower Manhattan Expressway was the victim of more or less conventional political decision making by an elected official responding to public pressure, then Westway floundered in courthouses where the government was repeatedly tripped up. "My sense is," Bobby Wagner said, "we weren't as smart as the other side."

By then, the government had spent fifteen years and more than $200 million on Westway, and there was little tangible to show for it. The original good intentions had largely gone awry on the proposed 330-acre site and the adjacent corridor that the project was supposed to make safe for development. Instead of landfill, a sprawling park and submerged expressway, the project had generated only a growing accumulation of bills for land acquisition and legal fees and a poisonous cynicism fed by what one frustrated state official denounced as a "procedural infinity." Even if the project originally had merit, New Yorkers were handed few hints over the years that the elected and appointed officials in charge were sufficiently well motivated and armed to carry it out. A skeptical public, planners lamented, no longer understood what was good for it.

Eulogies at the time mourned the loss of New York's will and ability to conceive and build great public works. Others insisted that market forces would eventually revive the far West Side waterfront with or without Westway. Governor Mario Cuomo, a staunch supporter of the project, immediately suggested that the city would survive without Westway, dismissing its impact as that of "a walnut in the batter of eternity." Bobby Wagner described the defeat of the project as "a fascinating case study that only Evelyn Waugh could do justice to, but in terms of the city's future, a footnote." They suggested that Westway was *sui generis*. They were unwilling to elevate its demise into a public policy watershed. But, in a way, it was.

Westway was a victim of government arrogance. In response to Robert Moses's excesses, layers of procedural and legal constraints had been imposed on public works. Consequently, those projects were subjected to more environmental review, more judicial oversight and more second-guessing. Highways faced an especially high hurdle, because for all the parks and beaches and housing Moses built, the expressways he bulldozed through unsuspecting neighborhoods to transport people to those parks and beaches and housing defined his legacy as an urban predator.

Since Westway would burrow under landfill in the Hudson, it raised unique environmental concerns. Regardless of those concerns, what most worried skeptics was a suspicion that Westway was simply a subterfuge for rapacious development along the river. It was publicly supported by virtually every power broker, but, even among government officials in Westway's camp, it was resisted by a number of officials with their own environmental and transit agendas and by a bureaucracy that seemed incapable of executing a project of that magnitude.

As one version of the development after another was revised to overcome judicial, biological and political objections, the project was transformed from a visionary, if vastly overblown road map for a revitalized West Side into a temporary boulevard of broken dreams.

———

To ensure that he would never be dismissed as a lame duck who could be trifled with because he might not run again, Koch would half-jokingly proclaim that he would be "mayor for life." But even he recognized that within another decade, by the end of his third term, he would be judged, in part, by whether he was able to produce some physical legacy in tawdry Times Square.

Sturz and Koch were determined that the slow death of Westway would not be repeated in the heart of Manhattan. Deep down, the most intellectually honest Westway supporters understood that the project had been scuttled as much by its friends as by its foes. "In my view," said Mitchell Bernard, who with Albert Butzel represented the anti-Westway plaintiffs, "what undid Westway was the arrogance of the government."

But Times Square was different. It's the centerpiece of the city, its palpitating heart (or, at the time, perhaps some less publicly venerated organ). Its renewal offered potential to celebrate an ascendant city. It was not just about attracting tourists and theatergoers, prettifying a ghastly eyesore or generating vitally needed tax revenue from new office towers and their occupants. "Development," said Martin Gallent, a City Planning commissioner, "not only provided new sources of municipal revenue, it served, in a very concrete and visible way, to symbolize New York's fiscal recovery and renewed vitality."

It also represented "a manhood question," as Sturz puts it, a palpable test of whether a broken and broke city could surmount parochial concerns to be great again. Even after the city had sacrificed some of its New Deal legacy during the fiscal crisis to gain back its credit, there was a desperate need to generate revenue to pay for a social welfare burden that was growing unabated. "New York will always be a magnet for immigrants from all over the world, many of whom are fabulous and provide a continuing renewal," Sturz says. "We are also a place where poor people get their start, but, until they do, it costs an awful lot to keep them going."

Sturz viewed Times Square as the vehicle to keep those people going by generating the tax revenue to support them.

———

In the Times Square that Herb Sturz inherited in the 1980s, no new building had been built on West 42nd

Street's (and probably the city's) worst block for forty years. Sturz was determined to demonstrate that the city government cared, that it was cognizant of the link between disorder and crime and felt compelled to do something about it. To meet his goal would take an imaginative combination of what Sagalyn defined as privatized financing, public works improvements and the legal authority to impound private property.

The stage setting for getting the project underway could not have been more complicated. It involved an arranged marriage between a regulator (the City Planning Commission), two entrepreneurial government agencies (the state Urban Development Corporation [UDC] and the city's Public Development Corporation, led by its able president, Philip E. Aarons) and a variety of private developers. And for all the flexibility Sturz enjoyed for years as an outsider unbeholden to anyone, he was considerably more muscular in dealing with the Times Square project as an insider, both in his own job and through Weisbrod.

"The real power," Lynne Sagalyn concluded, "lodged with Herb Sturz."

The Koch administration had inherited a redevelopment proposal called The City at 42nd Street, a more playful version for redesigning the blighted area, which included a plan for a fifteen-story indoor Ferris wheel. But Koch saw the proposal, which had been developed by his predecessors, too far outside the city's purview, too concentrated in the hands of a single developer and too removed from his own ground-level vision of what his constituents wanted. It was, in his mind, too Florida. He preferred, he explained, "seltzer instead of orange juice."

"It was glitzy, but didn't seem to have the economic engines," Sturz remembers of The City at 42nd Street. He was delegated to inform the high-powered foundations and businesses that had embraced The City at 42nd Street—a

group chaired by John Gutfreund of Salomon Brothers—
that their plan had been overtaken by events. "When I became planning chairman," Sturz says, "I found that their
plan was dead, but no one had told them." As Sturz remembers it, at a breakfast in his private dining room at Salomon, Gutfreund was furious at the news, threatened that
"I'm going to humiliate and embarrass you, get you, get the
mayor" and stormed out. But Koch stuck by Sturz. "Herb
made the recommendation to Koch to kill The City at 42nd
Street," Carl Weisbrod recalls. "It was a really tough decision, but he thought there shouldn't be a sole-source development in the middle of Manhattan. He was unwilling
to hand over 13 acres of Midtown to private interests without a competitive process. But he came pretty quickly to
the notion that you had to do *something* big. He embraced
the central thesis—that significant change in Times Square
would only occur through major economic development
and that required public control of 42nd Street itself."

To replace The City at 42nd Street, at Sturz's urging,
Koch reluctantly teamed up with the state Urban Development Corporation, the muscular agency that Governor
Nelson A. Rockefeller had established overnight in 1968
following the assassination of Martin Luther King Jr. to
override local opposition to low-income housing. The
mayor's goal was to plan still another version of the Times
Square redevelopment that would invoke the state's powers of condemnation to lure private financing. "I knew the
city couldn't do it without eminent domain," he explains.
The new plan would be more than a holding action or a
tactical attack waged sex shop by sex shop. Instead, it
would offer a bold redevelopment plan that would incorporate some of the features of The City at 42nd Street—
sans Ferris wheel (although a smaller version would be
built inside a Times Square Toys"R"Us store). Strategically,
the plan rested on a theoretical but plausible application of

urban anthropology. As Sturz put it at the time, "We're confident that good uses will drive out the bad."

After Sturz pulled the plug on The City at 42nd Street, he joined with the state (which was armed with the legal powers and financial resources that the city lacked) to draft redevelopment plans, solicit proposals from private developers and win approvals from the city's Board of Estimate (the powerful amalgam of citywide and borough-wide elected officials, later invalidated by the United States Supreme Court for defying the principle of one person, one vote) for what Sagalyn described as "a clever packaging of the city's limited resources."

The broad outlines were announced in 1980 by Koch and Richard A. Kahan, president of the Urban Development Corporation. Movie houses on the lawless block of West 42nd Street would be restored as legitimate theaters; four office towers, a hotel and a giant wholesale merchandise mart for the garment industry and the wholesale computer market would be inserted into the cityscape. More than two dozen developers bid on one part of the project or another. But the California developers selected to build the merchandise mart defaulted, casting a pall over the entire plan. William J. Stern, a brash, millionaire campaign contributor to the new governor, Mario Cuomo, was subsequently named to head up the Urban Development Corporation. Stern, Cuomo would explain, was not a bull in a china shop. "He's an elephant in a china shop," Cuomo said. But Sturz eventually won him over, much the same way he had charmed Police Commissioner Leary and Justice Botein. "Herb," Carl Weisbrod would say admiringly, "has the ability to manipulate people in the best sense of the word."

Stern demanded that the state control the redevelopment corporation's board and voided an earlier agreement that gave the city and state equal representation. Koch was prepared to scuttle the deal altogether, but Sturz pleaded with him not to. Any other course would be difficult to defend, and in the popular perception, the mayor might appear to be bullying the governor, who had been elected after defeating Koch only months earlier in the Democratic gubernatorial primary. By the summer of 1983, with the state embracing one developer for the $400 million merchandise mart and the city favoring another and with the nearby Garment Center plunged into darkness by a power blackout, the deal collapsed.

By then, the only thing that everyone agreed on was that Times Square was in limbo and a dump. But it was still unclear whether the city or the state would take the lead in its revival or whether private developers would fill the vacuum.

Despite what he viewed as his defense of the city's sovereignty, Koch came under pressure to go back to the bargaining table. Cuomo was importuned to intervene to solve a dispute in which, he maintained, the city and the Urban Development Corporation were mired in postures that were "technically defensible, but practically problematic." As an intermediary—the two officials had met privately only once in the eight months since Cuomo was inaugurated—Cuomo enlisted David Garth, the media consultant who had managed Koch's campaigns against Cuomo for mayor and for governor. Their challenge was to reconcile means and ends. As Sagalyn wrote, regulation had only a limited effect on spurring private development. Moreover, government's goal in Times Square went beyond "uncoordinated construction of new tax-generating office towers" to "create a fulcrum of economic stimulation." Driven by the Sturzian paradigm of public-private partnership, the project would also "generate (and require) private investment to renovate historic theaters and to modernize the Times Square's labyrinthine subway station."

The mayor and governor reached an agreement that created a consortium of developers and, in effect, gave the city a veto over the entire Times Square project. Koch agreed to a unique financial approach for the project that was a direct outgrowth of the city's fiscal limitations: UDC would use its power of eminent domain to acquire properties, private developers would directly pay for the land acquisition costs and they would be guaranteed to recover costs beyond a certain amount. The city would be protected from incurring onerous capital costs. Developers were granted aggressive tax incentives to take major risks and make long-term commitments. As Howard J. Rubenstein, the respected major domo of public relations in New York, observed: "The collective force of need and desire took over."

The Cuomo-Koch summit also led to a constructive relationship between Sturz and Stern. Sturz got what he wanted, and Stern got more than his share of the credit. "The city is a creature of the state, yet for the most part Times Square was city driven," Weisbrod says. "In the end, the city prevailed."

"It was Sturz," Sagalyn wrote, "who brought in UDC, kept control, defined the roles of each side, and was responsible for bringing in the people who would subsequently execute the project, Carl Weisbrod and his hire, Rebecca Robertson" (who was originally recruited by Sturz). From the beginning, Sturz recognized that the City Planning Commission's regulatory role over zoning might prod developers from East Midtown to Midtown West, and might serve as a catalyst for a visible shift in private investment, but that zoning alone—like crime prevention, by itself— would not meet the city's agenda for Times Square. He also perceptively identified all the constituencies for change and against it and their competing agendas. Stern's successor at the Urban Development Corporation, Vincent

J. Tese, puts it simply: "It would not have happened without him."

On November 8, 1984, Koch and Cuomo personally
presented the Times Square plan to the city's Board of Estimate. They spared no hyperbole. Presiding over the
board personally for the first time in five years, Koch
equated the project with the Pyramids. Cuomo's attendance marked the first time in a generation or more that a
governor had attended a meeting of the board (state officials had, more modestly, perhaps, compared the project to
the Parthenon). After adjustments that critics and competing developers would deride as too little, too late (plans
to protect neighboring residents and manufacturers in the
Garment District against displacement, regulations to retain Times Square's vitality), the redevelopment would be
approved largely intact. It was, Sturz observed, the natural
culmination of any giant project that the board deliberated
on. "It's the democratic dialectic," he said.

Over the next five years, the project was challenged
by forty-seven separate lawsuits. Stephen A. Lefkowitz,
a Columbia law professor working for the city, called it
the most complicated assemblage of land by municipal
government—seventy or so sites belonging to several dozen
owners—since Lincoln Center for the Performing Arts a
generation earlier. On May 8, 1986, delivering a landmark
decision in an enduring debate over eminent domain, the
New York State Court of Appeals, the state's highest court,
unanimously dismissed six legal challenges and upheld the
Times Square redevelopment plan. The opinion by Judges
Judith Kaye and Bernard Meyer affirmed the state Urban
Development Corporation's power to condemn the thirteen acres containing seventy-six parcels of property that
included sex shops, cheap movie theaters and fast food
outlets. (In her decision, Kaye also addressed a suit brought

by MFY Legal Services, an expanded version of the poverty law center that Sturz and Weisbrod had been involved in, and suggested that instead of earmarking money from developers to subsidize subway and theater renovations, those subsidies should be shifted to housing for poorer residents who would be displaced by gentrification in the neighborhoods adjoining Times Square.)

With an eye toward the proposed $2.5 billion overhaul of Times Square—billed as the nation's biggest urban redevelopment at the time—the *Times* invoked the lessons of Westway. "The law's delay was deemed by Hamlet a fairly good reason for self-destruction, even before urban renewal," an editorial recalled. "But as the sponsors of Westway and any number of projects have learned, it is a particularly powerful weapon in the cacophony of New York."

Sturz sums up the legacy of the project this way: "It's easier to kill than to create." In Times Square, he was determined not to repeat his predecessors' mistakes.

Chapter 13

The New
Times Square

One of the worries among advocates for the poor was that redevelopment of Times Square would wipe out the dwindling number of single room occupancy hotels, which, for better or worse, had become the last place that many New Yorkers could call home before resorting to overcrowded and dangerous city shelters. Their fears were not unfounded. In 1985, under cover of darkness, Harry Macklowe, a prominent developer and art patron, partially bulldozed several vacant buildings on West 44th Street off Times Square to beat a proposed city moratorium on the demolition of SRO hotels. The moratorium was to take effect the following night, and, in the rush to raze the buildings, proper safety precautions weren't followed. Macklowe, himself, was never charged in the illegal demolition although his development firm and one of its vice presidents were indicted.

Later that year, the city threatened to withhold permission to occupy the apartments in another Macklowe building on East 72nd Street because details had been modified in violation of a permit and without the commission's approval. After negotiations with Sturz and the commission, Macklowe agreed to pay for a $5 million renovation of a mile-long esplanade along the East River. The city extracted that quid pro quo not because Macklowe was brazen, but because he got caught again. "We weren't able to do that because of what he had done on 44th Street, but because of what he had done on 72nd Street," Sturz explained. Five years later, after Sturz visited the elegant thirty-eight-story hotel that Macklowe had erected on the 44th Street site, he was asked whether it represented an improvement over the low-cost, if shabby, housing that it had replaced. "I don't think that's the relevant question," Sturz replied. "Rather, it's the process one goes through. It's means and ends. And sometimes means become ends in themselves."

While Macklowe was perpetrating his private version of urban renewal, Sturz was consulting with other city and state officials to transform Times Square from a frightening place back to the more wholesome tourist and entertainment destination it had been decades earlier when teenaged girls (and their mothers) screamed for Frank Sinatra at the Paramount, families could afford first-run films on 42nd Street and tourists would gawk at the colossal waterfall that advertised Bond clothes and later Pepsi-Cola. "We want to bring fantasy back to Times Square," Sturz said, "and replace much of the grim reality that currently exists."

Government could play a role in the transformation, he believed. The new office towers, festooned with flashy advertising, would draw an influx of more upscale workers, but what about after five P.M.? "There aren't enough people in Times Square at night," Sturz reasoned. "We want to change that by enhancing the chaotic liveliness of the area." As builders assembled sites for future development, officials conjured up ways to encourage business related to theater, to television studios and production and to the ancillary demand for restaurant, retail and hotel space that those businesses would generate. The challenge was to balance development that would pay the rent but would also provide a vista that would keep the vibrancy of Times Square from being swallowed up in a black hole at the bottom of a sterile canyon. To replace a block dotted by sex shops and pornographic movie theaters, the developer William Zeckendorf Jr. commissioned Alan J. Lapidus, son of the architect who designed some of Miami Beach's gaudiest but most venerated hotels, to create a garish, uniquely New York version (the Crowne Plaza on Broadway) that would be enveloped in the glow that originally earned Broadway the sobriquet of the Great White Way. "It proves," Sturz said, "that you can do something economically viable that opens up light and air and keeps the rhetoric of Times Square's light and energy a reality."

In Times Square, though, the light and air and space that Sturz envisioned were largely being sacrificed, first to John Portman's hulking Marriott Marquis hotel and later to the glitzy office towers that, to be sure, helped pay the freight. "Had I been there from the beginning, I would not have approved the hotel design," Sturz later said. "The Portman—the Marriott Marquis—is a monstrosity. But, I think, the Portman has helped bring vitality to Times Square." For all the architectural criticism the Marriott generated, it was the highest valued hotel property in the city even two decades later.

The Marriott Marquis produced one unexpected benefit. In order to build it, two Broadway theaters were razed. The uproar over their demolition led to the creation of the mayor's Theater Advisory Council, which in 1983 recommended an innovative zoning proposal that Sturz and the Koch administration embraced. The council proposed that in return for promises to preserve individual theaters, owners be allowed to sell millions of square feet of "air rights"—the difference between the area of a building allowed on a particular site and the structure actually occupying it—to owners of property in a broad swath of Eighth Avenue from 42nd Street to Columbus Circle at 59th Street.

———

The new Times Square didn't necessarily open space, but it encouraged crowds. By the end of 2008, across the street from the Marriott there would even be a place for the public to sit in Times Square, on a red, glowing glass stairway—New York's biggest stoop—built expressly for that purpose. When Rebecca Robertson pointed out that 42nd Street was now a place where families could at last walk with their kids, Marshall Berman retorted that, yes, "it was nice, but my parents had used 42nd Street as a place to get away from their kids." Yet even Berman acknowledged: "More people have come in, many people have been moved around, but, contrary to expectations, nobody has been pushed out. Now it is clearer than ever that there is room for everybody—this space can hold them all."

Elaborating on what he called the democratic dialectic, Sturz later acknowledged that he was rarely swayed by community opposition to Times Square or any other major project. "Most of it, in my view, was knee-jerk," he says. "I was driven by the need, as I saw it, for jobs, the need for people to earn a living, the need to pay welfare benefits, the need to have police officers, the need to have teachers." More development generally meant more density, but whatever the rosy recollections that colored the debate over Times Square, it was never a sparsely populated sanctuary that was suddenly transformed by crowds of office workers. Times Square was always about crowds, and Sturz personally considers them integral to the city and its vitality: "There is a continuous tension between preservation, stabilization and development. I tried, during my years, to reconcile that balance. But I would rather err on the side of inclusion. Cities stagnate and die without a continual, fresh influx of people."

———

"Policy," Carl Weisbrod says, "is the product of planning and politics," and nowhere was that truer than in Times Square. As befitted such a mythical place, the revival would remain shrouded in an apocryphal cloak that various worthies would don when it suited them to claim credit. In fact, it evolved in fits and starts, the result of a communal and sometimes loosely orchestrated effort.

In the 1990s, the law enforcement strategies of Mayor Rudy Giuliani's police commissioners and the expanded force he inherited from his predecessor, David Dinkins, contributed mightily to an environment in which midtown Manhattan and other parts of the city would prosper. But Giuliani himself often received inordinate credit for presiding over ribbon cuttings for emblematic projects that had begun years earlier with Koch and Sturz. (One such instance occurred in 1994, a month into his first term when Giuliani immediately glommed the spotlight and claimed credit for luring Michael Eisner and Disney to Times Square, which, as Wayne Barrett wrote in *Rudy!*, had occurred under the Dinkins administration and by the architect Robert A. M. Stern and by Marian Heiskell of the *New York Times* family.)

Lynne Sagalyn recalls that "the transformation was 20 years in the making," that Disney's commitment to the

New Amsterdam Theater was, indeed, a catalyst for other commercial ventures, but that the pioneer was Cora Cahan, president of Heiskell's nonprofit New 42nd Street, Inc., who replaced pornography with quality children's fare. In 1995, her New Victory Theater opened, to be followed by the New Amsterdam, renovated and operated by Disney, the ten-story New 42nd Street Studios with dance, theater and music rehearsal space, two new hotels and more tourist attractions. Governor Cuomo (with the support of Sturz and Koch) would later appoint Weisbrod as president of the 42nd Street Development Project, an appointment that, as Robert Stern wrote, "brought new optimism and energy to the project." (Weisbrod would be succeeded by Rebecca Robertson, a former city planner, and she, Cahan, Gretchen Dykstra, who headed the Times Square Business Improvement District, and Fred Papert, who developed Theater Row farther west on 42nd Street as an incubator for Off-Broadway, were instrumental in the redevelopment, and a range of other characters— including Jean-Claude Baker, whose Chez Josephine restaurant has survived for years as a lonely outpost of civil society—helped beat the odds.)

The office towers finally proceeded, too (for The New York Times, Condé Nast, Ernst & Young, Reuters and Skadden Arps and by major developers, including the Durst Organization and Rudin Management). Douglas Durst, a respected Times Square property owner and developer who had opposed tax breaks for his competitors, eventually took advantage of those breaks to build a gleaming office tower of his own. He said of Rebecca Robertson: "We litigated against her for a good many years, and it was a difficult time. But now working with her, it's terrific."

Land values and rents soared. In 1980, the twenty-four-story Candler Building, a white terra-cotta office tower on 42nd Street between Seventh and Eighth Avenues that was built early in the twentieth century by the founder of Coca-Cola, was bought for $1.3 million. Five years later, it was sold for nearly $15 million. Less than a decade later, after the ground floor was renovated to house a glitzy McDonald's, it was sold for more than $60 million.

The notion that Times Square was transformed with minimal public investment was a myth. True, some of the financial risk of rising condemnation costs for land acquisition was shifted to private developers. But by the beginning of the 1990s, John H. Mollenkopf, a City University political scientist, estimated that tax and other benefits amounted to an "implicit city equity" of $400 million in 1985 dollars, in return for the new office towers, nine refurbished theaters, as many as 24,000 jobs and an estimated $400 million in payments in lieu of taxes over the next twenty years. Mollenkopf concluded that the "positive business environment" created by Sturz and his colleagues helped New York compete for regional and national office space, was instrumental in creating new downtowns in Brooklyn and Long Island City and contributed to "the postindustrial transformation of the New York City economy." In *The Devil's Playground*, his historical tribute to Times Square, James Traub wrote that no single place in America "demonstrates the renaissance of the old downtowns more impressively than Times Square itself, which passed through pornography and pathology to emerge, once again, as the capital of popular culture."

There has been no end to the redevelopment of Times Square, with the last original parcels only now finally being developed and other projects sprouting more or less on their own to the west and north. "Without the rejuvenation of Times Square," Weisbrod said, "there would be no talk today about developing the far-west side of Manhattan.

Without the rejuvenation of Times Square, today's positive image of New York would not have been possible."

Sturz's persistence had made a difference.

———

In 1986, after seven years, Sturz resigned from the Planning Commission, having served longer than any previous chairman. "That's a long time, with problems coming at you every day, being in the administration for nine years and feeling that some of the life had gone out," Sturz reflected. "Looking around the Blue Room at the commissioners who were there from the early days and, of course, the new ones, I came to feel there was a falling off in quality." Koch responded to the resignation graciously and with what seemed like genuine gratitude. "Your intellect, energy and powers of persuasion brought a consensus to the most controversial issues," the mayor wrote. "That is a rare ability not easily found or duplicated." Years later, Koch would look back and still be impressed by Sturz's "unusual" and versatile mind. "As mayor," he said, "I was fortunate to have that remarkable brain at my side. He was the city administration's lead person on Times Square and that plan would never have gotten off the ground without his leadership and zeal."

If he wasn't necessarily a member of the mayor's small inner circle, Sturz surely enjoyed Koch's confidence. He expressed the hope that he would be able to move several projects along before he left, including the development proposed at Hunters Point, Queens, on the East River. He regretted not having devoted more resources to waterfront planning and to making the harbor more accessible, to seeking alternatives that would have relieved subway, bus and vehicular congestion in Manhattan (he also envisioned a light rail line along the old Conrail right of way—part of which has been preserved as the High Line Park—connecting the West Side to New Jersey via the George Washington Bridge and linking to cross-town to Queens).

His biggest disappointment was the collapse of the deal with the state to sell Rikers.

But he could tout as accomplishments the first tangible progress in the proverbial clean-up of Times Square, the beginnings of a shift in development to Midtown West, the belated protections of space and light on the East Side (imposing his own design aesthetic, he encouraged builders of the tower just east of Saks Fifth Avenue to limit its height to the elevation of the adjacent tower on Madison—resulting in relatively low ceilings in the new building), the explosion in residential development of former manufacturing lofts that would contribute to a population boom in lower Manhattan and Brooklyn. He could point to other, less immediately concrete successes, like putting the "planning" back in City Planning and expanding its strategic purview to include, among other things, the creation of the Office of Immigrant Affairs and, in his earlier jobs in government, the legacy of a Juvenile Justice Department and the Victim Service Agency. "In my seven years, to the best of my recollection, I never lost a vote within the commission," Sturz says. "In part, it was our knowing how to work with people, with the commissioners, forging consensus, working out problems, doing good staff work, being able to anticipate questions, to answer them clearly." To Sturz, winning over the seven-member commission was not the final step. "If City Planning devoted the time and effort and commitment to take an affirmative action on an issue, it should then take the responsibility for its enactment into law." In all that time, too, he says, of the thousands of recommendations to the Board of Estimate,

perhaps a half dozen—none of them major ones—were
rejected.

In an interview for Columbia's oral history of the Koch
administration, conducted years after he had left city government, a seemingly disillusioned Herb Sturz deftly defined some of the distinctions between the public and
private sectors:

> My experience is that most bureaucrats, then and now,
> prefer not to make decisions. One is not fired, generally,
> for not doing anything; it's easy to just send memos back
> and forth and attend meetings. A real problem in city
> government is that staff productivity is measured on pro-
> cess, not product. If staff makes phone calls, if they attend
> meetings, if they write memos, then staff believes it's do-
> ing a good job. This is across the board, and very discour-
> aging. After a while, it becomes a cynical way to hold
> onto your job. It becomes a way of life. Too many people
> in government end up fearing and hating people outside
> of government. A great strength of government workers is
> the sense of camaraderie—you versus them. Even then,
> you will have internal warfare among agencies and back-
> biting. It's like white corpuscles coming together to fight
> off a foreign organism. I tried hard, in my years in govern-
> ment, not to regard the private sector as the enemy. I
> guess this stems from the years I worked in the nonprofit
> field. By and large, there's so much distrust of the outside.
> Many city officials believe that all virtue is within govern-
> ment. They are the holders of truth and decency. Their re-
> sentment manifests itself by simply not doing anything.

Part VI

The Benefactor

Chapter 14

A Planner
Faces Reality

Eager to practice what he had been preaching about re-sponsible development, Herb Sturz contemplated a plunge into the real estate industry when he left City Planning. "In my gut I never considered myself anti-development," he explains. "I basically think of myself as pro-development with great sensitivity to what kind and what scale and what a neighborhood can take." But an even better option presented itself (and, anyway, Fritz Schwarz, for one, cautioned about the potential for real or perceived conflicts of interest if Sturz transformed himself immediately from city official to developer). Instead, in 1986, he was invited by Max Frankel, the incoming exec-utive editor of the *New York Times,* and by his old friend Jack Rosenthal, who was succeeding Frankel as editor of the editorial page, to join the *Times'*s editorial board.

"I needed someone who knew the stuff and was known to know the stuff," Rosenthal recalls. He and Frankel were seeking a successor to Roger Starr, a onetime campus Trot-skyite who had evolved into a New Dealer and finally into a neoconservative. Starr had become thoroughly disillusioned with the cost of good intentions. He was a former housing commissioner in the Beame administration and probably best remembered for igniting a firestorm for suggesting that the city "accelerate the drainage" in its slums by reducing municipal services to poor and typically black and Puerto Rican neighborhoods. The proposed "planned shrinkage," inspired by a Rand Corporation study and reflecting both the city's declining population and financial condition, was immediately disavowed by Mayor Beame and subjected Starr to denunciation as "racist" and "genocidal." ("Although my phrase 'planned shrinkage' will run a poor second to 'benign neglect' in the unappreciated phrases derby," Starr wrote later, "it will remain the most prominent label in the file of my government service.")

Sturz was all about shrinking problems, not people or their opportunities. For a while, at least, journalism, to which Sturz was returning for the first time in a quarter century, offered a welcome respite from the public planning arena and just the right mix of intellectual and professional challenges. His editorial praising community programs by Geoffrey Canada's Rheedlen Centers for Children and Families in Harlem helped muster local and national support for the Beacon Schools initiative through which more than three dozen public school buildings in New York and others from Chicago to California have been transformed into twenty-first-century versions of settlement houses. At the *Times*, Rosenthal says, Sturz was "a little surprised to discover he could have an influence about a lot of things." But that influence came only with patience and tireless persistence. He was, as Michael Weinstein, his former *Times* colleague and now chief program officer of the Robin Hood Foundation, says, "the most persistent person I know." Rosenthal recalls him as "restlessly constructive every day."

Sturz could have been comfortably ensconced with his fellow editorial writers in a lofty tenth-floor aerie that suggested the detachment of a medieval monastery (monks never had it so good), but his insatiable curiosity to see things for himself would invariably inspire excursions into the real world that would often take form from the jottings of his editorial notebook. He visited the International High School in Queens, a windowless basement on the campus of LaGuardia Community College, where the 310 students hail from thirty-seven nations and speak thirty-two languages. "Something special is going on at this Board of Education alternative school," he wrote, noting that the dropout rate among the high-risk students was less than 4 percent compared with nearly 30 percent citywide and then explaining why the school seemed to be working and how its success might be replicated. He took a bus to the Atlantic City casinos—"a mobile nursing home," the driver called it—and he surprised himself by concluding that "there are worse ways to spend a dollar, or a day." He met Kalif Beacon, an itinerant musician who founded a makeshift soup kitchen manned by volunteers on the Lower East Side ("street people, taking care of themselves—and extending that care to others"), and Sidney Flax, a World War II veteran who, by traveling by ambulette to a Veterans Administration hospital in Queens three mornings a week, was part of an experiment in cost-effective health care that Sturz concluded could be replicated. He audaciously proposed ("the idea is not far-fetched," he assured readers) that jail guards help gather information on how much bail inmates awaiting trial could actually raise (about a quarter of the 10,000 pretrial detainees were being held on $1,000 bail or less) so judges could set a reasonable cash alternative.

Sturz also used the signed editorial notebook feature in the *Times* to indulge in what, for him, was an unusual,

even whimsical, public self-awareness. He wrote, with the
detachment of third-person anonymity, that he and Elizabeth, described only as a "sensibly Spartan" couple, had
decided to finally junk their fifteen-year-old Volvo and get
a new one, but were seduced by an engaging Toyota sales-
man who "quickly wove a spell that erased all thoughts of
a stripped-down, basic car." Three hours later, the couple
left the showroom and, "savoring the end of their austerity,
glided into the ether of the American Dream—Japanese
style." (Clearly smitten, they briefly considered a Lexus.)

Sturz summoned up his wife's recurring bout with a
stubborn case of Lyme disease to meditate on health care:
"Elizabeth's health insurance covers her home care, but
most such care is not covered by private insurance or
Medicare. That means some patients are kept in hospitals
longer than necessary in order to stay covered. In other
cases, patients go home without the care they badly need."
And he wondered out loud about diseases like Lyme and
Legionnaires' disease and AIDS, which seemed "to have
come recently from nowhere. Does it reflect a mutation of
microbes? A change in human immunity? Some subtle
shift in the environment? Good questions. And so is the
one the beach house friends were asking each other: What
did we do to deserve this?"

If one of Sturz's greatest assets was his willingness to
fail, another was his willingness to question things that
most other people took for granted. "What is always best
about Herb," Jack Rosenthal says, "is his impatience with
conventional wisdom."

In 1987, the conventional wisdom was that while the
Williamsburg Bridge between Brooklyn and Manhattan
wasn't falling down, about $250 million needed to be in-
vested in replacing cables that thrifty engineers had failed
to galvanize when it was built in 1903, to prevent its cor-

rosion and possible collapse. Sturz did not think in terms of quick fixes. He proposed a whole new bridge, one with elevated subways speeding through glass tunnels that "would muffle sound while offering an incomparable view." It might cost a billion dollars but would be built in New Yorkers' own "fantastic and pragmatic" image. Years before Bill Clinton popularized the phrase, Sturz dubbed it a bridge to the twenty-first century. Thinking still bigger, he suggested tolls be imposed to pay for maintenance (the Williamsburg bridge became toll-free in 1911, with predictable results) and that the city consider turning it over to private developers. Invoking Mark Helprin's stirring allegorical novel *Winter's Tale*, Sturz recalled that "a great white horse escapes from a stable in Brooklyn, trots across the new Williamsburg Bridge and pauses to contemplate bridges 'that spanned not only distance and deep water but dreams and time.'" Sturz exhorted: "Let that horse carry New Yorkers, galloping, into the 21st century."

"It was fanciful," Rosenthal recalled, "but an example of his willingness to think big and not be a functionary of mediocrity and ambition." For Sturz's birthday that year, Rosenthal had given him a copy of *Winter's Tale*. The novel is about a man who changes the world and an engineer, an exile from heaven, who hopes to build the ultimate in bridges, one that will ultimately return him there—"to tag this world with wider and wider rainbows," the bridge builder explains, "until the last is so perfect and eternal that it will catch the eye of the One who has abandoned us, and bring Him to right all the broken symmetries and make life once again a still and timeless dream." His purpose? "To stop time, to bring back the dead. My purpose, in one word, is justice." City officials' agenda also could be summed up in a word: corrosion. The bridge was fixed, not replaced, but Sturz had at least succeeded in firing New

York's imagination in a decade when it seemed as if the city's future was behind it.

From the Times building on West 43rd Street, Sturz was also especially well-situated to survey the results of his handiwork at City Planning. In a reflective editorial notebook titled "A Planner Faces Reality," Sturz would write lyrically of "a rare, almost archeological moment in history, one that gives me personal pangs—perhaps of pride, perhaps of anxiety." There was no doubt by then that East Midtown had stabilized while Midtown West was undergoing volcanic change. But plenty of questions persisted: Would looming skyscrapers and office workers overwhelm Times Square's traditional venue as the city's town square, as the Crossroads of the World? If "good uses" supplanted "bad ones," would that leave the area less tawdry, but dead after dark? Could the special character and effervescence of the Great White Way be mandated by government regulation requiring lights and signs? "Perhaps the central question is whether a revitalized mixed-use commercial and entertainment district can strengthen both west midtown's economy and its soul," Sturz wrote. "The answers won't be evident until the buildings take shape, lights and signs go on, and office workers, tourists and those just there for a good time begin to rub elbows." Two decades later, Times Square may be a bit less soulful—more orange juice than seltzer—but it is a lot safer, and booming.

————

After two years, Sturz had tired of sermonizing. Moral suasion took you only so far. "If I wrote an editorial, I really cared and wanted it to make a difference," he says, "and one of the reasons I left was that many weren't making a difference." He had served in government long enough to have absorbed the lesson Barry Gottehrer, a City Hall troubleshooter, had learned during the Lindsay administration—that not only bureaucrats, but their bosses, become so exposed to human failings and bombarded with second-guessing that they cloak themselves in a protective shell of defensiveness, self-righteousness and even obliviousness. They can become impervious to criticism no matter how constructive or sustained. As an editorial writer, Sturz pursued his criminal justice agenda, but from the outside. And how many editorials would his colleagues, to say nothing of the readers, endure about sick prisoners being inhumanely handcuffed to hospital gurneys?

"I wrote four editorials on women being shackled," he recalls. "People would say, 'what's the good, you're just throwing away space,' but I know enough about government to know you have to keep hammering. Persistence is a form of intelligence."

In late 1988, after years of preaching, Sturz decided to expand his practice into private development. After years at City Planning of drafting the game book for other players to follow and of second guessing them from the editorial board, Sturz wondered if he could meld good intentions with economic success. The answer emerged from a partnership with two entrepreneurs who could afford the gamble, William Zeckendorf Jr., the developer who built Worldwide Plaza on Manhattan's West Side and an apartment complex on Union Square, the Crowne Plaza in Times Square (and whose father was a legendary owner and builder of trophy properties in, among other cities, New York and Los Angeles), and Howard Stein, who was mulling uprooting his Dreyfus Corporation from Manhattan and moving to New Jersey. The Stein-Sturz collaboration, a Dreyfus subsidiary, was called the Trotwood Corporation, named after Sturz's standard poodle (a complement to the iconic Dreyfus lion) who shared the name bestowed on Dickens's David Copperfield by his eccentric aunt.

Sturz's short odyssey a few blocks east, from the *Times* to Dreyfus on the 55th floor of the MetLife Building, was typically idiosyncratic, convoluted and deeply rooted in personal relationships. While he was still at the Planning Commission, the Port Authority had proposed two residential and commercial developments, one in Hoboken and the other somewhere in New York City. Sturz steered the city development to Hunters Point, Queens, a largely derelict industrial location that boasted a great view and proximity to Manhattan. It had been eyed for housing since the early 1980s, but its most visible landmark remained a giant Pepsi-Cola sign. Only a visionary would consider it a dream site on which to create a new neighborhood, a community so close to midtown that "you could turn the East River into a lake" instead of a psychological barrier between the boroughs.

"I never had a remote dream that I would be involved in its actual development," Sturz says. While he was still at the *Times*, the Steins invited the Sturzes and the Zeckendorfs for a weekend at the Steins' beach house in Southampton. "What an affirmation if Dreyfus stayed in New York City and helped develop Hunters Point," Sturz recalls. "By Sunday evening we put together the idea of developing this at-the-time barren, forsaken and unzoned land. I was sufficiently intrigued to join the effort."

Trotwood and its partners (Hunters Point Associates, which would take in two Japanese partners and become MO Associates) would build and manage Citylights, a forty-two-story federally insured cooperative where tax deductions on loans and maintenance were intended to make living more affordable. It was the first of four buildings planned as the first phase of a seventy-four-acre development in Hunters Point across from Manhattan named

Queens West by Governor Cuomo (it is on the east bank of the East River but is in western Queens) and constructed under the auspices of an Urban Development Corporation subsidiary. Citylights's design was by Cesar Pelli & Associates and SLCE Architects.

When the forty-two-story 522-unit co-op opened in 1997, a two-bedroom, air-conditioned apartment in a building with indoor parking and a health club could be had for as little as $25,000. The price tag would require an annual income of about $52,000. "We believe the apartments should be accessible to the firefighters, schoolteachers and cops who work in the city," Sturz reasoned. Twenty percent of the apartments were reserved for low-, moderate- and middle-income households (and those apartments were offered at lower prices and with lower maintenance fees). The bargain-basement prices were set to attract pioneers to a fairly desolate site only five minutes by subway to Manhattan's East Side. Sturz persuaded the Federal Housing Administration to guarantee a mortgage loan, a first for a cooperative, which allowed for long-term financing. "It was the most ingenious financing I knew," Zeckendorf recalls. The low-equity financing, the *Times* reported, "neatly dovetails with the wishes of liberals, who look for the most housing bang from a government buck, as well as those of conservatives, who emphasize the virtues of owning over renting." Sturz envisioned replicating the low-equity finance formula to build low-to-moderate income housing on abandoned or donated land subsidized by the sale of tax-exempt bonds—the sort of innovative thinking that would set the stage for his association with George Soros and the construction of hundreds of thousands of houses in South African townships.

To help instill a sense of community and stability in what might otherwise become a mecca for speculators, the developers insisted that 70 percent of the initial buyers designate Citylights as their primary residence and that a 50 percent "flip tax" be imposed on profit from resale within two years.

The attraction of additional projects to the site at market-rate rentals was, in large part, a tribute to Trotwood's success in luring middle-class homesteaders to a building credited with high-quality construction and extra amenities, but on desolate waterfront. Five thousand prospective buyers signed up before the waiting list was closed. Today, the cheapest rent for a two-bedroom market-rate apartment in the rest of the project is $4,000 a month. A two-bedroom co-op can cost $850,000 or more. Slowly but steadily, Queens West has become a neighborhood with 2,000 occupied apartments and more on the way.

———

As rewarding as for-profit development could be, for Herb Sturz it could never be challenging enough to sate his intellect or his inborn conscience as a social engineer and entrepreneur. For nearly half a century, Sturz has been practicing his profession without pausing to give it a name or define it. Academics can't resist, though. And, perhaps in classifying his brand of do-gooder more specifically, by dissecting Sturz's strategy, they might help make his accomplishments more replicable.

With social problems demanding innovative solutions, a unique blend of individuals is rising to the occasion. According to J. Gregory Dees, director of the Center for Advancement of Social Entrepreneurship at Duke University, "increasingly societies are realizing that private citizens, acting in entrepreneurial ways, blending business tools with relevant social expertise, are the best hope for finding those solutions. These citizens are social entrepreneurs."

Herb Sturz emerged as a catalytic social entrepreneur years before Harvard and NYU and Stanford and Duke and other institutions began incorporating programs dedicated to the concept. The term itself is widely credited to William Drayton, a former management consultant and federal environmental official. In 1980, he founded Ashoka (named for a king of ancient India) to promote what the organization describes as "individuals with innovative solutions to society's most pressing social problems. They are ambitious and persistent, tackling major social issues and offering new ideas for wide-scale change." "Rather than leaving societal needs to the government or business sectors," says Drayton, "social entrepreneurs find what is not working and solve the problem by changing the system, spreading the solution, and persuading entire societies to take new leaps. Social entrepreneurs often seem to be possessed by their ideas, committing their lives to changing the direction of their field. They are both visionaries and ultimate realists, concerned with the practical implementation of their vision above all else." Drayton credits Sturz for his unusual "conceptual ability" and as a pioneer, "role-modeling, ice-breaking, being a mass recruiter of local change-makers. At the end of the day, if you want the world to change you've got to get other people to take our model and run with it."

"The true visionary," says Lynn Barendsen, the Harvard professor who runs the GoodWork Project, "recognizes an opportunity and transforms it into a mission." To paraphrase Barendsen, business entrepreneurs make dollars, but social entrepreneurs make change.

"The social entrepreneur," Sally Osberg and Roger Martin wrote in their case for definition, "should be understood as someone who targets an unfortunate but stable equilibrium that causes the neglect, marginalization, or suffering of a segment of humanity; who brings to bear on this situation his or her inspiration, direct action, creativity, courage, and fortitude; and who aims for and ultimately affects the establishment of a new stable equilibrium that secures permanent benefit for the targeted group and society at large."

But Professor Paul Light of New York University cautions against defining social entrepreneurship "so broadly that it becomes just another word that gets bandied about in funding proposals and niche building. Other terms such as innovation have gone that route, and may never be rescued from over-use. At the same time, social entrepreneurship should not be defined so narrowly that it becomes the province of the special few that crowd out potential support and assistance for individuals and entities that are just as special, but less well known."

The first recorded backlash against social engineering may have occurred nearly 2,000 years ago when Juvenal complained that Roman leaders were quelling civic unrest by placating the populace with bread and circuses. In 1899, the *New York Times* heralded the emergence of an entirely new profession, the social engineer. Its founders, Josiah Strong and W. H. Tolman, persuaded American industrialists that it was mutually beneficial for them to provide amenities for their employees. In the beginning, as befitted the new profession's name, most of the amenities those engineers developed were physical. And, early on, before the profession degenerated into a handy epithet for government meddling and experimentation by highbrow interlopers, before the New Deal raised the specter of socialism or, in the aftermath of the Great Society, even liberals began to question the cost of good intentions, social engineers were welcomed by enlightened industrialists. An American-sponsored plan to transform poor Jews in Russia and Eastern Europe into farmers in the late 1920s was endorsed by John D. Rockefeller Jr. as "a notable and creative example of social engineering."

Since then, social engineering has grown more sophisticated, graduating into an entirely new sphere that smacked less of state-sponsored planning and more of venture capital (and underwritten creatively by, among others, Atlantic Philanthropies and the Skoll, Edna McConnell Clark and Robin Hood Foundations). It is, as Sturz would attest, in terms of preparation and in practice, not a specific field. Rather, as Andrew Wolk, a Massachusetts Institute of Technology professor and founder of Root Cause, which supports social innovation, says, it is "the practice of responding to market failures with transformative, financially sustainable innovations . . . like business, using markets to drive innovation and productivity; like government, responding to market failures by providing public goods and services; and like nonprofits, engaging individuals to achieve social goals."

One myth about social entrepreneurship is that it's brand new. But it isn't. Think of it as a continuum, from Florence Nightingale, from Jane Addams, who popularized the settlement house movement in the late nineteenth century, to Wendy Kopp, who, a hundred years later, in 1989, transformed a dreamy undergraduate thesis about recruiting graduates of elite colleges to educate poor children into Teach for America, a thriving program that now has 17,000 alumni, or to Muhammad Yunus, the Nobel Peace Prize–winning "banker to the poor" whose Grameen Bank turned microfinance from an untested theory thirty years ago into a household word in the Third World, or to Herb Sturz.

Another misconception about social entrepreneurship is that it is synonymous with bigger government. It isn't.

Nor is it about substituting the private sector for what most reasonable people would agree are government's core responsibilities. Rather, in most of its incarnations, social entrepreneurship can be an extraordinarily effective device to leverage the government's potential to deliver public services with the private sector's potential for investment and innovation. "It is not that government is too small or too big," says Louisiana Lieutenant Governor Mitch Landrieu. "It needs to work better."

Herb Sturz has epitomized the movement to make government work better, by being unafraid to fail. As America turned from the Great Society into a nation more concerned with doing well than doing good, Sturz has personified the cautionary advice of John Gardner, the founder of Common Cause, that good intentions aren't good enough. Failing to deliver on those intentions, to acknowledge failure and to shift course, Gardner said, in a warning largely unheeded by social reformers in the 1970s and 1980s, is pious and damaging. "Damaging," he said, "because it uses up well meaning dollars, because it breeds discouragement in people who just feel 'we're working so hard and we're just not getting anywhere.' There's something about lofty ideals that are at odds with clean-cut self-evaluation. You know, 'How can you criticize us when our ideals are so great?'"

Sturz has embodied James Joyce's maxim that a genius makes no mistakes, that his "errors are the portals of discovery." He remains a pragmatic optimist. In the expanding pantheon of social entrepreneurs, he has distinguished himself in other ways, too, and in the process has redefined the field.

One is his sheer longevity. The fledgling nonprofit that he and Louis Schweitzer founded nearly fifty years ago has launched some thirty successful and independent spinoffs, each imparting its own lessons about success and failure, each culminating in a tipping point, which sparked more challenging questions and, ultimately, more answers. Driven by a broad programmatic synergy, those spin-offs attracted talent, expanding the public and private funding pool, and helped isolate potentially fatal mishaps without affecting Vera's overall reputation.

Another distinction is the breadth of societal challenges he has taken on, from the burdens of unreasonable bail that kept people accused of crimes and presumed innocent from getting out of jail to the subprime mortgage crisis, which exploits people lured into the dream of ownership and who are now getting evicted from their homes.

In contrast to many other social entrepreneurs, he viewed government never as an adversary but as a collaborator. He began by seeking public funds to prod public institutions, then as a public official overseeing the integration of innovative social ventures into government and finally as a benefactor to launch new partnerships between the public and private sectors and to underwrite them.

"I know of no one else who has undertaken such a wide range of activities," says Stanley N. Katz, the Princeton scholar of philanthropy. "He has also been better at leveraging government resources than most."

Herb Sturz and Louis Schweitzer might not have anticipated Google.org, created as a for-profit enterprise to invest in social entrepreneurship and lobby government. They might not have envisioned that social entrepreneurs would win Nobel Prizes or that universities would establish interdisciplinary programs to teach social entrepreneurship. But they knew they were dealing with gaping holes in the social fabric that demanded innovative solutions. In defining a social entrepreneur, the author David Bornstein describes a person who sounds a good deal like Herb Sturz. The profession, Bornstein writes, "does not require an elite education; it requires a backpack. The corpus of knowledge in social entrepreneurship comes from first-hand engagement with the world—from asking lots of questions and listening and observing with a deep caring to understand."

Sturz has been a pioneer in doing just that. In *How to Change the World: Social Entrepreneurs and the Power of New Ideas,* Bornstein writes, "Where governments and traditional organizations look at problems from the outside, social entrepreneurs come to understand them intimately, from within. Through a persistence of looking they discover the mistaken assumptions that lead policy makers astray. Because they do not have armies or police forces behind them, they work to elicit change rather than impose it, so they build human capacity rather than encouraging dependency." Sturz has relentlessly applied his inductive reasoning to those problems.

Whatever it was called before, social entrepreneurship has now entered the lexicon of presidential politics. In 2008, Barack Obama, echoing the terminology of social entrepreneurs, committed himself to enlisting "the grass roots, the foundations, the private sector and the government" to "invest in ideas that work; leverage private sector dollars to encourage innovation; and expand successful programs to scale." He even vowed to establish a national social entrepreneur agency "to make sure that nonprofits have the same kind of support that we give small businesses." David Gergen, director of the Center for Public Leadership at Harvard's Kennedy School of Government, calls social entrepreneurship "the most important movement since the civil rights movement."

Chapter 15

A Winter's Tale at
the Bonfire of the Vanities

By the early 1990s, Sturz was approaching sixty-five. But rather than retirement, he was contemplating new challenges and conjuring up new solutions that he would continue to improvise through Vera and its offspring and through an entirely different vehicle, a privately funded think tank committed to a public policy agenda as eclectic as Sturz's and—in contrast to the original incarnation of Vera—brimming with resources generated by the financier George Soros. In the more than three decades since Vera began as an instrument to reform and rationalize the bail system, Sturz would wander down other less traveled roads, too. Invariably, though, like the bridges in *Winter's Tale*, they would lead to a single goal: Justice.

In 1991, Sturz appealed to Peter Goldmark Jr. at the Rockefeller Foundation for a grant to create a local branch of the Criminal Court that would seek justice for crime victims as well as for criminals, and hold the perpetrators accountable, in the neighborhood where the crime occurred. Under the existing system, low-level arrests were typically processed at the local precinct station house for subsequent arraignment in Criminal Court downtown, a process that averaged twenty-four hours, but of course often took longer. The torrent of cases meant, Sturz said, that "turmoil is the norm."

Sturz concluded his appeal to the Rockefeller Foundation on a note of desperation: "New York City is not a happy place these days. Many persons are discouraged; they believe things are bad and growing worse. There is a feeling that it is virtually impossible to get anything done in the city." If anything, Sturz was guilty of understatement. Just a few years earlier, Mayor Koch's Commission on the Year 2000, which was chaired by Bobby Wagner and on which Sturz served, concluded that "crime today in New York is so much more extensive and violent than even in the recent past—say the 1950s—that the minor reductions in crime are dwarfed by the enormity of the problem." The random, stranger-to-stranger crimes worried people most. Bad enough, the commission found, that New York, with 3 percent of the nation's population, accounted for 18 percent of all the robberies in the United States. Even so-called minor offenses were taking their toll. They "perpetuate a sense of disorder and lawlessness to both criminals and law-abiding cities. . . . If drug dealers can operate openly in midtown, then so can thieves and muggers. The connection is as clear to the law-abiding as it is to criminals." The commission acknowledged that "police are often reluctant to arrest petty offenders because they feel the offenses are minor within the context of the city's violent crime, and because they know the offenders will probably go unpunished, making the arrest futile." But, the report said, "indifference to petty crimes undermines community efforts to combat them." The commission praised "determined and thorough" groups like Vera that run "well administered and strict" alternative programs.

By the early 1990s, crime had gotten worse. Give 1977 first prize in the category of most dramatic performances. By some measures, cumulatively, for sure, a little more than a decade later, New York seemed to be setting new standards for depravity. The early 1990s evoked the culmination of a Russian novel with primal forces unleashed years earlier inevitably colliding in a benumbing finale. The city's very survival seemed at stake. In 1990, the murder toll reached a record 2,245 (tenth per capita among the twenty-five largest cities, but nearly equal to one St. Valentine's Day Massacre every day). The *New York Post* appealed plaintively to Mayor Dinkins: "Dave, Do Something!"

Since 1977, the city had spiraled downward into isolated but horrendous cases of racial vitriol and violence with the white-on-black murders in Howard Beach, Queens, and Bensonhurst, Brooklyn, the brutal Central Park jogger assault and the Crown Heights race riots. Jeremy Travis, then the Police Department's counsel, remembers his boss, Commissioner Ward, returning from Los Angeles and warning, "I've seen something out there called 'ice,' and when it hits New York it's going to undo everything we've done." Ice was crack cocaine, and it did undo everything. In 1990, the city became a grim theater of bizarre juxtapositions. A rosy television interview with Parks Commissioner Betsy Gotbaum at the Alice in Wonderland sculpture in Central Park ended abruptly when the body of a homeless man who had been stabbed to death bobbed to the surface of the nearby sailboat pond. And that, as it turned out, was an otherwise garden-variety crime in a year when the murder victims would include eighty-seven people who died in a social club arson fire in

the Bronx, the stabbing of a twenty-two-year-old Utah
tourist who was defending his mother from muggers, targets of a serial killer who called himself Zodiac, livery drivers slain in their cabs and, defying the convention that
there are no innocent bystanders, young children killed in
the crossfire of gun battles among drug dealers.

For a while, the city was building more jail cells than
apartments. The extremes of wealth and poverty were impossible to ignore. They inspired Tom Wolfe's *Bonfire of
the Vanities* and the 1988 Tompkins Square riot against
gentrification (and the "police riot" that erupted in response). In 1990 the top fifth of Manhattan households
made thirty-two times more than the bottom fifth, or a
bigger income gap than in Guatemala.

Drawing a contrast with urban unrest in earlier decades, former Mayor Lindsay coined a new term for the
daily dose of random crime inflicted by disaffected young
people raised in poverty. He called it "a slow-motion riot."
A film titled *King of New York* proclaimed, "Not everyone
who runs a city is elected." The film was about a drug lord.
And New York's senior senator, Daniel Patrick Moynihan,
wrote that while Americans were still rattled by peaks in
crime, "these are peaks above 'average' levels that 30 years
ago would have been thought epidemic. . . . We have been
re-defining deviancy so as to exempt much conduct previously stigmatized, and also quietly raising the 'normal' level
in categories where behavior is now abnormal by any earlier standard."

————

Where other people saw problems, Sturz, while working
full-time on Queens West, seized an opportunity. The
courts downtown and the correctional system were

clogged. Misdemeanor arrests were virtually ignored. Community and business leaders were angry with the bureaucracy's inability to cope with rising crime and its devastating economic consequences. Politicians were desperate, willing to try almost anything, especially if they could be shielded from the blame and could share in the credit, however unlikely. Of all the places to experiment, Times Square offered the greatest potential for tangible impact and also posed the risk of embarrassing failure if its elasticity allowed another serial killer to slip through the cracks. But in Times Square, Sturz, through his myriad roles in and out of government, was wired into a matrix of public and private resources that, together, could make things happen that would otherwise be impossible. "One thing that made the redevelopment of Times Square so strikingly different from typical urban renewal projects," Benjamin Chesluk, a cultural anthropologist, wrote in *Money Jungle*, "was its collection of self-conscious, highly publicized efforts to 'reach out' to marginal groups and include them in its transformation."

The Midtown Community Court was conceived over breakfast between Sturz and Gerald Schoenfeld, chairman of the Shubert Organization, and a larger-than-life booster for the tourist-dependent Theater District. The business of live Broadway theater and of the ancillary restaurants and hotels that cater to their audiences depends, in contrast to television or even the movies, not only on the price of admission and the appeal of what is being performed onstage but on the environment outside. "Gerry was rightfully bemoaning over bagels at the Pierre the toll crime had taken on Times Square and on Broadway theater ticket sales specifically," notes John Feinblatt, who would be recruited to run the court. "My friend Herb said that maybe the thing to do was to try an experiment, which was to have a community-based court right in the middle of Times Square."

Nobody believed that a community court would solve the crime problem, although it might make a dent. It could, at worst, paper over the most visible symbols of deterioration—the street theater of panhandlers and homeless people huddled on subway gratings. At best, it might even prevent violence by intervening in the lives of troubled individuals before they plunged into an irreversible pathological spiral. With *Les Misérables* (whose hero spends years in prison for stealing a loaf of bread) already a theatrical hit nearby, but with so many other vacant venues, what better place to stage a real-life version of crime and punishment than inside a Broadway theater? "Give me a theater," Sturz told Schoenfeld, "and I'll get you a court." Schoenfeld enthusiastically offered the Longacre (which had opened with *It Takes a Thief* and last hosted *Ain't Misbehavin'*) rent-free for three years. But Actors Equity balked, because, with a number of legitimate theaters already having been razed by real estate developers and others being threatened, the loss of still another for something as incongruous as a courthouse seemed extravagant. The owners of adjacent stores and restaurants balked, too, fearing that the daily parade of prostitutes, panhandlers and assorted miscreants in the heart of the Theater District would detract from public confidence rather than instill it. (Sturz countered, to no avail, that police officers routinely accompanying prisoners to court and appearing there to testify would produce an entirely different effect: "I argued it would be the safest block in the city," he says.)

Within the criminal justice system, the resistance to change would reflexively be prompted by concerns over turf. Judith Kaye, however, and her predecessor as chief judge, Sol Wachtler, were famously open to experimentation, an exception in the government's most insular and independent branch. Generally, in a climate where everyone was concerned about rising crime, judges were disinclined to expose themselves any more than necessary to public accountability and to second-guessing. Defense lawyers were unwilling to cede jurisdiction over their clients to a system in which judges could exercise considerably more discretion. Prosecutors, too, were reluctant to relinquish their prerogatives over criminal cases to the courts.

Robert M. Morgenthau, the venerable Manhattan district attorney, was hostile to a proposal that would potentially dilute his prosecutorial resources and his clout in the centralized court system. Public defenders were no less antipathetic. "It sounds like a machine for securing guilty pleas," said Archibald R. Murray, executive director of the Legal Aid Society. Frederick H. Cohn, who monitored the assigned counsel program for indigent defendants in Manhattan, expressed concern about the pretrial interviews, in which defendants would be asked, among other questions, whether they used drugs or were employed. "The pedigree interview that elicits information for sentencing is a serious derogation of clients' rights before an attorney has access to the defendant," Cohn complained.

At the other end of the political spectrum, the nationwide trend toward strict sentencing guidelines and the imposition of mandatory punishment was a direct reaction to concerns that judges were exercising too much personal prerogative. The proliferation of special interventionist courts offering a greater array of sentencing alternatives would grant the judiciary even greater discretion. From another perspective, some critics wondered whether, however well-motivated, the courts would turn the promise of being judged by one's peers on its head. Typically, the judges rendering unfettered determinations and dealing directly with "clients" (rather than through their lawyers) were likely to be white, male and middle-class and, at least demographically, quite different from their clientele.

Some supporters of the three-year experiment offered, at best, a backhanded endorsement, fearing that criminals would merely be displaced to adjoining neighborhoods. Others labeled the project elitist, suggesting that it was being tested first in a community with outsized political clout where business could afford to help subsidize the government's investment.

But Sturz had also mustered a broad coalition of proponents, criminal justice officials who were grasping at almost any proposal that held out some promise of moderating soaring crime rates. Among them were Sol Wachtler, Police Commissioner Lee P. Brown and, importantly, Robert Keating, administrative judge of the city's Criminal Courts (who saw a fortuitous confluence in the revival of the magistrate's court just as the city was promoting community policing). Countering Frederick Cohn's criticism, Keating explained that under the existing system, judges operated pretty much in the dark when it came to determining a defendant's fate. "We don't know how serious the disease is or what it is," Keating said. "Do we treat it with a Band-Aid or with surgery?" If failure is an orphan, the community court experiment still had enough parents to hold out the promise of success. The Citizens Crime Commission, a monitoring and advocacy group supported by business, recommended it. Matthew T. Crosson, the state's chief administrative judge, envisioned community courts throughout the city. Sturz galvanized political support by enlisting the business and civic communities, embodied in the energetic and imaginative Times Square business improvement district. Arthur Sulzberger Jr., who would become publisher of the *New York Times*, chaired the business improvement district's board, which was studded with other muscular executives. Its stated goal, as articulated by its president, Gretchen Dykstra, was both broad-minded and practical, given the fierce competition for public services and the paradoxical concern that government intervention was likely to do more harm than good. The court, she argued, would help discourage antisocial behavior, not merely displace it—a strategy, built on consensus rather than divisiveness, that might be summed up as not-in-anybody's-backyard. Its jurisdiction would extend to the Midtown North and Midtown South police precincts, which accounted for more than a third of the misdemeanor arrests in Manhattan.

It didn't help, though, that Morgenthau was antagonistic. He and Sturz weren't exactly rivals, but they competed over some of the same turf. "Most people, for example, who work in criminal justice have very limited access to editorial writers, which he surely did, as did I," Sturz says. "As well, to Washington. I had networks that I'd built over the years. It is probably not surprising that he and I should have had difficulties." Ultimately, over a bottle of wine with Bobby Wagner in Morgenthau's King Street apartment in Greenwich Village, he and Sturz made peace. At a critical juncture when, as Sturz recalled, the support of court officials and the mayor "were shaky in the extreme, to put it mildly," Arthur Sulzberger hosted a lunch that unequivocally placed the *Times*'s corporate imprimatur on the project. "We may not have won the New York County District Attorney entirely over that day," Sturz remembers, "but his opposition softened, support for the court stabilized and momentum built."

Rather than in a theater, the court moved into a former courthouse. On a Sunday in the fall of 1993, while the weather was teasing most New Yorkers with the fleeting vestiges of summer, Sturz found himself in a grimy, Renaissance Revival building on West 54th Street in Hell's Kitchen just west of Times Square with Chief Judge Judith Kaye. That Kaye's vision of her job, as the chief administrator of the state's clogged, cumbersome judicial system, included helping to paint an entirely new court conceived by Herb Sturz spoke to her gung-ho inclination to support a project she believed in by whatever means necessary. The Midtown Community Court embodied all the talents that Sturz could bring to bear on a challenging criminal justice logjam.

The concept of a Midtown Community Court was older than the building. The very site of the courthouse on West 54th Street had been bought by the city a century earlier under legislation introduced by State Senator George Washington Plunkitt, the shoeshine stand bard of Tammany Hall, who became famous for unabashedly seeing his opportunities and taking them. Terra-cotta representations of justice still adorned the building.

"To it come all the common woes of the common people, a constant stream of human trouble," Mildred Adams wrote in the *New York Times* in 1930. "The West Side Court boasts a proportion of confidence men, fur-clad women whose escorts somehow cannot keep out of fights, sleek youths with occupations as uncertain as their places of residence." But by 1962, the West Side Magistrates Court and its counterparts in other neighborhoods were consolidated, merged into centralized, largely anonymous courthouses downtown where the stream of cases was growing into a torrent that commanded an entirely new goal—efficiency. Downtown, far from where most crime was committed, justice was homogenized, meted out with all the customized fine-tuning of an assembly line. Precisely because the old Magistrates Courts were so personal—at the end of the day, virtually everybody involved in the proceedings was a neighbor—they were considered subject to unjustified leniency toward people from within the community. Reviving local courts raised just the opposite concern, though: Would New Yorkers in gentrifying neighborhoods, frustrated by the irrelevance to their everyday lives of the criminal justice system downtown, be less forgiving?

———

Sturz hired John Feinblatt, a former Legal Aid lawyer and deputy director of the Victim Services Agency, to administer the Midtown Community Court. Foundations, corporations and the city government contributed $1.4 million to renovate the building into a facility that by its very appearance spoke volumes about its mission. The contrast with squalid conditions downtown was manifest. (The city initially committed $475,000 a year; another $2.5 million was raised by the Fund for the City of New York from, among others, the Times Square Business Improvement District, the Rockefeller Foundation and the Shubert Foundation; and another $1.6 million was promised for drug treatment and for a research study by the National Center for State Courts.) The court is bright, modern, computer-equipped with custom software, accompanied by space for counseling and social services and screening for sexually transmitted diseases. An acupuncturist ministers to drug addicts.

To help design the court, Sturz hired Amanda Burden, a Planning Commission member (who would become the commission's chairwoman) whom he had known when she was at the Urban Development Corporation. "I went to him the day after I got my master's degree at Columbia and I said, 'O.K. I'm going back to public service,'" Burden recalls. "Out of the blue, he said, 'don't look at another thing, I have a project to start a new kind of court in Times Square. You would be perfect at setting this up with John Feinblatt, who you're going to meet this afternoon." She stayed for eight years as the court's planning director, designing innovative programs for offenders that included watering street trees that otherwise would have wilted on midtown's blistering sidewalks over the summer. Instead of being confined in dreary pens behind steel bars, defendants at the court await arraignment in rooms secured by clear glass panels. "It was a kind of softening of justice, but in no way being soft on justice," Sturz notes.

————

The court opened for business in 1993 adjudicating misdemeanor cases—prostitution, peddling, fare-beating, minor drug possession and shoplifting—which had either been overlooked by the police or had clogged court calendars and detention cells. The "desk appearance tickets" issued by police officers for misdemeanors were still derided by cops as "disappearance tickets" since nearly half of those served failed to appear as scheduled downtown. Because the Midtown Community Court was so self-contained, its success or failure would be relatively easy to gauge compared to the sprawling criminal justice system in general. Feinblatt and his staff could assess whether cases were being adjudicated efficiently, swiftly and with certainty; whether apprehension and punishment offered sufficient opportunity to provide counseling, treatment and other interventions (or whether some miscreants, prostitutes, in particular, considered arrest as an acceptable occupational hazard).

With the Midtown North station house right next door, there would be plenty of feedback from cops on whether adjudicating their cases in a community court was more meaningful than shoveling more statistics into an insatiable black hole downtown. Because the court's staff worked in the community, they would know very quickly whether residents, commuters, office workers, storekeepers, business-people, and property owners noticed any improvement in the quality of their lives and attributed that improvement to the efficacy of the court.

———

In a system where justice used to be dispensed, formally and informally, at the neighborhood level, calling the Mid-town Community Court a community court was a bit of a misnomer—unless community was defined broadly to en-compass a vast and diverse swath of Manhattan's West Side, 350 blocks that included Chelsea, Clinton, Hell's Kitchen, Times Square and the Theater District. Tens of thousands of people lived there, and every day hundreds of thousands more commuted in. Swarms of sightseers and theatergoers injected the more or less organized chaos with an even more unpredictable dynamic. Still, this fluctuating population qualified as a community, defined by a cohe-siveness and intimacy compared to the distant and faceless judicial machinery downtown. "Even if the community court has no cohesive geographic community," David C. Anderson, a Ford Foundation analyst and former colleague of Sturz at the *Times* editorial board, concluded, "it honors the idea of community in two ways: it holds low-level criminals fully accountable for their crimes while helping them deal with their problems, and it helps to control the chronic misconduct that poisons the experience of daily life for residents, businesses and visitors alike."

Even so-called victimless crimes inflicted a toll, on the morale of the front-line cop, on the social service providers who, like the individual victims, were often left on the sidelines and on blocks and entire neighborhoods. As John Feinblatt put it, "the community is the victim. The community wants to be paid back for the crime, and the community also knows we ought to solve problems at the root of the crime." The formula was familiar. Sturz had followed it with Easyride and with Wildcat. "You take people who are looked at as the problem," he says, "and turn them into part of the solution."

———

Sturz approached the community court project with typical zeal, pulling out all the stops. "What he does behind the scenes is always invisible, no fingerprints, but powerful and relentless," Burden says. "His most brilliant ideas are based on common sense" (which, as Ralph Waldo Emerson said, is "genius dressed in working clothes"). "I went to the police commissioner and got the department to agree to use police officers to approach ill, down-and-out people in Times Square, to approach them to bring them in for help, for care, on an absolutely voluntary basis," Sturz recalls. "How did I learn how that worked? Simply by going up five flights of stairs with some cops and seeing who's there, just going out and approaching people." A twenty-year-old woman, sentenced to four days of community service in the midtown court's mailroom (which provides services for various nonprofit agencies in the neighborhood), served her sentence, but was arrested again for prostitution. The next solution was to get her and her three-year-old daughter out of town. The court's social service team arranged for her to plead to an outstanding warrant, reached out to her mother, who agreed to take her. The Travelers Aid Society paid for one-way bus tickets. "I said, 'You want some help?'" says Sturz, recalling his first encounter on the street. "She said, 'What I really want—I guess, at this point—is for you to send me home to Dayton, Ohio.' And we arranged for her to go home the same day."

By statistical and more intangible measures, the Midtown Community Court was generally judged to be a success. From October 1993 through December 1994, the court arraigned nearly 12,000 defendants. Among those who were sentenced to some form of community service, about three-quarters finished their assignments (if the sentence was a single day of service, the process from arrest to fulfillment of sentence could be completed within twenty-four hours), compared with the average two-thirds failure rate of defendants sentenced downtown to community service. About one in six who were sentenced to drug treatment, counseling or other social service or community programs voluntarily continued in those programs after completing their sentences.

If processing could be streamlined and routinized as time went on, the original premise of the community court would be preserved and enhanced. More sophisticated computer software for monitoring individual defendants and overall caseloads was developed. More opportunities for counseling, physical and emotional health care and employment (in keeping with Sturz's conviction that those few minutes in court represent "a teachable moment") could prove to be transformative. And the court's reputation for swift, certain, fair, constructive and visible accountability would establish it as a judicial line to, and bulwark of, the community. Paul Shectman, counsel to the Manhattan district attorney, praised the drug treatment options and concluded that ability to do same-day community service meant more defendants completing their sentences. Indirectly delivering a similar verdict on the court, a defense lawyer, Kenneth L. Olsen, recommended to clients like unlicensed street vendors who were likely to be recidivists to "stay downtown" where sentences were typically less strict.

The Midtown Community Court further formed a partnership that might have seemed innovative for the judicial branch, but it evoked the constructive collaboration that made the original Manhattan Bowery Project so successful by empowering the police not only to respond to crime but to prevent it. Vera had been a leading pioneer in problem-solving justice and in alternative sentencing.

Later in the 1990s, police officers in midtown Manhattan, wearing, in warm weather, shorts and blue polo shirts (dressed to identify themselves as cops but to be less intimidating), would go out regularly with a Street Outreach Services worker from the community court in a green SOS T-shirt. On one night at three A.M., Dave Connolly, a recovered alcoholic and SOS worker, was introduced by the cops to two elderly men sprawled on a piece of cardboard. One was a sixty-nine-year-old Korean War veteran. "Why don't you get your benefits?" the outreach worker asked. "You could get money. You could get an apartment instead of being out here at three o'clock in the morning." When the man replied that he had tried to, but had gotten the runaround, Connolly interjected: "We kick ass and take names later. We know how to get things done for you." The man took Connolly's business card and agreed to give him his name and social security number. When a prospective client showed up in his office, Connolly or one of his colleagues negotiated a treatment protocol tailored to his priorities. According to Connolly, "I'll say, 'all right, you're unemployed, you have no identification and you're living on the streets. So, prioritize. First, we should get you a place to stay. Then we should get some of that identification back, because that's going to help get you a job. And then ultimately we should get you a job with a focus on permanent housing.'"

On paper, the partnership may have seemed unusual, even unnatural. But Sturz's hunch a generation earlier about the relationship had been vindicated for the very same reasons by the Bowery project. "Too often," David Anderson wrote, "police were arresting the same people again and again for the same offenses. The cops understood more than anyone the importance of helping such offenders confront the real issues: substance abuse, homelessness, mental illness or sexual exploitation." To be sure, probation and parole officers were more likely to have effectively married the duties of social workers with law enforcement officers, but cops? At what point do they belong in the business of intervening to prevent crime? And does their very presence transform the role of the accompanying counselor or outreach worker into an implicitly coercive posture? (However coercive or not, the police presence generally did prove to be a motivating factor. "It makes compliance go up," Connolly said.)

———

The Midtown Community Court was not the first of its kind. In Hollywood, local courts were created to deal with prostitution and similar crimes. In Miami, drug courts diverted first offenders to treatment. But given his access to both policy and opinion makers, Sturz's court would be

hailed as "the most ambitious effort to dispense justice lo-
cally in the nation." And it would become a prototype,
spawning scores of versions around the country that would
be modeled on the principle that John Feinblatt had articulated at the very beginning, that "justice ought to be
restorative." The Midtown Community Court, he said, "will
actually pay back the community where the crime took
place and where justice will be local, visible, and it will
be swift."

The progeny modeled on the Midtown Community
Court have largely disproved the skepticism that the neighborhood in which the original court operated and the financial backers it attracted had given it elitist airs. The
concept of the self-contained community court inspired a
community court that bordered a crime-infested public
housing project in Red Hook, Brooklyn, before expanding
to outposts in Harlem, the Bronx and beyond. Special
problem-solving courts were subsequently spawned in
New York and around the country to cope with some of
the specific underlying conditions that contributed to
crime—drug addiction, homelessness, domestic violence
and mental health. Opening in 2000 in a former parochial
school, the Red Hook Community Justice Center, championed by District Attorney Charles J. Hynes, was billed as
the nation's first multi-jurisdictional community court, diverting some cases that would otherwise have been handled
in the criminal, housing or family courts. David Bookstaver,
a spokesman for the state's Office of Court Administration,
described it as "a small-town court in a big city." In a former
courthouse on East 121st Street, the Harlem Community
Justice Center opened a juvenile intervention division at
the beginning of 2002.

———

The Midtown Community Court's legacy would go well beyond that of progenitor for imitators and models that improved upon the original. In true Sturz style, the experiment on West 54th Street would lead to a permanent partnership in 1996 between New York's Unified Court System and the Fund for the City of New York to make justice, as Jonathan Lippman, the state's chief administrative judge, put it, "not some far-away abstraction, but something meaningful." That partnership, embodied by a Center for Court Innovation, would become an incubator for developing the means to administer justice more effectively and a vehicle to test, monitor and implement alternatives— from mandated drug treatment rather than incarceration for nonviolent offenders, to anger-management counseling for perpetrators of domestic violence, and medication coupled with therapy for mentally ill defendants.

"If you were to distill this down to its essence, it's about improving public confidence in the criminal justice system," said Greg Berman, who succeeded John Feinblatt.

———

Feinblatt would move on to run the Center for Court Innovation (and eventually be recruited by Mayor Bloomberg to be the city's criminal justice coordinator). The center, like so many other Sturz-inspired think tanks, is part petri dish, part clearinghouse and part cheerleader for the concept of problem-solving courts around the world and, at home, the reform of a civic institution that, despite historic declines in crime across the country, was suffering from a crisis of confidence. "The list of complaints is long: courts are too slow, judges are out of touch, the needs of victims are ignored and offenders continue to commit the same crimes again and again," Feinblatt and Berman wrote in

Good Courts. Their goal has been consistent with Sturz's other efforts to institutionalize reform—combining social engineering and entrepreneurship to systemically change perception and practice, in this case, to address the issues that brought people to court in the first place. To carry out its mission, the Center for Court Innovation recommended smaller and specialized jurisdictions that respond to patterns of crime and punishment; innovative partnerships to integrate services into the menu of sentencing alternatives; sufficient profiles of defendants and of the impact of their crimes on a community; and rigorous monitoring to ensure that defendants and the courts were held accountable for individual decisions and for their broader implications.

————

In 2007, the Center for Court Innovation convened a unique, introspective roundtable in keeping with Sturz's philosophy of being unafraid to fail. The discussion was called "Learning from Failure," and it was an unusual attempt to distill innovation out of criminal justice experiments that fell short. Michael Jacobson, Vera's director, pointed out that government is not very tolerant of failure and that, as Sturz would be the first to say, one person's failure is another's opportunity:

> Failure depends upon where you stand. I think of the issue of technical parole violations. To me those are failures, but if you ask parole officials they will say, "No, that is a success. We caught that guy before he was going down a slippery slope and slammed him back into prison." Not a speck of research says this is even remotely true. Take a place like California. There are 120,000 people on parole

in California and each year they send back 70,000 for technical violations. They go back for an average of two and a half months at a total cost of almost a billion dollars. So you ask someone like me, and I say, who would spend a billion dollars sending 70,000 people back to prison for three months? Who could possibly say that if we have a billion dollars to spend on law enforcement, what we want to do is catch 70,000 parolees after they test positive for drugs and slam them back into prison for two and a half months? But for parole officials in California, it's a success. You are getting people off your caseload. You're doing good law enforcement work. And you are minimizing your political risk.

Since the first drug court opened in Florida in 1989, followed four years later by the Midtown Community Court in Manhattan, thousands of problem-solving courts have been established in the United States and other countries with quantifiable results. The Midtown Court is credited with reducing prostitution by 56 percent and illegal vending by 24 percent and improving compliance with community service sentences by 50 percent. A Manhattan drug court, by offering treatment to addicted parents, reduced the average time children spent in foster care, from four years to less than one. In Red Hook, the approval rating for the criminal justice system more than doubled since the community court opened.

From serving hot soup to offering English-language courses at night to defendants, the Midtown Community Court would continue to expand its reach and to experiment. And, like so many of Sturz's other projects, each of which could proudly stand alone with its own vision and agenda, the court would become part of a more ambitious design, its squares woven into an almost seamless tapestry.

Sturz's role, officially, was as an unpaid adviser, which, again, was in keeping with his no-fingerprints style, but belies his actual influence.

Begun as a small group of researchers conjuring up a single experiment, the Midtown Community Court would grow in a decade into an organization with more than 150 employees and well over a dozen distinctive demonstration projects. It spawned scores of variations that, after a decade, included 9 mental health courts, 196 drug courts, 7 community courts, 3 sex offender management courts and dozens of domestic violence courts. Inspired by the Midtown Community Court envisioned by Sturz and Gerald Schoenfeld, other versions would spread to Atlanta, Austin, Dallas, Denver, Hartford, Indianapolis, Memphis, Minneapolis, Philadelphia, San Diego, Seattle, West Palm Beach and Washington, D.C. Sturz's prototype would be replicated beyond the United States. A decade after the Midtown Community Court opened for business, Britain's highest judicial official visited it and declared himself so "utterly delighted" that he decided to import the model to Liverpool. Others have opened in South Africa and Australia.

The Center for Court Innovation propagated its expertise, too, advising innovators in every county of New York State and in Armenia, Britain, Canada, China, New Zealand and South Africa and began a pilot curriculum on problem-solving justice at Fordham Law School. Greg Berman attributed the growth and adoption of the program to two principal forces—forces that were at the heart of every successful project that Sturz had a hand in. "The first is a clear set of values," Berman observed. "In all of our work, we have sought to help the justice system become more problem-solving and more thoughtful about the outcomes that it achieves for victims, defendants and communities.

Beyond our vision, the key to our institutional success has been the demonstrable results that our projects have achieved." The causal reductions in crime and drug abuse, the concomitant increases in public safety and society's trust in the judicial system, were not mere abstractions. "Behind the numbers," Berman noted, "are real people: victims of domestic violence who no longer fear for their lives; ex-offenders who have gotten back on track, and community residents who have reclaimed public parks from drug dealers."

Chapter 16

"As Long As I'm Doing Something That Matters"

In 1994, Sturz was building Citylights, promoting home ownership in Queens, and launching the Midtown Community Court in his spare time, when he was invited to join two nonprofit boards. Both invitations were initiated at the recommendation of Aryeh Neier, the president of George Soros's Open Society Institute (OSI), which had just given the two nonprofit groups grants. Years earlier, when Sturz was at Vera, Neier was executive director of the New York Civil Liberties Union and persuaded Sturz to make participation in the Manhattan Bowery Project's detoxification regime voluntary. "He was not rigidly committed to a particular approach," Neier remembers. "He addressed the civil liberties issue and still made the program effective."

Sturz called Neier for lunch and briefed him on the Queens West project and its innovative financing (which had been the subject of a *New York Times* story that caught Neier's attention). Neier talked about Soros's interest in the housing crisis that Nelson Mandela faced as he was just assuming the presidency of the African National Congress and the opportunities for home ownership in a nation struggling to overcome the legacy of apartheid. Neier invited Sturz to lunch with Soros, who worried that democracy would not survive in South Africa without affordable shelter. Two weeks later, in February 1994, Sturz found himself in South Africa for the first of many visits.

"My job," he recalls, "was to go over and get a feel for how it could be done." The problem was not only how, but who? Sensing the incredible obstacles, Sturz wanted the best candidate, regardless of race. Further, he wanted a person open to new ideas and less bound by the conventional wisdom or freighted by the baggage of why things hadn't worked in the past. "Go with the amateur," Sturz advised. "It's all the things you don't have to unlearn."

The relative amateur, in this case, was Cedric de Beer, a white urban planner who had been imprisoned for his political activities during apartheid. He was tapped by Sturz as the operational deputy but was suddenly promoted when the chief executive officer decided at the last moment not to take the job. Very quickly, de Beer transformed himself into a consummate housing professional. de Beer remembers that Sturz's partner in Trotwood, Fred Harris, once told him: "I work out the numbers and the technology; Herb works out the people." As director of urbanization for the Johannesburg City Council, de Beer inherited a vague vision about how to finance housing during the tumultuous conflict between the African National Congress and its allies and the apartheid apparatchiks who were clinging to power.

The original premise behind the proposed low-cost housing finance company was that the vast number of homeless blacks would need financial assistance, that community-based contractors and not-for-profit organizations would need access to capital. These developers had no access to capital, and banks, wary of the highly politicized housing environment and clueless about how to under-write those entities, would need a risk buffer to, as Sturz put it, "embarrass them" into extending credit.

Sturz and Fred Harris conducted several field visits to South Africa in an attempt to embrace, firsthand, the prob-lems, the players and the potential solutions as Sturz had three decades earlier in New York City's detention pens and on the Bowery. As de Beer vividly recalls, Sturz and Harris "witnessed a land invasion as homeless people claimed their piece of the new South Africa, setting up an informal settlement overnight on state-owned land; they were threatened with violence for photographing a single-sex hostel just north of Johannesburg in Alexandra Town-ship, a hotbed of political conflict in the pre-election period; they visited extremely poor and dysfunctional areas, where the prospects for an orderly process of housing delivery seemed most unlikely; and they were introduced to the reality of whole communities refusing to make rental and utility payments as part of the ongoing struggle for power: a refusal that spilled over into massive boycotts of mortgage payments by the first generation of black home owners." Despite the breathtaking depth of research and the com-mitment of the new national government, those field visits might have prompted ordinary people to give up. Instead, de Beer says, they fostered "Herb's extraordinary capacity to encourage people to get things done, to see what is possible, rather than to dwell on what might go wrong."

Even with loans guaranteed by the nonprofit National Urban and Reconstruction Agency (NURCHA), the oli-gopoly of banks were balking at the risk involved in offer-ing up loans for housing developments in South Africa's turbulent political climate. With the banks pulling back, Soros agreed to commit $5 million to operating costs and $50 million in guarantees matched with securities NURCHA raised from other sources, including the new South African government. With the risk removed, Soros figured, working capital could be unlocked to produce thousands of homes that would eventually be paid for with already allocated public funds. "George called and said he was coming the next day," Sturz recalls. "I said I still don't know enough. But do it." Soros's commitment was front-page news.

By early 1995, de Beer was named managing director of NURCHA. "Through this complicated and sometimes turbulent process," de Beer says, "one constant was the calm and reassuring presence of Herb Sturz."

Eventually, NURCHA would become much more than a loan guarantor. It trained small contractors, generated its own capital. It became a lender itself and went beyond low-income housing to build community centers and gated communities for an emerging black middle class. NURCHA, according to one study, has not only been hailed as the South African government's leading housing program, but "almost single-handedly fostered the emergence of a new generation of developers and contractors"—most of them women and blacks, for whom credit would otherwise have been inaccessible. By 2007, the 200,000th house delivered with NURCHA financing was built, one of nearly a thousand projects valued at nearly $1 billion. (NURCHA's land acquisition strategy that provided a foundation for the housing and community facilities in South Africa has been replicated in New York to help developers of affordable housing compete for building sites. In 2006, on the basis of his success in South Africa, Sturz teamed with Housing

Preservation and Development Commissioner Shaun Donovan to help initiate a $230 million New York City Land Acquisition Fund. The fund has been replicated in other cities and was honored in 2008 with an Innovations in American Government award from the Ash Institute at Harvard's Kennedy School.)

"There is no doubt in my mind that Herb Sturz is one of two or three people whose contribution was absolutely essential to NURCHA's successful establishment and functioning," de Beer says. "He truly does have a magic touch when it comes to getting people to work together."

———

George Soros, unlike Quincy Wilbur, the quixotic protagonist in Herb Sturz's screenplay "The Peacemaker," is not "the richest man in the world." But close enough. The story that Sturz collaborated on nearly sixty years earlier proved on several levels to be remarkably prescient.

The concept of entrepreneurship—personified by George Soros and Quincy Wilbur—dates to the eighteenth-century French economist Jean-Baptiste Say. In French, it means "undertaking." Soros, a very practical man, is reluctant to apply the word to social causes. "A business entrepreneur has a bottom line," Soros says. "In a social entrepreneur, it is much harder to judge an easy criteria of success." And, in some respects, it may be much harder not only to judge success but to achieve it.

"Sturz manages to work within the system, but what systems tend to do is maintain themselves and protect themselves," Soros explains. "His concept is that the private sector is meant to be a catalyst, an innovator, and then the public sector has to basically deliver."

The stated goal of Soros's institute is "building a global alliance for an open society." Quincy Wilbur had something similar in mind.

When Sturz, between college and graduate school, collaborated on the screenplay for "The Peacemaker," he never imagined he would some day work for one of the richest men in the world. But "The Peacemaker" foreshadowed two character traits that would define Herb Sturz's career. Wilbur (or his literary creators) was blessed with a healthy cynicism. ("We are peace-loving men and all that," one world leader says in the screenplay, "but let us deal with Peace when we come to it, and not try to precipitate events we have no control over.") And, Wilbur's greatest contributions come when he has what the authors proclaim "AN IDEA." His mightiest weapon was his imagination.

———

Gara LaMarche, the former director of OSI's programs in the United States, recalls that in 1998, "Soros's money was burning a hole in his pocket—we weren't spending it fast enough. He wanted to do something for New York City." Sturz offered up the perfect solution. He created The After-School Corporation (TASC).

"I'd been circling this idea for years," Sturz says. It had been percolating since he was in Teachers College and then worked at the school for troubled children, when he was deputy mayor and created the Department of Juvenile Justice and at City Planning, when he established the New York City Volunteer Corps.

> Over the years, I'd seen kids roaming the subways and streets, had read during my criminal justice days that the hours between three and six P.M. were when kids were

most likely to get into trouble—whether as perpetrators or victims. I was aware of the burden on working, often single parents and children who didn't have anything to do after school other than hang out or become couch potatoes. One morning, I realized that there were a bunch of hit-or-miss after-school efforts, but few of sustainable value for kids and families. The important thing was to develop something of quality that could go to scale.

An after-school program, Sturz recalls, "doesn't have a lot of natural haters, but also not a lot of supporters." Sturz galvanized the supporters and wasted no time filling the vacuum in Soros's agenda. As LaMarche tells it, "Herb, almost instantly, at breakfast sketched out his idea for after school. It was simple, but creative, done to scale and in partnership with community-based organizations so they would have some political ownership of the program. It would help working parents, raise academic performance, improve public safety. I wouldn't say he invented after-school programs but he came into it at a pivotal point and is making it universal."

Sturz's vision for The After-School Corporation also challenged the canard that Sturz did big things, but sometimes in a small way. "In after-school—given the world of the Board of Education, and a million, one hundred thousand kids—to do a kind of cameo experiment wouldn't work," he says. "If you can't show scale, and get to it, you have no purchase, you have no interest."

TASC was founded with a five-year $125 million challenge grant from the OSI. Sturz was the founding chairman of the board. The need for affordable or free after-school programs for children in New York City had been obvious for decades but had been smothered by competing priorities. America was no longer an agrarian society. The school calendar did not have to conform to the seasons for sowing and reaping and the school day did not have to terminate abruptly in early afternoon so youngsters could scurry to farms and factories. With more parents working, many schoolchildren were likely to return to empty homes. TASC's goals were to make after-school programs more available, to improve their quality and to create a critical mass of high-caliber programs that would transform the popular perception of after-school programs from custodial babysitting or a luxury of enrichment available only to those few who could afford it into a public responsibility.

When TASC was launched, the quality of after-school programs in New York City was, at best, uneven. Financing was unreliable, given the budgetary pressures local schools faced for their regular curriculum. As its president, Lucy N. Friedman explained, TASC began as an intermediary, strengthening links between schools with their local community organizations, and funders and education specialists with service providers. And just as Vera had nursed so many offspring, the Open Society Institute—personified by Soros—served as an incubator for TASC. "I wanted this to be a seminal thing, something to last for the long-term," Sturz says. "He and I both knew that just helping a program here and a program there wasn't going to do it."

TASC embraced programs that operated inside public schools three hours every day, complemented but did not duplicate academic, arts and sports and community service programs already operating (from cooking nutritious meals to creating comic books), were run by a full-time coordinator on-site, served between 150 and 400 students, maintained a staff-to-student ratio of ten-to-one and provided snacks or supper to any student who wanted them.

By the end of its first decade, TASC and Friedman had demonstrated that a well-run, large-scale program was capable of also providing a nurturing and intimate environment. TASC had revolutionized how after-school programs were funded in New York, struck a unique collaboration with the community groups that delivered after-school programs and the education staff and officials without whose cooperation the goals of the program could never have been accomplished, much less surpassed. TASC programs reached more than 200,000 youngsters, and their ability to leverage matching funds (the original $125 million pledge was contingent on a three-to-one match), helped to more than double public funding to nearly $300 million. TASC created training academies and protocols to help expand and replicate its programs and teamed with the Afterschool Alliance (which, with Sturz's guiding hand, became an independent organization in its own right), to lobby for universal after-school programs for the estimated 14 million children—nearly one-third of all students—who now care for themselves after school.

Following the Vera model, TASC submitted itself to rigorous research and accountability, which strongly suggested a correlation between enrollment in after-school programs and better attendance and grades. TASC's board was a virtual who's who of well-connected people, each of whom, according to the Sturzian matrix, was poised at just the right button if it needed to be pressed (in this case, the board eventually included his old friend Jay Kriegel; Leon Botstein, the president of Bard College and conductor of the American Symphony Orchestra; Stanley S. Litow, president of the IBM Foundation and former deputy schools chancellor of New York City; Geoffrey Canada, president of the Harlem Children's Zone; Esther Dyson, the digital technology entrepreneur; Victor Gotbaum, the former municipal union leader; Jennifer J. Raab, the president of Hunter College of the City University of New York; and

Diana Taylor, the former New York State superintendent of
banks who is chairwoman of the Hudson River Park Trust
and is Mayor Bloomberg's regular companion).

Beginning at Vera, Sturz demonstrated a legendary ability to detect talent—talent that people sometimes didn't
know they had. Perhaps because TASC was his first big
venture with the Open Society Institute and so much of
George Soros's money was at stake, Gara LaMarche recalls, TASC "suffered a bit in the early years, because Sturz
included people only in his circle. Eventually, Herb let go,
but he left very little to chance in the governance." Another
handicap, one that Sturz had never had to face before, was
the difficulty in raising money from other sources because
Soros had committed so much himself. "Other people felt
we didn't need it," Sturz says. TASC did, though, and managed to leverage Soros's original investment, raising $3 for
every $1 Soros invested and leveraging that into a $60 million annual appropriation for after-school programs generally in the city budget. "At the end of the day, George got
a program institutionalized without a continuing need of
his philanthropic dollars," says Michael Weinstein of the
Robin Hood Foundation. "That's the name of the game."

By creating a program model that could economically
serve a large pool of students, building a network of after-
school staff trainers and identifying and supplying a rich
after-school curriculum, TASC raised the bar for what children could be expected to do in the three hours *after*
school. Schools and their program partners in community
organizations responded by focusing more on the quality
and relevance of the programs they operated, including
science, college preparation and a supported work model
for teenagers at risk of dropping out.

TASC has managed to match Soros's original $125
million by leveraging more than $375 million in public
and private funds. Since it began a decade ago, annual pub-

lic support for after-school programs in New York City increased from $60 million to an estimated $295 million. TASC spurred the expansion of these programs. Before, only 10,000 New York youngsters attended daily programs that include arts, sports, community service and academic enrichment. Now, 140,000 do.

————

Vacationing in Paris in the early 1970s, rummaging for something to read in English, Sturz came across *The Coming of Age* by the French existentialist writer Simone de Beauvoir. The book, which discusses the mistreatment of older people in society and the loneliness with which they sometimes struggle, inspired him to start Easyride, to transport the homebound, solitary elderly to the world outside their door. "It was the first time I thought seriously about the problems of aging people," says Sturz. "What struck me in the book was the poignancy of what it was to grow . . . older, to lose friends and access, to face ageism. I decided that I'd try to do something about it."

Early in 2005, Sturz and Jack Rosenthal (by then the president of the New York Times Company Foundation), who were both well beyond customary retirement age (and both maintaining a quarter-century-long tradition of attending opening day together at Yankee Stadium), were struck by a demographic disconnect. More Americans were living longer; more had mentally and physically healthy lives; more retired better educated and with learned and acquired skills. Yet the value of well-educated and retired older Americans was being woefully wasted. Few opportunities exist for retirees to engage in public service.

Characteristically, they decided something needed to be done to address this gaping inefficiency. Rosenthal envisioned ReServe and would become its driving force and

chair its board (Sturz is vice chairman). To improve the
lives of older people, it was founded on two premises: retirees would eagerly apply those skills at nonprofit and
public agencies for pay, and enough enlightened agencies
would seize the opportunity. Both hypotheses proved cor-
rect. City departments, including Consumer Affairs, the
Downtown Alliance, which nurtures businesses in lower
Manhattan, Goddard Riverside, a respected social service
agency, and Vera spin-offs—including TASC, the Center
for Court Innovation and a new Vera Guardianship Project
(which acts on behalf of incapacitated individuals)—were
among those that embraced ReServe and the collective
experience it offers at a bargain. Begun with a grant from
the Blue Ridge Foundation, founded by John A. Griffin, a
hedge fund manager, ReServe steers retirees to jobs that
pay $10 an hour for a maximum of 15 hours a week (they
are not eligible for pensions or other benefits). Employers
can pay participants directly or contract with ReServe to
handle the payroll at $14 per participant an hour. By
mid-2008, ReServe had matched 450 participants, three-
quarters of them college graduates and more than four in
ten with master's degrees, with 110 nonprofit agencies.

Paid volunteerism might have an ironic ring to it, but
there's a rationale behind the philosophy. "For most of the
participants," Claire Haaga Altman, ReServe's former executive director, explains, "it is not about the amount they are
paid but the fact that they are paid." Having retired from
his law firm, Fritz Schwarz volunteers for a modest stipend
at New York University's Brennan Center for Justice. "An
organization and a person are simply more committed to
each other when the person is paid," he says.

"With 8,000 Americans a day turning sixty," Sturz says,
"I could not tell you right now where ReServe is going to
end up." But considering the pace at which it is expanding

and being replicated, the program appears to be feeding a hunger. "It is inertia," de Beauvoir wrote, "that is synonymous with death."

"These individuals still have a lot to teach and contribute, and they aren't satisfied just sitting around until they die," Sturz says. "They want to live until they die."

―――――

Sturz is still teaching and contributing, too. And learning. In 2007, at the suggestion of George Soros, he plunged into the subprime mortgage crisis, interviewing borrowers, lenders, brokers, bankers, prosecutors and advocates and absorbing the arcana of law and high finance that he'd previously known little about. The Open Society Institute committed $10 million over two years to help prevent foreclosures and, if they could not be prevented, to mitigate their negative impact on neighborhoods, including $2 million to a neutrally named Center for New York City Neighborhoods established by Mayor Bloomberg and Christine Quinn, the city council speaker, in December 2007. Bloomberg and Shaun Donovan, the housing commissioner, recruited Sturz as chairman of the center's board to help stanch the flood of foreclosures by providing counseling and legal services. Echoing Koch, Bloomberg observes, "If Herb Sturz isn't the consummate Renaissance man, he's pretty close to the mark. He's an intellectual, a creative thinker, and a practical visionary."

―――――

After serving for twelve years on the board, Sturz is a senior adviser at the Open Society Institute, which operates, Gara LaMarche explains, like a monarchy in which board members are either too reticent to publicly challenge Soros or savvy enough to pick their fights. "I don't think Herb's style is to rock the boat or to be a grandstander," LaMarche says. "I'm essentially making a compliment. Herb is not a man who believes that the most effective way to accomplish something is by making statements." But Sturz's reluctance to squander political capital on inconsequential or lost causes would evaporate when the stakes were raised. At one board meeting, members debated how to address the nation's record prison population. As LaMarche tells it, Lani Guinier, the Harvard law professor,

> was mainly interested in theory and principle. Herb was more, like, if we cut the prison population by tinkering with technical parole violations, which is one reason why so many people are incarcerated. It wasn't that Herb didn't care about the justice. The idea that you had to make a major theoretical statement didn't appeal to him. You can accomplish programmatic goals, it turns out, in a more efficient way if you don't emphasize ideology, without changing the hearts and minds of every politician. You can call that incremental, I guess. But it is like Barack Obama's vision of the world. Herb is not a centrist. His is not the Third Way. He's a pragmatist.

Being self-effacing—personally and professionally—is also Sturz's defense pragmatism. Over the years, spinning off individual programs meant that Vera itself became less of an institutional target. "It keeps down visibility," Sturz points out. Spin-offs also benefit from a wider pool of potential board members to lend their expertise and to cheerlead and open doors. The staff is endowed with greater responsibility and its own stake.

Sturz also avoided Pyrrhic victories and defeats. In 2002, he was appointed by Mayor Bloomberg to a charter revision commission charged, in part, with eviscerating a potential rival, the city's public advocate, Betsy Gotbaum. Gotbaum was a former employee and Sturz's friend. Still, he voted with the mayor, on principle (he believed that in the event of a mayoral vacancy, the public advocate, whatever the worth of the office, should serve as the interim mayor only a short time before a special election) and on pragmatism (he needed the mayor's support for myriad other projects). His vote was not pivotal anyway. "Practical considerations totally outweighed his friendship," Carl Weisbrod says. "He took the accommodationist point of view rather than loyalty. And let's say he was being practical."

Yet for all the whirring gears as he plots the mental chess moves he taught himself during high school when he was homebound with polio, for all his instinctive skill at evaluating the motivation of others, what you see in Herb Sturz is pretty much what you get. He does not put on airs. He is refined, but not fancy. He reads novels in between more weighty tomes. His sun-drenched home office, in a cozy, unpretentious Park Avenue apartment that he and Elizabeth have lived in for three decades, is cluttered mostly with books and papers, rather than with the customary trophies and testimonials and stiff portraits with public officials. When he greets people, he reflexively and unapologetically extends his slack right hand.

People have been shaking his hand a lot lately. At Harvard, the Kennedy School's Innovation in American Government Awards program has recognized several Sturz-inspired projects, including the New York Acquisition Fund, which offers loans to developers of affordable housing through several partners, including the Local Initiatives Support Corporation. In 2006, Sturz was among the finalists for the first Purpose Prize, a grant by Civic Ventures, a San Francisco–based think tank that recognizes Americans over sixty whose "encore careers" as social entrepreneurs produce the "greatest return on experience." ReServe was also cited by Civic Ventures with its Break-Through Award for innovatively partnering with government agencies to deliver services to a wider constituency. But the Purpose Prize jury was frustrated that, given Sturz's most recent ventures, there was no category for lifetime achievement. "Clearly ReServe was not a post-retirement career," said the author David Bornstein, a member of the jury, "but a new focus area in a life devoted to problem solving and institution building."

Sturz will turn eighty on December 31, 2010. He used to buy books that he hoped to get to when he got around to retiring. Now, he says, he buys books to read. Today, he hopes to continue working "as long as I'm doing something that matters." He has no plans to retire. "Herb," says Carl Weisbrod, "is as much in the game as ever and much of the games he's in are games he manufactured." Gara LaMarche adds, "He has this self-propelled career. There's nothing for him to retire from."

Always Connect

When Herb Sturz and Louis Schweitzer met serendipitously in 1960, neither could have imagined that their initial collaboration would develop into a fruitful union that would eventually produce dozens of offspring. Schweitzer died in 1971, but in over nearly a half century, Vera and its offshoots have profoundly improved the delivery of services and redefined the debate over criminal justice and social welfare in the United States and now also overseas.

"Picking only one thing," Sturz's friend and former colleague, Fritz Schwarz, notes, "Vera is an incredible accomplishment, when you think about going from an editor of a boys' magazine to a highly innovative head of a criminal justice agency."

Sturz "is someone to whom mayors and presidents turn when they want to appraise social policy—and make it happen," according to Jack Rosenthal. "Herb threads filaments of self-interest from person to person into webs of accomplishment."

When Sturz is asked how he seamlessly wove disparate threads together, he can answer almost by rote, producing a deceptively simple rule book of maxims that would serve any innovator well: "'Surround' problems. Talk with everyone, whether centrally or peripherally engaged. Test insights and facts against each other. Read. Observe. Learn by intervening. Initiate pilot efforts; most depend on both public and private sectors to succeed. Articulate goals in unthreatening language. Give credit to public agencies. They need it. That's where the dollars are."

What have those dollars bought? Nearly fifty years since his award-winning series in *Boys' Life* transformed Sturz from an accomplished writer and editor into a full-time, certified reformer and social entrepreneur, he could claim credit for an incredible list of accomplishments. Asked to itemize the achievements that he values most, he puts aside his customary modesty for a moment: "Devising alternatives for easing the lives of skid row derelicts, addicts, homeless and home-bound, persons in jail awaiting trial, kids on the streets after school, victims of crime." To accomplish those goals, Sturz "created an array of self-sustaining nonprofits that build up and carry forward cutting-edge reforms led by entrepreneurial individuals who develop their own initiatives, creating a dynamic for constructive change. And in the course of doing so, thousands have committed their careers to the public interest."

Even if, as Gara LaMarche laments, from the Bowery to South Africa, in classrooms around the country and courtrooms all over the globe, virtually none of the beneficiaries of Herb Sturz's vision have heard of him, the protégés whom he implanted and inspired who regard Sturz as their mentor enrich his legacy.

He, in turn, has his own heroes (whom he shrewdly lists alphabetically). They include his wife, Elizabeth, who was there from the beginning, Louis Schweitzer, George

Soros, Jack Rosenthal, Carl Weisbrod, Jay Kriegel, Burke Marshall, Robert F. Kennedy, the author Susan Sheehan, who has chronicled the plight of the underclass, Willie Mays, the star outfielder of the former New York Giants (who redeemed Sturz's faith in underdogs by winning the World Series), Cedric de Beer and other colleagues such as Amalia Betanzos, Ed Geffner, Paul Samuels, Fritz Schwarz, Dan Freed and Patricia M. Wald, who later served with distinction as chief judge of the U.S. Court of Appeals for the District of Columbia.

Sturz has instilled them with his credo in times when social reform seemed attainable and in times when it did not. His record is all the more impressive considering the challenges he took on, the times in which he pursued them, the risky solutions he advanced and his counter-intuitive strategy of divesting subsidiaries when they succeed. There were a few mistakes, of course, or missteps, although he learned from them, too. The biggest setback in a professional career that spanned more than half a century was when he was fired as deputy mayor—a demotion in name only, as it turned out. When asked what Sturz has done wrong in his life or could have done better, Fritz Schwarz replied, "Like Eisenhower said when he was asked about Nixon's accomplishments, give me a week and I'll think of one." Gara LaMarche points out: "In entrepreneurship, there's a high probability of failure. If you asked in Herb Sturz's case what the failures are, that would be a hard question to answer."

"When you think of the things he attempted, but didn't succeed at, there are very few," Carl Weisbrod notes. "The root question to Herb is, were there things that he never attempted? Is it like a prosecutor with a 100 percent conviction rate? Were there more things he didn't attempt because they would have taken too long or wouldn't succeed?"

There is no denying that, beginning with bail reform, Sturz has been instrumental in fundamentally altering practice and public perception of a broad range of society's toughest problems. The United States may be the only developed nation in which bail is still partially a private prerogative subject to the discretion of bondsmen, but the parameters of who is eligible and when are very different from the system that existed when Vera was born nearly fifty years ago. "Herb revolutionized a system that was un-changed in 400 years of American jurisprudence," Jay Kriegel says. "His approach has been incremental; the results—in that case—were revolutionary, in others, profound."

"Many of Herb's ideas are simple and relatively small," Nick Katzenbach, the former attorney general, says. "They don't seem grand enough for political appeal and aren't likely to be taken up by government agencies. But they work, and sometimes grow into programs of significance."

His friend Peter Goldmark Jr. says Sturz has "incubated and launched more ingenious social change experiments and in tougher contexts than any other living American—by a large margin. He is the Michael Jordan of social change over the last half century in the area of domestic American policy. His fingerprints, programmatic offspring, and re-form children and grandchildren are all over the domestic landscape."

Crime victims and potential targets are being afforded safe havens. Alcoholics are treated as victims, not criminals. Outpatient methadone programs have transformed many addicts into functioning human beings. More public and private institutions are benefiting from an infusion of retired people who are being compensated for their expe-rience and expertise. More American children are partici-pating in constructive after-school activities, and that those programs need to be provided is being elevated to a universal premise. In 2008, when Project Renewal celebrated its fortieth anniversary, a forty-eight-bed experimental detox unit on the Bowery had grown to thirty-five programs with 600 employees and a budget of $40 million serving thousands of homeless New Yorkers. Hundreds of thousands of South Africans are living in houses that would not exist except for NURCHA.

"He is unique," says Joel L. Fleishman, a public policy professor at Duke, "in the number of successful, socially beneficial organizational start-ups to his credit."

David Bornstein, author of *How to Change the World: Social Entrepreneurs and the Power of New Ideas*, describes Sturz as a "serial social entrepreneur" armed with singular skills that have enabled him to leverage private efforts at reform to reimagine government. "The way you achieve greatest impact is not by building a parallel system, but by getting into the DNA of government and the vast maze of existing institutions," Bornstein says. "Getting systems to change is very tough—harder than building something new. It takes a different set of skills and a different vision. You have to understand those systems deeply, have to respect them and the people in them, have to know how to appreciate and influence others, because you are trying to bring change in areas beyond your control. One of the core behavioral definitions of entrepreneurship is leveraging resources you don't control. That seems to be key to Sturz's approach: Borrow, or redirect, an army."

For a man most people haven't heard of, Sturz has made an enormous difference, divining the means and motives to change perceptions, to galvanize unlikely partnerships and to bring the intellectual and political resources to bear on seemingly intractable challenges, combining an agile mind with a carefully calibrated moral compass to navigate from a vague, even fanciful, idea to an enduring, replicable solution. "He has an exquisite sense of the possible," Weisbrod has said, "and, unlike most creative people, he has the ability to turn his creativity into practical programs."

Sturz has also been endowed with the intellectual tools not only to have invented an entire new dimension of social entrepreneurship but to have excelled in it. For a personally unassuming man who operated for decades unobtrusively, largely in the dark, Sturz has cast a remarkably broad shadow. Two of his closest friends have attributed him, interestingly, with the qualities of a successful spy. He is capable of insinuating himself into other people's heads to plumb *their* motivations, and of planting a cadre of agents both to carry out his mission and to call on as needed. Both friends said they meant the comparison as a compliment.

"Herb is the reincarnation of someone who's head of the CIA," Fritz Schwarz (who was counsel to the Senate Select Committee on Intelligence, the Church Committee, in the mid-1970s) notes. "He is never going to forget what he wants to get accomplished. But he also has the good will and the charm, so when he comes to me, I don't care that he also has an agenda. If he were a different kind of person, you wouldn't like it."

Weisbrod credits Sturz with a remarkable ability to create a network "almost like a spymaster who places moles in various organizations and ten years later they flower."

Stephen Lefkowitz, the lawyer who helped fend off the legal challenges to Times Square's revival, invokes another shadowy figure to describe Sturz's talent: T. S. Eliot's "McCavity the Mystery Cat," the one who escapes detection. Sturz, like McCavity, is "the Hidden Paw."

The only thing about Sturz that is out-sized, that goes well beyond what might have been expected or even what a person with comparable potential might have accomplished, is his legacy. It is all the more remarkable because Sturz did not begin with, and never visualized, a road map of where his curiosity might lead him. "I didn't have a vision, but I didn't think I'd be working for *Boys' Life* forever either," Sturz says. "When I started Vera I didn't know where it was going. I knew I cared about the problems."

Nor did he know where he would wind up when he audaciously wrote to John Steinbeck in 1953, connecting the land turtle's perilous journey across the highway to the Okies' equally determined crossing to the other side of a continent. One prominent critic, Frederick J. Hoffman, had branded the inner chapters of *The Grapes of Wrath* "some of the most wretched violations of aesthetic taste observable in modern American fiction." Sturz, however, was mesmerized by what Steinbeck described as his "psychological trick" of endowing an ordinary turtle—"turning aside for nothing," seeding new life along its path with the barley beards and clover burrs and wild oat heads that rolled from its back and fell to the ground, crushing a pesky red ant, straining to right itself after being flipped by the front tire of a careening truck—as an allegory for a larger struggle.

And, after all, what was the story of Tom Joad, who delivers the turtle as a gift for his kid brother, but a story of prisoner re-entry, an inmate released with government-issued shoes that pinched his feet but did not cramp his spirit to return to fit into society? As a kid, Sturz rooted for last-place teams. "It's not just about compassion," he explained, "it's what we do to help the downtrodden, the weary, rather than how we change the system." And if improving their lot individually eventually produced systemic change, all the better.

John Steinbeck once elaborated on the aphorism that people make plans and God laughs at them. "A journey is a person in itself; no two are alike," he wrote. "And all plans, safeguards, policing and coercion are fruitless. We find that after years of struggle that we do not take a trip; a trip takes us." Still, in everyone, consciously and sometimes not, a moral compass suggests a direction if not always a destination. "It wasn't luck that I learned about bail reform," Sturz says, "but you knew it had to be luck that I met Louis Schweitzer and he was interested in bail at the same moment that Robert Kennedy became attorney general."

If he had stayed in Spain as a novelist, if he had not so graphically reminded Americans as an editor at *Boys' Life* of the gift of the Bill of Rights, if he had not read Simone de Beauvoir's *The Coming of Age* in Paris, it is safe to say that our lives would be the poorer for it.

For nearly a half century, Sturz's intellectual curiosity, energy and embrace of daunting challenges combined with his grasp of human nature and commitment to see his endeavors through have produced a remarkable record of achievement. He has not radically changed the world, but, by dint of a kind of genius, he has improved the lives of untold numbers of people—the prostitute whom he sent back home to Ohio, the defendants in Brooklyn and Britain and Russia who, unable to make bail, might have languished in prison, the kids who would have been home alone after school watching television—or worse—instead of playing sports or learning a musical instrument or brushing up on biology; the black South African who would otherwise have been relegated to raising a family in a corrugated hut; the ex-inmate who, because his record was expunged, was able to get and hold a job as the head of Argus Community, the program for teenagers and adults that Elizabeth Sturz founded in the Bronx; the woman provided with a safe haven from her abusive husband; the former addict who might have died from AIDS or hepatitis or have robbed or killed to support his habit; the crime victim who otherwise might have been forgotten by an overwhelmed bureaucracy stretched so thin that it becomes more concerned about crime than about justice; Gloria Spagnoli, a retired social worker who, through ReServe, counsels seniors at Goddard Riverside Community Center; Dr. Bob Morgan "leaning over the bed of a patient who probably had never been cared for" and even the countless authors (and critics) who have been heartened by Sturz's recollections of the transformational correspondence from John Steinbeck, the first man to take him seriously.

Immortality takes many forms. Under a protective sheet of Plexiglas on her desk, Elizabeth George, the author of the Thomas Lynley mysteries, keeps a copy of John Steinbeck's 1952 letter to Herb Sturz. "I find his comments about critics particularly smile-producing," George wrote. While critics view writers as "groping their way up the staircase of immortality," Steinbeck observed, "most good writers I know have no time for immortality."

Sturz wrote Steinbeck that he was moved most by "the poetry, the toughness and integrating beauty" of the inner chapters of *The Grapes of Wrath*, chapters that some critics derided. He was especially taken with the third chapter, by the metaphorical land turtle's tortuous, but tenacious trajectory dodging obstacles as he struggles to traverse a treacherous strip of concrete. The other side, of a highway, of a fence, of a mountain, physical or figurative, always holds promise, for all creatures. Sometimes it is about survival, but what distinguishes human beings, Steinbeck wrote, is that beyond the bare requisites of reproducing, "man wants to leave some record of himself, a proof, perhaps, that he has really existed. He leaves his proof on wood, on stone, or on the lives of other people. This deep desire exists in everyone, from the boy who scribbles on a wall to the Buddha who etches his image in the race mind. Life is so unreal. I think that we seriously doubt that we exist and go about trying to prove that we do."

"Man," Steinbeck wrote, "unlike any other thing organic or inorganic in the universe, grows beyond his work, walks up the stairs of his concepts, emerges ahead of his accomplishments."

After Sturz survived polio as a teenager, he decided to become more serious, to make his life more meaningful, perhaps to leave a record of himself on the lives of other people. He found the gumption to seek validation directly from Steinbeck and he got it. "It gave me incredible confidence," he recalled, "that I really could accomplish whatever I put my mind to." Over fifty years, he has never stopped growing, never stopped working, never stopped accomplishing.

———

If you ask Herb Sturz to reflect on his accomplishments in fifty years as a social engineer and a social entrepreneur, he will more likely tell you what he did that day at lunch. Which says a lot about him, how he works and how much he's accomplished. On one day the question was posed, he was juggling two daunting challenges. The first dealt with the subprime mortgage mess. As chairman of Mayor Bloomberg's Center for New York City Neighborhoods, he was meeting with housing officials to see what steps—from weeding gardens to literally fixing broken windows—could be taken to mitigate the impact of foreclosures in communities with a critical mass of properties that had been abandoned or foreclosed. "A silent heart attack," he called it. At the same time, pursuing his goal of double social utility, he was conferring with officials of the city's Human Resources

Administration to determine whether, and how, Wildcat workers could be enlisted to perform that maintenance. How could banks and other private institutions be enlisted as partners? How could the city's cumbersome competitive bidding process be bypassed or abridged in time to forestall further deterioration, vandalism or panic selling by vulnerable neighbors?

The second challenge that day dealt more directly with criminal justice. It was prompted by a speech that Jeremy Travis had delivered not long before to the bar association. Travis talked about the vast number of New Yorkers—most of them black, Hispanic, male and young—who were stopped and frisked and the impact of those encounters on the community's perception of the police. A former Lindsay administration colleague, Fred Nathan, invited his cousin, Michael Cardozo, the city's corporation counsel, to lunch, during which Sturz gently pointed out that the police stopped and frisked 600,000 people the year before, but only about 10 percent were arrested. "600,000," Sturz repeated. "Doesn't that seem like a lot?" Another lunch followed, this one with the deputy police commissioner for legal matters, who happened to be a Vera alumnus. Nudging unrelentingly, Sturz pokes and prods until the system responds.

It was never easy, not during the post-Watergate era when even liberals were suspicious of government, not during the Reagan administration when budget cutting was a vehicle for shrinking government, not during the Bush years when Washington expanded the federal bureaucracy by investing in homeland security (and foreign wars) and in bailing out companies that contributed to the subprime crisis, and not even during the early days of the Great Society programs when Sturz began forging public-private partnerships that challenged government prerogatives. Remembering Vera's earliest ventures in criminal justice with City Hall's blessing, Sturz recalls Burke Marshall marveling: "It was insane that Wagner and the courts let us in."

But they did. And with that first opening, Sturz embarked on a career that would be validated again and again by what he brought to the table: starting always on the ground knowing what you don't know and nimbly adapting to the fact that the goal line will keep shifting in the course of making anything happen that matters, transforming problems into elements of the solution. Sturz approached every challenge with a singular strategy: discovering government's enlightened self-interest.

He would repeatedly apply the same methodology to his many social experiments: "Expand the scope of people's lives, opening opportunities perceived hopelessly distant or forever closed. Help make life fairer and achieve more decent treatment of society's 'losers,' cost-effectively and measurably. Turn liabilities into assets."

His philosophy, he says, "applies to place as well as persons—whether a South African township or Times Square." Any number of Herb Sturz's catchphrases reveal his mind at work. One, the simple sign that hangs on the wall of the Herb Sturz–Burke Marshall Conference Room at the Vera Institute in Manhattan, speaks volumes. It reads: "Learning by doing."

Herb Sturz has followed his own advice. Like Steinbeck's gutsy land turtle, he relentlessly pursued his goals, not always sure where he would wind up, but deftly dodging obstacles, willing to stick his neck out and sowing seeds of new life in his wake. Struz connected. He did things. He kept learning. And then he did some more.

Acknowledgments

This book would not have been possible without the cooperation, energy, candor, indulgence and genius of Herb Sturz. Whatever benefits the book provides to others, I'm grateful that it
presented an opportunity for Herb and me to get to know each
other better.

Three other principals made this book possible and their support is enormously appreciated: Peter Osnos, the astute founder of
PublicAffairs; Jack Rosenthal, my wise friend and fellow *Times*-
man; and Gara LaMarche and his generous colleagues at Atlantic
Philanthropies.

Thanks to my other partners in this project, including the
present and former officials of Vera and its offspring and of
the other ventures with which Herb has been associated—
especially Carl Weisbrod and Jeremy Travis—who very graciously
took the time to collect and contribute their recollections and to
vet my research, including:

Claire Haaga Altman, Cedric de Beer, Greg Berman, Mary
Ellen Boyd, Stan Brezenoff, Amanda Burden, Kate Chieco, John
Feinblatt, Joel Fleishman, Lucy N. Friedman, Peter Goldmark,
Betsy Gotbaum, Bill Grinker, Michael Jacobson, Fred Harris, Nick
Katzenbach, Jay Kriegel, Stephen Lefkowitz, Ken Marion, Rose-
mary Masters, Aryeh Neier, Anne Rankin, Paul Samuels, Ellen
Schall, George Soros, Bill Stern, Elizabeth Lyttleton Sturz, Mindy
Tarlow, Franklin Thomas, Patricia M. Wald, Michael Weinstein,
and Robert V. Wolf.

Charles R. Morris contributed thorough and insightful research into Vera and Herb Sturz.

Through their reporting, my *Times* colleagues, especially Martin Gottlieb, David Dunlap, Charles Bagli, Leslie Eaton, Leslie

Kaufman, Jan Hoffman, Sara Rimer, Paul von Zielbauer and Joyce Purnick, contributed mightily to an appreciation of the issues. I very much appreciate the unflagging support, encouragement, professionalism, and friendship of my editors, in particular, Joe Sexton and Jim Dao.

Thanks, too, to others who took the time to be interviewed, including Ed Koch, Mario Cuomo, Robert Morgenthau, Victor Gotbaum, Marian Heiskell, John Mollenkopf, Howard Rubenstein, Michael Mushlin, Gerry Schoenfeld, William Zeckendorf Jr., Cora Cahan, Joel L. Fleishman, David Bornstein, Vincent Tese, Natalie d'Arbeloff, Elizabeth's daughter Anna Wood; and to ever-helpful archivists and researchers, especially Jeff Roth of the *Times*; Dr. Richard K. Lieberman, director of the La Guardia and Wagner Archives at La Guardia Community College of the City University of New York; Brian G. Andersson, commissioner of the New York City Department of Records and Information Services; Leonora Gidlund, director of the Municipal Archives; David Smith of the New York Public Library; and to Jeff Zachowski.

At PublicAffairs, thanks especially to Susan Weinberg; to my unfailingly gracious editor, Morgen Van Vorst; to Whitney Peeling, Melissa Raymond, Meredith Smith, and Norman MacAfee for their professionalism, thoroughness and commitment.

At the Open Society Institute, none of this would have been possible without Amy Anderson.

My deepest gratitude to Shelby White, for her support and hospitality, and to Karen Salerno, Paul Neuthaler, Richard Mittenthal, Patsy Glazer, Marty Matz, and Elizabeth Grant (they know why they're here).

Above all, thanks to Mike, Will, and Sophie Roberts, and especially to Marie, for their endurance, confidence (they helped transform the subject of this book from "Herb who?" to folk hero) and affection, and for making me laugh.

A Note on Sources

This book is about a man who has affected countless lives, but whom not many people know—even by name. Which means not much has been written about him before—about who he is, where he comes from, what shaped him and his agenda, how he operates, what he's accomplished—either in popular publications or more esoteric journals.

He could have written this book but chose not to. So the author relied on a documentary trail and on the recollections and perceptions of friends, adversaries, people intimately involved in the cause of social justice and others deeply affected by it. Herb Sturz cooperated fully and was completely accessible, but the author's analyses and conclusions were not subject to his review.

Some of the background about the organizations with which he has been affiliated (including the Vera Institute of Justice, the Center for Court Innovation, The After-School Corporation, Re-Serve, NURCHA) comes from their analyses and annual reports. Charles Morris's valuable early research into Sturz and his record were enormously helpful.

Most of the direct quotations and anecdotes in the book are from personal and written interviews with the sources themselves. Those individuals include Herb Sturz, Lynn Barendsen, Cedric de Beer, Greg Berman, David Bornstein, Stan Brezenoff, Amanda Burden, Mario Cuomo, Natalie d'Arbeloff, John Feinblatt, Joel Fleishman, Lucy N. Friedman, Peter Goldmark, Betsy Gotbaum, Victor Gotbaum, Bill Grinker, Fred Harris, Marian Heiskell, Michael Jacobson, Nick Katzenbach, Ed Koch, Jay Kriegel, Gara LaMarche, Stephen Lefkowitz, Ken Marion, Rosemary Masters, John Mollenkopf, Robert Morgenthau, Michael Mushlin, Aryeh Neier, Anne Rankin, Jack Rosenthal, Howard Rubenstein, Gerry

Schoenfeld, George Soros, Bill Stern, Elizabeth Lyttleton Sturz, Mindy Tarlow, Vincent Tese, Franklin Thomas, Jeremy Travis, Patricia M. Wald, Michael Weinstein, Carl Weisbrod and William Zeckendorf Jr.

In addition, a number of alumni of Vera and its offspring generously contributed written reminiscences, vetted the recollections of others or both. They include Claire Haaga Altman, Greg Berman, Lucy Friedman, Mindy Tarlow, Jeremy Travis and Carl Weisbrod.

Much of the material on New York City's fiscal crisis, the Summer of Sam, the Lindsay, Beame and Koch administrations and the tortured route of the Westway project is drawn from my own contemporaneous reporting, first for the *New York Daily News* and then for the *New York Times* (and extensive interviews with, among others, Mario Cuomo, Daniel Patrick Moynihan, David Rockefeller and Robert F. Wagner Jr.). Other newspaper sources include the *New York Post*, the *Wall Street Journal* and the *Bayonne Times*.

Periodical articles referenced include Daniel Patrick Moynihan's seminal essay, "Defining Deviancy Down" (*American Scholar,* Winter, 1993); Herbert Sturz, editor, "America's Heritage: The Bill of Rights" (reprinted from *Boys' Life*); George L. Kelling and James Q. Wilson, "Broken Windows" (*The Atlantic,* March 1982); Roger L. Martin and Sally Osberg, "Social Entrepreneurship: The Case for Definition" (*Stanford Social Innovation Review,* Spring 2007); Cyril D. Robinson, "A Proposal for a Heroin Maintenance Experiment in New York City: The Limits of Reform Strategy" (*Contemporary Crises,* 1978); and Candace McCoy, "Caleb Was Right: Pretrial Decisions Determine Mostly Everything" (*Berkeley Journal of Criminal Law,* forthcoming Fall 2008, http://web.gc.cuny .edu/criminaljustice/pages/faculty/Calebwasright.pdf.pdf.).

Archival sources consulted include a trove of personal papers belonging to Herb Sturz (including a copy of the screenplay for "The Peacemaker," by Natalie d'Arbeloff and Herb Sturz); the Koch Collection at the La Guardia and Wagner Archives of La-

Guardia Community College of the City University of New York, which included official correspondence documents; and the Lucille Lortel papers at the Library for the Performing Arts at Lincoln Center.

Among the books that provided background and additional insights were:

Henry J. Aaron, *Politics and the Professors: The Great Society in Perspective* (Washington, D.C.: Brookings Institution, 1978).

Wayne Barrett, *Rudy!: An Investigative Biography of Rudolph Giuliani* (New York: Basic Books, 2000).

Simone de Beauvoir, *The Coming of Age,* translated by Patrick O'Brian (New York: Putnam, 1972).

Greg Berman and John Feinblatt, *Good Courts: The Case for Problem-Solving Justice* (New York: The New Press, 2005).

Marshall Berman, *On the Town: One Hundred Years of Spectacle in Times Square* (New York: Random House, 2006).

David Bornstein, *How to Change the World* (New York: Oxford University Press, 2007).

Robert A. Caro, *The Power Broker: Robert Moses and the Fall of New York* (New York: Alfred A. Knopf, 1974).

Benjamin Jacob Chesluk, *Money Jungle: Imagining the New Times Square* (New Brunswick, N.J.: Rutgers University Press, 2008).

T. S. Eliot, *Old Possum's Book of Practical Cats* (New York: Harcourt Brace Jovanovich, 1982).

Daniel J. Freed and Patricia M. Wald, *Bail in the United States* (Washington, D.C.: National Conference on Bail and Criminal Justice Working Paper, 1964).

Josh Alan Friedman, *Tales of Times Square* (New York: Doubleday, 1986).

Michael Goodwin, editor, *New York Comes Back: The Mayoralty of Edward I. Koch* (New York: Museum of the City of New York/PowerHouse Books, 2005).

Barry Gottehrer, *The Mayor's Man* (Garden City, N.Y.: Doubleday, 1975).

Roberta Brandes Gratz, *The Living City* (New York: Simon and Schuster, 1989).

David Halberstam, *The Fifties* (New York: Villard Books, 1993).

Edward I. Koch (with William Rauch), *Mayor* (New York: Simon and Schuster, 1984).

Leaders in Government Symposium, *The Koch Administration: "How'm I Doin'?"* (Stony Brook: State University of New York, 2002).

Paul C. Light, *The Search for Social Entrepreneurship* (Washington, D.C.: Brookings Institution Press, 2008).

Robert J. MacCoun and Peter Reuter, *Drug War Heresies: Learning from Other Places, Other Times and Other Vices* (Cambridge: Cambridge University Press, 2001).

Martin Mayer, *The Lawyers* (New York: Harper & Row, 1967).

John H. Mollenkopf, *A Phoenix in the Ashes: The Rise and Fall of the Koch Coalition in New York City Politics* (Princeton, N.J.: Princeton University Press, 1992).

Sylvia Nasar, *A Beautiful Mind: A Biography of John Forbes Nash, Jr., Winner of the Nobel Prize in Economics, 1994* (New York: Simon & Schuster, 1999).

Jacob A. Riis, *The Battle with the Slum* (New York: Macmillan, 1902).

Lynne B. Sagalyn, *Times Square Roulette: Remaking the City Icon* (Cambridge, Mass.: MIT Press, 2001).

Charles L. Schultze, Edward R. Fried, Alice M. Rivlin and Nancy H. Teeters, *Setting National Priorities: The 1973 Budget* (Washington, D.C.: The Brookings Institution, 1972).

Frederick F. Siegel (with Harry Siegel), *The Prince of the City: Giuliani, New York, and the Genius of American Life* (San Francisco: Encounter Books, 2005).

Roger Starr, *The Rise and Fall of New York City* (New York: Basic Books, 1985).

John Steinbeck, *The Grapes of Wrath* (New York: Chelsea House Publishers, 1988).

Robert A. M. Stern, David Fishman and Jacob Tilove, *New York 2000: Architecture and Urbanism Between the Bicentennial and the Millennium* (New York: Monacelli Press, 2006).

Robert A. M. Stern, Thomas Mellins and David Fishman, *New York 1960: Architecture and Urbanism Between the Second World War and the Bicentennial* (New York: Monacelli Press, 1995).

Elizabeth Lyttleton Sturz and Herbert Sturz, *Reapers of the Storm* (London: D. Dobson, 1958).

Herbert Sturz, *Midtown Development Project: Draft Report* (New York: Department of City Planning, 1980).

James Traub, *The Devil's Playground: A Century of Pleasure and Profit in Times Square* (New York: Random House, 2004).

Robert F. Wagner Jr., editor, *New York Ascendant* (New York: The Commission on the Year 2000, 1987).

William H. Whyte, *The Social Life of Small Urban Spaces* (Washington, D.C.: Conservation Foundation, 1980).

William H. Whyte, *City: Rediscovering the Center* (New York: Doubleday, 1988).

James Q. Wilson, *Thinking About Crime* (New York: Basic Books, 1983).

Index

Abzug, Bella, 233
Accountability, 105, 126, 180, 273, 279, 286, 287, 292, 305
Actors Equity, 278
Adams, Mildred, 282
Adam's Rib (Herschberger), 18
Addiction Research and Treatment Corporation, 114
Adolescents/teenagers, 20, 26, 31, 34, 36, 37, 48, 70, 143, 227, 228, 323. *See also* After-school programs; Juveniles
Afterschool Alliance, 305
After-school programs, 6, 110, 210, 302–307, 316
Agriculture Department, 6
AIDS/HIV, 103, 106, 110–111, 177, 260, 320
Air rights, 248
Alcoholism, 5, 8, 83, 87, 94, 99, 109, 110, 111, 112, 316. *See also* Drunkenness; Manhattan Bowery Project
Allen, Frank, 53. *See also* Committee on Poverty and the Administration of Criminal Justice
Allen, Michael (Reverend), 83
Altman, Benjamin, 173
Altman, Claire Haaga, 308
Altman, Roger, 173
American Bar Association, 22, 55
American Friends Service Committee, 17
Americans with Disabilities Act, 110
"America's Heritage: The Bill of Rights" (Sturz), 22–23, 27, 32, 38
America Works, 137
AmeriCorps, 211
Anderson, David C., 285–286, 289
Ares, Charles, 52

Argentina, 20
Argus Community, 320
Arrests. *See under* Criminal justice system
Arson/Arson Strike Force, 150, 183–184, 275
Arthur Liman Policy Institute, 111
Ashoka organization, 267
Atlantic City, 259

Baby boomers, 35
Badillo, Herman, 171–172
Bail, 3, 7, 8, 25–28, 40, 69, 170, 220
    vs. bond, 26
    bondsmen, 42–43, 47–48, 59, 68, 316
    collateral for, 47
    consequences of bail system, 37–38
    data concerning, 54, 57–58, 61, 67
    federal bail reform bill, 68 (*see also* Reforms: bail reform)
    and imprisonments, 61, 62
    inability to make bail, 26–27, 42, 50, 65, 72, 77, 259 (*see also* Criminal justice system: detentions before trial *and* correlations between bail and sentencing issues)
    origin and history of, 27–28
    questions/research concerning, 42, 52–53, 76
    risks concerning, 47–48, 50, 56–57, 59, 61, 71
    See also Manhattan Bail Project; Reforms: bail reform; Vera Institute: underwriting own bail fund
Baker, R. Palmer, 89, 90, 91, 97, 101, 107

Baltimore, 126
Barendsen, Lynn, 14, 267
Baron, Roger, 58, 65, 66–67, 72
Barr, Stringfellow, 32
Barrett, Wayne, 199
Bartholet, Elizabeth, 104, 107
Battery Park City Authority, 144
Bayonne, New Jersey, 11, 12, 13
Bayonne Times, 12, 21
Bazelon, David, 52
Beacon, Kalif, 259
Beacon Schools initiative, 258
Beame, Abraham D., 131–132, 133,
        150, 152, 154, 156, 169, 197,
        208, 225, 258
Beeley, Arthur Lawton, 28
"Before the Mellowing Year" (Sturz),
        20
Bellamy, Carol, 136, 197
Berger, Meyer, 31
Berkeley, Norborne, Jr., 124, 137,
        165
Berkowitz, David. *See* Son of Sam
Berman, Greg, 291–292, 294–295
Berman, Marshall, 224, 230, 248
Bernard, Mitchell, 2326
Bernstein, Richard K., 216
Betanzos, Amalia, 142, 145, 315
Bill of Rights, 22–23, 29, 31, 32, 33,
        112, 320
Black Panthers, 49
Blacks, 39, 108, 114, 116, 166, 187,
        200, 202, 203, 209, 210, 258,
        300, 323
Bloch, Abraham M., 49
Bloodletting (therapeutic), 118–120
Bloomberg, Michael R., 144, 206,
        291, 309, 310
Blue Ridge Foundation, 308
Bonfire of the Vanities (Wolfe), 276
Bookstaver, David, 290
Bornstein, David, 271–272, 312, 317
Botein, Bernard, 40, 41, 63, 64, 67,
        69, 72, 74, 75, 90, 239
Botstein, Leon, 305
Bouza, Anthony, 157
Boyd, Mary Ellen, 146
Boys' Life, 22, 28, 32, 38, 112, 320
Bradley, Bill, 124
Brecht, Bertolt, 30
Brennan, William J., 29, 52

Breslin, Jimmy, 141, 149–150, 152
Brezenoff, Stan, 133, 163
Britain, 4, 145, 209, 294, 320
Broken-windows theory, 229–230
Brookings Institution, 5, 104–105
Brown, David, 157
Brown, Edmund G., Jr., (Jerry), 207
Brown, Lee P., 280
Brown, Michael, 206
Brown, Richard A., 148, 153
Buckley, James, 136
Buckley, William F., Jr., 208
Buffalo, New York, 109
Bundy, McGeorge, 118, 119
Burden, Amanda, 283–284, 286
Bush, George W., 6, 323
Butzel, Albert, 236

Cahan, Cora, 250
Califano, Joseph, 107, 140
California Conservation Corps, 207
Campbell, Gordon, 179
Camp La Guardia (Orange County,
        NY), 86–87, 100
Canada, Geoffrey, 258, 305
Candler Building, 250–251
Cardozo, Michael, 323
Carey, Hugh L., 180, 198, 202
Caro, Robert A., 7
CASES. *See* Center for Alternative
        Sentencing and Employment
        Services
Castro, Fidel, 30
Catskills hotels, 87
Cavanagh, James A., 132
Cecil Hotel (Harlem), 102
Center for Alternative Sentencing
        and Employment Services
        (CASES), 70–71
Center for Court Innovation,
        291–292, 294, 308
Center for Employment
        Opportunities, 146
Center for New York City
        Neighborhoods, 309, 322
Center for the Study of Democratic
        Institutions (Santa Barbara),
        33
CETA. *See* Comprehensive
        Employment and Training Act

Chase, Gordon, 118
Chesluk, Benjamin, 277
Chess, 14, 125
Chile, 4, 145
Citizens Crime Commission, 280
Citylights, 264–266
City University of New York, 122
Ciuros, William J., Jr., 181–182
Civic Ventures Purpose Prize,
    311–312
Civilian Conservation Corps, 207
Civil liberties/libertarians, 31, 33,
    39, 51, 95
Civil Rights Law (1964), 108
Class-action lawsuits, 108
Clinton, Bill, 6, 211
Cohn, Frederick H., 279
Columbia Teachers College, 20
Coming of Age, The (de Beauvoir),
    307, 320
Commager, Henry Steele, 33
Committee on Poverty and the
    Administration of Criminal
    Justice (Allen Committee),
    53–54, 55
Common law, English, 27
Common sense, 81, 155, 212, 286
Communism, 32, 39
Community court, 7. *See also*
    Criminal justice system:
    Midtown Community Court
Comprehensive Employment and
    Training Act (CETA), 129, 175
Computers, 147, 171, 180, 283, 287
Connolly, Dave, 288–289
Constitution, 28, 29. *See also* Bill of
    Rights; Sixth Amendment;
    Eighth Amendment;
    Fourteenth Amendment
Cooperatives, 103, 264, 265
Cosell, Howard, 183
Council on Drug Addiction (New
    York State), 113
Cove, Peter, 137
Crack cocaine, 275
Crawford, Morris D., Jr., 233
Crime, 35, 39, 44, 156, 183, 184,
    207, 223, 225, 227, 237, 277,
    280
  alcoholism as a crime, 87
  crime victims, 7, 67, 78, 158,

273, 291, 316, 321 (*see also*
    New York City: Victim Service
    Agency)
former criminals, 104, 106, 108,
    109, 121, 123, 127, 138, 144,
    166 (*see also* Prison/jail
    populations: and prisoner re-
    entry)
juvenile crime, 180
law-and-order backlash to, 47
major vs. minor criminals, 106
minor offenses/misdemeanors,
    274, 277, 281, 284 (*see also*
    Disorderly conduct)
petty larceny, 77, 79
poverty as a crime, 50
restitution for, 175
sex offenders, 77
shoplifting, 77, 284
simple assault, 74, 77, 79
victimless crimes, 286
violent crime, 70, 180, 274, 275,
    276, 278 (*see also* Domestic
    violence)
See also under Drug addiction
Criminal justice system, 3, 7, 17, 28,
    29, 38, 43–44, 154
arraignments, 57, 67, 74, 86, 153,
    274, 287
arrests, 69, 72, 74, 75, 76, 78, 79,
    150, 152, 186, 227, 273–274,
    277, 281, 285, 323 (*see also*
    Drunkenness: arresting
    drunks)
backlog of cases, 72
community service sentences,
    286, 287, 288, 293
correlations between bail and
    sentencing issues, 51, 54, 62
and dangerousness as criterion for
    release of accused, 154–155
and defendants' roots in
    community, 58, 61, 66, 75, 76,
    78, 153, 155
detentions before trial, 26, 34,
    36, 37, 41, 51, 55, 62, 64, 67,
    68
dismissal of charges, 69
failure to appear at trial, 60, 63,
    64, 65, 67, 68, 148, 155
and inability to afford lawyer, 40

Midtown Community Court,
    277–291, 293–294
overcrowded facilities, 72, 75
parolees, 186, 292–293
Red Hook Community Justice
    Center, 290, 293
and release on own recognizance,
    57, 58, 60, 61, 62, 64, 73, 153
and right to counsel, 53
speedy trials, 27, 28, 72 (*see also*
    Sixth Amendment)
summons issued, 75–76 (*see also*
    Manhattan Summons Project)
supervised release for felony
    defendants, 148
suspended/reduced sentences, 51
See also Bail; New York City:
    Rikers Island *and* Tombs;
    Police
Crosson, Matthew T., 280
Cuba, 30
Cuomo, Mario, 156, 234, 239, 240,
    241, 242, 250, 265

Dan, Susan, 97, 98
D'Arbeloff, Natalie, 18–20
Davis, Bob, 172
Davis, Gordon, 200
De Beauvoir, Simone, 307, 309, 320
De Beer, Cedric, 298, 299, 300,
    315
Dees, J. Gregory, 266
Defense lawyers, 54, 59, 62, 279,
    288
Denatured alcohol, 83
Department of the Aging (federal),
    139
Derelicts, 82, 118. *See also*
    Manhattan Bowery Project
De Rochemont, Louis, 18, 20–21
Des Moines, Iowa, 173
Detentions. *See* Criminal justice
    system: detentions before trial
Detoxification programs. *See under*
    Drunkenness
Detroit, Michigan, 226
Devil's Playground, The (Traub), 251
Devine, William J., 200
Dewey, John, 15, 164
Dimon, Jamie, 142

Dinkins, David, 132, 169, 203, 249
Disabled/handicapped people, 108,
    110, 124–125, 131, 138, 139,
    140, 141, 210
Discrimination, 106–111
Disney Corporation, 230, 249–249
Disorderly conduct, 74, 75, 79
Domestic violence, 146, 176, 178,
    179, 290, 291, 295
Donovan, Shaun, 309
Douglas, William O., 52
Drayton, William, 267
Dreyfus Corporation, 263
Drug addiction, 8, 36, 48, 70, 77,
    94, 95, 100, 110, 121, 210,
    283, 287, 290, 293
and crime, 112, 113, 115, 117,
    121, 127
and domestic violence, 178
former/recovering addicts, 99,
    104, 106, 108, 111, 123, 125,
    126, 128, 131, 133, 138, 144,
    165–166, 288, 320 (*see also*
    Methadone)
Drug laws, 84, 109
Drug testing, 111
Drunkenness, 72, 74, 82
arresting drunks, 83, 86, 87, 92,
    289
detoxification programs for, 88,
    91, 94, 98, 99, 317
See also Alcoholism; Manhattan
    Bowery Project
Durando, Ernie "The Rock," 11
Durst, Douglas, 250
Dykstra, Gretchen, 250, 281
Dyson, Esther, 305

Eastern Paralyzed Veterans
    Association, 140–141
Easyride, 138–141, 166, 286, 307
Edelstein, Julius C. C., 134
Education, 71, 105, 106, 110, 112,
    145, 166, 203, 248, 259, 307
high school dropouts, 207, 208,
    210, 306
Eighth Amendment, 23, 27, 28, 31
Eisner, Michael, 249
Elderly people, 8, 138, 139, 140,
    210, 211, 212, 307–309, 316

Ellinghaus, William, 124
Employment, 94, 96, 97, 99–100,
    106, 121, 137–138, 139, 140,
    178, 186–189, 212, 248, 289
  discrimination in hiring, 108,
    110, 111
  employed looters during 1977
    blackout in New York, 151
  municipal employees, 129, 132
  supported work programs,
    122–123, 137 (*see also*
    Wildcat Service Corporation)
  transition to full-time, 137, 142,
    143, 187
  welfare to work, 133, 134, 137,
    145
Entrepreneurship, 301, 315, 317. *See
    also* Social entrepreneurship
Ervin, Sam, 67
Europe, 20–21

Failure, 6–7, 270, 315
Farrell, Michael, 149
Federal Housing Administration, 265
Federalism, 29
Feinblatt, John, 175, 176, 277–278,
    283, 286, 290, 291–292
Female juvenile defendants, 71
Feminism, 18
Ferry, W. H., 33
Fifth Amendment, 108
First Amendment, 29, 31
Flax, Sidney, 259
Foote, Caleb, 28, 40, 50–51, 52, 54,
    62
Ford administration, 126
Ford Foundation, 33, 56, 57, 78,
    108, 118–120, 134, 143, 163
Fortas, Abe, 42
Fourteenth Amendment, 53, 108
Franco, Francisco (Generalissimo),
    21, 41
Frankel, Max, 257
Freed, Daniel J., 55, 63, 315
Friedman, Josh Alan, 224
Friedman, Lucy, 147, 174, 178, 179,
    210, 304
Fund for the Republic, 33
Funding issues, 3, 4, 92, 93, 98, 99,
    102, 107, 116, 122, 123,

    125–126, 130–131, 132, 139,
    140, 144, 149, 158, 171, 175,
    241, 270, 273–274, 283, 303,
    305, 306–307, 308, 309. *See
    also* Ford Foundation

Gallent, Martin, 236
Gallo gang, 26
Gardner, John, 270
Garth, David, 240
Geffner, Edward, 96, 98, 315
Gelb, Richard, 124
Genius, 81, 220, 270, 286
Genovese, Vito, 25
George, Elizabeth, 321
Gergen, David, 272
G.I. bill, 110
Gideon v. Wainwright, 53
Girl Scouts, 110
Giuliani, Rudolph, 73, 82, 145, 169,
    189, 249
Goals, 15, 33, 47, 58, 69, 104, 174,
    207, 210, 226, 240, 269, 273,
    281, 282, 304, 314, 322
Gold, Eugene, 173
Goldfeld, Bob, 93–94
Goldmark, Peter, Jr., 4, 273, 316
Goldstein, Abraham, 52
Good Courts (Feinblatt and
    Berman), 292
Gotbaum, Betsy, 130, 138–139, 275,
    311
Gotbaum, Victor, 130, 305
Gottehrer, Barry, 205, 263
Grameen Bank, 269
Grapes of Wrath, The (Steinbeck),
    1–2, 319, 321
Great Depression, 135
Great Society, 5, 7, 104–105, 268,
    270, 323
Griffin, John A., 308
Grinker, William J., 143, 164, 167
Grossman, David, 125, 126, 134
Guinier, Lani, 310
Gutfreund, John, 238

Haaren High School, 20
Hackett, David, 53
Halberstam, David, 5

Harlem Community Justice Center, 290
Harlem Urban Development Corporation, 102
Harnick, Sheldon, 163
Harris, Fred, 298, 299
Hawaii, 110
Hayes, Frederick O'R., 134, 182
Heald, Henry, 118–119
Health care, 97–98, 103, 110, 139, 140, 212, 259. *See also* Medicaid/Medicare
Hearst Advertising Service (New York), 18
Hebrew School, 13
Heiskell, Marian, 249
Helprin, Mark, 261
Herman, Susan, 178
Heroin, 114–117, 124. *See also* Drug addiction
Herschberger, Ruth, 18–19
Hess, Robert V., 103
Highways/expressways, 232, 233, 234
Hispanics, 108, 166, 187, 203, 210, 323
Hogan, Betsy Flower. *See* Gotbaum, Betsy
Hogan, Frank, 5
Hollywood, 289
Homelessness, 8, 82, 91, 93, 95, 96–97, 100, 101–102, 177, 194, 278, 289, 290
Home Relief, 125, 131, 135
Hood, Robert, 6
Hope, 94, 96
Hospitals, 212, 260
Hotlines, 178
Housing, 96, 97, 98, 99, 142, 177, 178, 184, 190, 209, 226, 238, 243, 265, 289
  city lofts, 214–215
  discrimination in, 110
  home ownership/foreclosures, 101, 189, 298, 299
  single room occupancy (SRO) hotels, 101–102, 245
  in South Africa, 297–301, 317
  and subprime mortgage crisis, 309, 322, 323
Housing and Services, Inc., 103
Howards End (Forster), 16

How to Change the World: Social Entrepreneurs and the Power of New Ideas (Bornstein), 272
Hruska, Roman, 65
Human nature, 3, 15, 165, 196
Human Nature and Conduct (Dewey), 15
Hunter College, Brookdale Center on Aging, 139
Huxtable, Ada Louise, 195, 197, 213, 215
Hynes, Charles J., 184, 185, 290

Imagination, 3, 302
Immigrants, 211, 236
Institute for Mediation and Conflict Resolution, 174
International High School (Queens), 259

Jacobs, Jane, 231
Jacobson, Michael, 292
James, W. H., 232
James, William, 16, 81, 219
James Madison Lecture on the Constitution and Bill of Rights, 29
Javits, Jacob, 136
Jewish Child Care Association shelter (Pleasantville, NY), 20
Jewish Science, 14
Job Links, 99–100
Johnson, Lyndon, 5, 55, 68, 104
Johnson, Sterling, Jr., 109
John V. Lindsay Academy, 145
Joyce, James, 270
Justice, 2, 5, 39, 42, 51, 64, 76, 188, 261, 273, 282, 283, 284, 290, 291
  sociology of, 53
Justice Department, 54, 55, 56, 63, 68, 92, 109, 123
Juvenal, 268
Juveniles, 37, 71, 179–180, 290. *See also* Adolescents/teenagers

Kahan, Richard, 231, 239
Kappner, Augusta, 209

Katz, Stanley N., 271
Katzenbach, Nicholas deB., 55, 114, 166, 169, 219, 316
Kaye, Judith, 242, 278, 282
Keating, Robert, 280
Kelling, George L., 229–230
Kelly, Frank, 33
Kelly, Raymond W., 149, 173, 189
Kennedy, John F., 22, 39, 63, 64
Kennedy, Robert F., 53, 55, 63, 64, 68, 315, 320
Kiernan, Betty, 85, 87
King of New York (film), 276
Koch, Edward I., 38, 145, 156, 157, 159, 163, 169–170, 171, 172, 179, 181, 182, 190, 194, 195, 197, 198, 200–201, 203, 206–207, 208, 230
    and Times Square, 214, 224, 235, 237–242, 252
    and Westway, 233
Kopp, Wendy, 269
Kriegel, Jay L., 6, 88, 124, 130, 167, 305, 316
Kross, Anna M., 36, 37, 39, 75
Kuhlman, Charles, 151

Labor Department, 122, 123
La Guardia, Fiorello H., 194
LaMarche, Gara, 4, 6, 7, 219, 302, 303, 306, 309, 310, 312, 315
Landrieu, Mitch, 270
Lapidus, Alan J., 247
Lasker, Morris E., 189–190
Law Enforcement Assistance Administration (federal), 73, 149, 173
Lawyers, The (Mayer), 44, 74, 86
Lazarsfeld, Paul F., 147
Leary, Howard, 165, 182, 239
Lee, Spike, 149
Lefkowitz, Stephen A., 242, 318
Legal Aid Society, 190
Legal issues, 177, 237, 239, 242, 323. *See also* Manhattan Bail Project; Pretrial Services Agency; Vera Institute: Legal Action Center
Lenya, Lotte, 30
Lewis, Anthony, 107

Light, Paul, 268
Liman, Arthur, 107, 109, 111
Lindsay, John V., 6, 73, 88, 113, 116, 163, 169, 205–206, 233, 263, 276
Lippman, Jonathan, 291
Litow, Stanley S., 305
"Little Yellow Dog, The" (Barr), 32
Logue, Edward J., 231
Looting, 150–151, 156
Lord, Day & Lord law firm, 89
Lortel, Lucille, 29–30
Loyalty oath, 17
"Lycidas" (Milton), 20
Lyttleton, Elizabeth, 21–22, 41

McCarthy, Joseph, 16, 22, 31, 32
MacCoun, Robert, 117
McCoy, Candace, 51
McGuire, Robert J., 157, 200, 201
Machiavelli, Niccolò, 164, 166
Macklowe, Harry, 245–246
Mailer, Norman, 18
Manhattan Bail Project, 55–69, 74, 83, 147, 208
    benefits of, 60
    dissatisfaction with, 59–60
    eligibility qualifications, 57–58, 65–66
    as pragmatic approach, 59
    and reminding about court dates, 60, 148
    states influenced by, 67
Manhattan Bowery Project, 8, 82–100, 122, 288, 289, 297
    board of directors, 93, 97
    housing programs of, 98, 99
    identity crisis in, 94–95
    management, 92–93
    medical director for, 90–91
    as Project Renewal, 96–100, 317
Manhattan Court Employment Project, 69–71, 112
Manhattan Summons Project, 76–79, 81, 84
Manpower Demonstration Research Corporation, 126, 137, 143
Marden, Orison S., 90
Marion, Ken, 17, 123, 124
Marriott Marquis hotel, 247

Marshall, Burke, 54–55, 90, 96, 107, 158, 315, 324
Marshall, Thurgood, 110
Martin, Roger, 267–268
Masonry Cleaners, 122, 125
Masters, Rosemary, 84–85, 86, 88, 89, 91, 93, 96, 100, 176
Matthews, Herbert, 22
Mayer, Martin, 44, 74, 86
Mead, Margaret, 33
Means/ends, 15, 104, 231, 240, 246
Medicaid/Medicare, 125, 138, 139, 140, 212, 260
Meiklejohn, Alexander, 15
Meirowitz, Samuel and Annie, 11
Menschel, Ronay, 182
Mental illness/institutions, 17, 70, 95, 100, 102, 289, 290, 291
Merola, Mario, 157
Methadone, 8, 108, 111, 112, 113–114, 115, 116, 122, 316
Meyer, Bernard, 242
MFY Legal Services, 243
Miami, Florida, 289
Milk, Harvey, 182
Milton, John, 20
Misdemeanors, 74, 77, 87
Mitchell-Lama Program, 103
Mollenkopf, John H., 251
Money Jungle (Chesluk), 277
Morgan, Robert (MD), 90–91, 96, 99, 100, 321
Morgenthau, Robert, 157, 180, 279, 281
Moses, Robert, 7, 196, 197, 219, 231–232, 234
Moynihan, Daniel Patrick, 133, 231, 276
Muggers, 73
Municipal Assistance Corporation (New York State), 81
Murphy, Michael J., 75, 76
Murray, Archibald R., 279
Murtagh, John M., 49–50, 83
Museum of American Folk Art, 217
Mushlin, Michael B., 190

Nathan, Fred, 323
Nathaniel Project, 70

National Conference on Bail and Criminal Justice, 63, 76
National Council on Crime and Delinquency, 53
National Institute on Drug Abuse, 108, 123
National Supported Work Demonstration Project, 134
National Urban and Reconstruction Agency (NURCHA), 299–301, 317
Neier, Aryeh, 4, 166, 167, 297
Netherlands, 145
New Amsterdam Theater *and* New Victory Theater, 250
New Deal, 7, 39, 48, 236, 268
Newman, Jon, 172
New Statesman, 22
New York City, 18, 31, 41, 54, 75
Access-a-Ride, 141
blackout of 1977, 150–151
Board of Correction, 36
Board of Estimate, 239, 242, 253–254
Bowery Mission, 89
Bronx, 98, 103, 150, 156, 157, 179, 218, 276, 290, 320
Brooklyn, 99, 156, 173, 184, 218, 233, 253, 275, 290, 320
Brooklyn House of Detention, 26, 36, 37
Center for Economic Opportunity, 144
Center for Employment Opportunities (CEO), 186–189
Children's Courts/Family Court, 40
city contracts, 125–126, 129, 134, 141, 149
City Council, 196
City Planning Commission, 183, 190, 193–195, 196–197, 199, 205–220, 225, 237, 238, 241, 252–254, 262
City Volunteer Corps, 129, 206, 207–211
Commission on the Year 2000, 206, 274
Court of Special Sessions *and* Magistrates Felony Court, 56, 83

Criminal Courts Building, 57
Criminal Justice Agency, 73, 149,
    150–151, 153, 155, 174
Criminal Justice Coordinating
    Council, 73, 88
Department of City Planning, 211
Department of Correction, 186
Department of Employment,
    125, 126, 134
Department of Housing
    Preservation and
    Development, 102
Department of Juvenile Justice,
    181
Department of Sanitation, 121
Department of Social Services,
    88, 92
Economic Development
    Corporation, 144
fiscal crisis in, 132, 133, 196, 236
42nd Street Development
    Project, 250
Garment District, 240, 242
Harlem, 20, 98, 102, 166, 190,
    201, 258, 290
Human Resources
    Administration, 101, 144, 179,
    180, 322–323
income gap in Manhattan, 276
Juvenile Justice Agency, 179, 253
Lower East Side, 259
Lower Manhattan Expressway,
    233
Mayor's Office of Midtown
    Enforcement, 99
Men's Shelter on East Third
    Street, 85, 88, 98, 99, 101
Midtown West, 241, 253
Narcotics Control Council, 116
in 1960s, 38
Office of Immigrant Affairs, 211,
    253
Office of Management and
    Budget, 197, 199
Office of Midtown Enforcement,
    176, 227
PlaNY2030, 206
Police Department, 76, 189 (*see
    also* Police)
Probation Department, 66,
    71–72, 180

Public Service Action Center,
    102, 103
Queens, 187, 209, 252, 259,
    264–266, 275
Regional Plan for (1929), 232
Rikers Island, 36, 37, 180, 182,
    185, 187, 197–200, 253
Skid Row, 82, 83 (*see also*
    Manhattan Bowery Project)
Staten Island, 218
Theater District, 247–248, 277,
    278
The City at 42nd Street, 237–239
Times Square, 7, 99, 176, 214,
    223–229, 230–231, 236,
    245–252, 253, 262 (*see also*
    Criminal justice system:
    Midtown Community Court;
    under Koch, Edward I.)
Times Square Development
    Corporation, 97
Tombs (Men's House of
    Detention), 37, 57, 72, 86
Transit Authority, 108, 111
vertical growth in, 213–214
Victim Service Agency (VSA),
    104, 146, 172–178, 253
Victim Witness Assistance
    Administration, 173
Williamsburg Bridge, 260–261
Women's House of Detention,
    63, 77
New York Herald Tribune, 22
New York magazine, 232
New York Post, 274
New York State Court of Appeals,
    242
New York State Division of Parole,
    187
New York Times, 56, 62, 77, 114,
    117, 140, 151, 182, 195, 210,
    243, 249, 265, 268, 282, 297
New York Times Book Review, 22
New York University Law School, 29
Nixon, Richard, 116–117, 126, 315

Obama, Barack, 272, 310
O'Brien, John P., 40, 78
Off-Track Betting Corporation, 123
Ohlin, Lloyd E., 90

Olsen, Kenneth L., 288
Onassis, Jacqueline Kennedy, 226
Open Society Institute (OSI), 297,
    302, 303, 304, 309
Ormento, Big John, 25
Osberg, Sally, 267–268
OSI. *See* Open Society Institute
Ott, Mel, 13
Outward Bound, 209–210

Panetta, Leon, 208
Panhandlers, 82, 97, 278
Papert, Fred, 226, 250
Paper Tigers, 122
Parole Restoration Project, 71
Paterson, Basil and David, 107
"Peacemaker, The" (Sturz and
    Herschberger), 18–19, 301, 302
Pennsylvania, University of (Law
    School), 28, 40, 50
Peron, Eva, 20
Philadelphia, 28, 51, 54
Philosophy, 15, 16
Pioneer Messenger Service,
    122–123, 128–129
Plattsburgh, New York, 67
Plunkitt, George Washington, 282
Poetry, 18
Poker, 163–164
Police, 17, 36, 76, 83, 85–86, 88, 90,
    119, 120, 128, 130, 138, 148,
    151, 152, 165, 170, 175, 197,
    225, 227, 229, 248, 274, 276,
    278, 286, 288, 289, 323
  accused of racially motivated
    brutality, 200, 203
  black, Hispanic, and women
    officers, 203
Police Academy, 218
police commissioners, 156–157,
158, 189, 200–203, 239, 249
Polygraph tests, 111
Pope, Dorothy, 33
Pornography, 223, 225, 226, 247
Portman, John, 247
Poverty/poor people, 2, 5, 21, 22,
    29, 31, 39, 40, 44, 51, 59, 105,
    133, 236, 276
poverty as a crime, 50
Powell, Lewis, 110
Power Broker, The (Caro), 7

Power issues, 7, 16, 18, 232, 237,
    299
  abuse of power by states, 29
  empowerment of derelicts, 91
Pragmatism, 16, 59, 310, 311
Pretrial Services Agency, 147–149,
    153, 173, 174, 201
  in Washington, D.C., 154
Primm, Beny, Dr., 114
Princeton University, 14, 195
Prison/jail populations, 35–36, 184,
    276, 310
  and prisoner re-entry, 184–189,
    198, 319
Pritchett, V. S., 22
Privacy laws, 110–111
Private sector, 3, 142, 254, 270, 271,
    272, 301, 314
Probation. *See* New York City:
    Probation Department
Project Renewal. *See under*
    Manhattan Bowery Project
Propaganda, 32
Prostitution, 47, 70, 72, 223, 224,
    225, 227, 278, 284, 285, 287,
    293
Puerto Ricans, 39, 150, 258
Pugach, Burton, 25–26
Punishment as therapy, 17

Quindlen, Anna, 195
Quinn, Christine, 309

Raab, Jennifer J., 305
Rangel, Charles B., 116
Rankin, Anne, 53, 54, 56–57, 62
Rappleyea, Robert (Reverend), 224,
    226
Ratensky, Samuel, 231
Ravello, Italy, 21
Ravens, Carl, 225
Ravitch, Richard, 226
Reagan, Ronald, 6, 207, 323
Reapers of the Storm (Sturz and
    Lyttleton), 22
Recidivism, 70, 186, 202
Reforms, 5–6, 66, 69, 135, 171, 314
  bail reform, 23, 41, 44, 49, 50,
    53, 67, 71, 72, 166, 316, 320
  prison reform, 39

Regan, Donald, 124
Rehabilitation Act of 1973, 108, 109
Rehabilitation process, 78, 94, 106
Religion, 13, 14, 19
ReServe, 307–309, 312, 321
Reserve Officers Training Corps
    (ROTC), 16
Reuter, Peter, 117
Rheedlen Centers for Children and
    Families (Harlem), 258
Riis, Jacob, 133
Riots, 72, 275, 276
Ritter, Bruce (Reverend), 228
Roberts, Burton D., 78–79
Robertson, Rebecca, 241, 248, 250
Robinson, Cyril D., 113, 115, 117
Rockefeller, Nelson A., 84, 109, 238,
    269
Rockefeller Foundation, 273–274,
    283
Rohatyn, Felix G., 81
Roosevelt, Franklin D., 207
Rosenthal, Jack, 4, 8, 55, 56, 58, 64,
    140, 167, 210–211, 257, 258,
    260, 261, 307, 313, 315
ROTC. *See* Reserve Officers Training
    Corps
Rubenstein, Howard J., 217–218, 241
Rudin, Lewis, 201
Rusk Institute of Rehabilitative
    Medicine, 139
Russia, 4, 320
Rykken, Richard, 147, 149

Safe Horizon, 146, 178–179
Sagalyn, Lynne B., 227, 237, 239,
    240, 241, 249–250
Salant, Richard, 124
Salisbury, Harrison, 33
Samuels, Gertrude, 77, 78
Scall, Les, 78, 147
Schaffer, S. Andrew, 149
Schall, Ellen, 172
Schlesinger, Arthur, Jr., 32
Schoenfeld, Gerald, 226, 228, 277,
    278
Schrank, Robert, 220
Schwartz, Allen, 181
Schwarz, F. A. O. (Fritz), Jr., 107,
    200–201, 257, 308, 313, 315,
    318

Schwarz, Min, 172
Schweitzer, Louis, 23, 29–32, 37, 38,
    39, 41, 43–44, 48, 56, 68, 73,
    89, 119, 270, 314, 320
    brothers William T. and Peter, 90
    death of, 313
    first meetings with Sturz, 33–34
    wife of, 29–30
Schweitzer, Louis (cabbie), 30
Scoppetta, Nicholas, 151, 153, 155,
    157
Scotto, Anthony, 124, 130
Self interest, 166–167, 184, 313,
    324
Setting Priorities: The 1973 Budget
    (Brookings Institution),
    104–105
Sex businesses, 225, 238. *See also*
    Pornography; Prostitution
Shamrock Construction, 99
Shapiro, Ken, 136
Shaw, George Bernard, 81
Shectman, Paul, 288
Sheehan, Susan, 315
Silver Gavel award, 22, 55
SingleStop program, 185
Sixth Amendment, 26–27, 28, 53.
    See also Criminal justice
    system: speedy trials
Slums, 133, 258
Smith, Michael, 158
Smith, William, 135, 136
Smith Barney, 142
Social engineering, 3, 4, 12, 23, 105,
    266, 268–269, 271–272, 292
Social entrepreneurship, 3, 14, 23,
    211, 219, 266–268, 292, 301,
    311–312, 317, 318
Social philanthropy, 32
Social Security, Supplemental
    Security Income (SSI), 124,
    131, 140
Son of Sam, 150, 152–156
Soros, George, 4, 265, 273, 298,
    300, 301, 302, 304, 306, 309,
    315
South Africa, 4, 265, 294. *See also*
    under Housing
Spagnoli, Gloria, 321
Spain, 21–22, 41
Spofford Juvenile Center (Bronx),
    179–180

SRO. *See* Housing: single room occupancy hotels
SSI. *See* Social Security, Supplemental Security Income
Starr, Roger, 257–258
States' rights, 27
Stein, Howard, 263, 264
Steinbeck, John, 1–2, 19, 319–320, 321–322
Steingut, Robert and Stanley, 135, 136
Stern, Robert A. M., 249
Stern, William J., 239, 241
Strasburg, Paul, 138, 172, 181
Street Outreach Services, 288
Strong, Josiah, 268
Sturz, Herbert, 2, 73, 74, 114, 117, 120, 136, 241
    achievements of, 320–321, 322
    bail reform strategy of, 42
    Bar Mitzvah preparation, 13
    birth/early life, 11, 12–14
    brothers, 15
    characterized, 6, 43, 164–169, 190, 219–220, 260, 270, 302, 310, 311, 317–318
    compared with Robert Moses, 7
    contracting polio, 14
    as coordinator of criminal justice, 181–190, 202
    as deputy mayor for criminal justice, 159, 170, 171–181, 183, 189, 197–198, 225, 315
    as director of City Planning Commission, 183, 190, 193–195, 206
    first meetings with Louis Schweitzer, 33–34
    governing boards served on, 156
    heroes of, 314–315
    hiring women, 84
    and illusions, 81–82
    and mantra "Only connect," 16
    maxims of, 314
    and motivations of others, 164, 166, 168, 194, 318
    on *New York Times* editorial board, 257, 258–263
    parents of, 11–13, 15
    as Planning Commission chairman, 206, 238, 252–254,

262 (*see also* New York City: City Planning Commission)
    in private sector, 263–267
    quantifying social engineering results, 12
    replacing himself as director, 58, 158
    wife Elizabeth, 21, 260, 320
Stutman, Leonard J., Dr., 119
Suicides, 74
Sullivan, Joseph (Bishop), 209
Sulzberger, Arthur, Jr., 209, 280, 281
Summer of Sam (film), 149
Summons, 75, 86. *See also* Manhattan Summons Project
Supreme Court, 29, 52, 53, 64, 108, 109–110, 239
Sviridoff, Mitchell, 118, 119, 120, 133, 136, 163
Sweden, 145

Talbot, Ernie, 99
Tales of Time Square (J. Friedman), 224
Taxation, 101, 142, 236, 250, 251, 264, 265, 266
Taylor, Diana, 306
Teach for America, 269
Teenagers. *See* Adolescents
Telephones, 148–149, 173
Tennis, 14
Terrorist attacks of 9/11, 179
Tese, Vincent J., 241–242
The After-School Corporation (TASC), 302–307
    board of directors, 305
Theater De Lys (Greenwich Village), 30
Thomas, Dylan, 18
Thomas, Franklin, 167, 206
Thompson, Jim, 147
Threepenny Opera, The (Brecht and Weill), 30
Times Square Roulette: Remaking the City Icon (Sagalyn), 227
Tolman, W. H., 268
Topper, Louis, 48
Transportation, 138, 142, 187, 198. *See also* Easyride; Highways/expressways
Traub, James, 251

Travelers Aid Society, 176, 287
Travis, Jeremy, 66, 72, 148, 151,
153, 154, 156, 173–174, 275,
323
Trilling, Lionel, 4, 15
Trotwood Corporation, 263–264
Trust, 62, 76
Truth, 16, 43, 44
Tufo, Peter, 199

UDC. *See* Urban Development
Corporation
Unemployment, 8, 132, 207, 289
Uniform Land Use Review
Procedure (ULURP), 212
Unions, 129–130
Unitarians, 16
United States Information Agency,
23
United States Postal Service, 108,
152
Urban Development Corporation
(UDC), 231, 237, 238, 239,
240, 241, 242, 265
Urban Mass Transportation
Association, 139

Venice, Italy, 30–31
Vera Institute, 43, 47–79, 88, 112,
133, 158, 173, 174, 187, 188,
195, 270–271, 273, 288, 308,
310, 313, 319, 323, 324
board of directors, 90, 106–107,
132
choosing name for, 45
cities influenced by, 64, 66–67
job creation unit, 137–138
Legal Action Center, 104,
105–112
management of spin-offs, 92–93
and methadone/heroin
maintenance programs,
113–117
Neighborhood Work Project,
186–187
programs/groups inspired by, 8
underwriting own bail fund, 48,
50
as "Very Easy Release Agency," 63
as Vera Institute of Justice, 90, 120

Vera Point Scale, 66, 149, 154
Vocational Development
Program, 187
See also Center for Alternative
Sentencing and Employment
Services; Manhattan Bail
Project; Manhattan Bowery
Project; Manhattan Court
Employment Project;
Manhattan Summons Project
Veterans Administration, 110
Village Voice, 199
Volunteers in Service to America
(VISTA), 175, 207
Vorenberg, James, 73

Wachtler, Sol, 278, 280
Wagner, Bobby, 194, 195–196, 200,
215, 225, 234, 274, 281
Wagner, Robert F. (senator), 48
Wagner, Robert F., Jr., 36, 48–49, 56,
83, 169, 324
Wald, Patricia M., 63, 84, 165, 315
Walker, Gary, 122
Walker, James J., 40
Wall Street firms, 142
Wall Street Journal, 136
Ward, Benjamin, 182, 201–203, 275
Warren, Earl, 63, 165
WBAI-FM (NY), 30
Weill, Kurt, 30
Weinstein, Michael, 120, 185, 258,
306
Weisbrod, Carl, 99, 136, 164,
168–169, 176, 193, 194, 208,
210, 215, 219–220, 223, 227,
237, 239, 249, 250, 251–252,
311, 312, 315, 318
Weiss, Ted, 233
Welfare issues, 112, 123, 135–137,
138
welfare mothers, 143, 144, 212
See also Employment: welfare to
work
Wepner, Chuck "The Bayonne
Bleeder," 11
Westway, 231, 232–236, 243
Whitaker, Craig, 231
White Barn Theater (Westport, CT),
30
Whyte, William H., 228, 229

Wilbur, Quincy, 18
Wildcat Service Corporation,
        123–146, 208, 286, 323
    board of directors, 124, 137
    funding pool for, 144
    and permanent employment,
        137, 143
    and rollover model, 141–142
    Wildcat Academy, 145
Williams, Harrison, 33
Willig, George, 150
Wilpon, Fred, 209
Wilson, James Q., 69, 229–230
Wilson, William Julius, 143–144
Winter's Tale (Helprin), 261, 273
Wisconsin, University of, 15–18
Wolfe, Tom, 276
Wolk, Andrew, 269
Women, 13, 84, 118, 143, 144, 145,
        146, 166, 178, 203, 212, 263,
        286–287, 300

World Series, 13
World Trade Center, 150
Wright, Bruce, 63
Wright, Frank Lloyd, 16
Wriston, Walter B. 132

Youth Foundation, 33
Youth Service Corps, 22
Yunus, Muhammad, 269

Zeckendorf, William, Jr., 247, 264,
        265
Zoning issues, 109, 110, 214–218,
        225–226, 241, 247–248

Sam Roberts, urban affairs correspondent for the *New York Times*, has written for the *Times* for more than twenty years, prior to which he was a reporter and city editor at the *Daily News*. His writing has appeared in the *New York Times Magazine*, the *New Republic*, and *New York Magazine*. Author and coauthor of several books, he lives in New York with his wife.

PublicAffairs is a publishing house founded in 1997. It is a tribute to the standards, values, and flair of three persons who have served as mentors to countless reporters, writers, editors, and book people of all kinds, including me.

I. F. STONE, proprietor of *I. F. Stone's Weekly*, combined a commitment to the First Amendment with entrepreneurial zeal and reporting skill and became one of the great independent journalists in American history. At the age of eighty, Izzy published *The Trial of Socrates*, which was a national bestseller. He wrote the book after he taught himself ancient Greek.

BENJAMIN C. BRADLEE was for nearly thirty years the charismatic editorial leader of *The Washington Post*. It was Ben who gave the *Post* the range and courage to pursue such historic issues as Watergate. He supported his reporters with a tenacity that made them fearless and it is no accident that so many became authors of influential, best-selling books.

ROBERT L. BERNSTEIN, the chief executive of Random House for more than a quarter century, guided one of the nation's premier publishing houses. Bob was personally responsible for many books of political dissent and argument that challenged tyranny around the globe. He is also the founder and longtime chair of Human Rights Watch, one of the most respected human rights organizations in the world.

. . .

For fifty years, the banner of Public Affairs Press was carried by its owner Morris B. Schnapper, who published Gandhi, Nasser, Toynbee, Truman, and about 1,500 other authors. In 1983, Schnapper was described by *The Washington Post* as "a redoubtable gadfly." His legacy will endure in the books to come.

Peter Osnos, *Founder and Editor-at-Large*